Exploring Social Behavior

Investigations in Social Psychology

Exploring Social Behavior

Investigations in Social Psychology

James A. Schellenberg
Indiana State University

Allyn and Bacon
Boston London Toronto Sydney Tokyo Singapore

This book is very broadly dedicated to all who are or have been children. In particular, it is dedicated to Robert L., Franklin M., Amy J., and Stephen A. Schellenberg. So much of our purpose for living—and so much of our wonder at the immense potentialities in being human—are provided by our children!

J. A. S.

Series Editor: Karen Hanson
Series Editorial Assistant: Laura Lynch
Production Administrator: Deborah Brown
Editorial Production Service: P. M. Gordon Associates
Cover Administrator: Suzanne Harbison
Manufacturing Buyer: Megan Cochran

Copyright © 1993 by Allyn and Bacon
A Division of Simon & Schuster, Inc.
160 Gould Street
Needham Heights, Massachusetts 02194

Library of Congress Cataloging-in-Publication Data
Schellenberg, James A.
    Exploring social behavior : investigations in social psychology / James A. Schellenberg.
    Includes bibliographical references and index.
    ISBN 0-205-13861-6
    1. Social psychology. I. Title
HM251.S2985   1993
302—dc20   92-22210
                                                      CIP

Printed in the United States of America
10 9 8 7 6 5 4 3 2   95

Contents

Preface   vii

Chapter 1
On Being Human   1

Chapter 2
The Mystery of Identity   17

Chapter 3
The Mystery of Conscience   43

Chapter 4
The Mystery of Intelligence   71

Chapter 5
The Mystery of Beliefs   99

Chapter 6
The Mystery of Attraction   125

Chapter 7
The Mystery of Aggression   141

Chapter 8
The Mystery of Crowds   161

Chapter 9
The Mystery of Social Order   175

Chapter 10
On Living with Mystery   203

Bibliography   209

Index   223

Preface

Human behavior is full of mysteries.

There are the little mysteries about particular persons or particular situations. Then there are the fundamental questions about the behavior of people in general. It is to the fundamental questions that we turn for the subject matter of this book. These questions include the following: How do we know who we are? How do we manage, usually, to behave so well? How are we able to become so intelligent? How do people develop the odd beliefs that we sometimes find them holding? Why are we especially attracted to certain people? What makes people sometimes so destructive? Why is behavior in crowds often so unusual? And how do we manage to live, generally peaceably, with others in a social order?

This book treats these fundamental questions about social behavior as mysteries—mysteries for which we are able to unravel parts of the answers to basic questions, but with many uncertainties remaining.

In pursuing these mysteries, we borrow broadly from the social and behavioral sciences. This book is not easily categorized in terms of disciplines such as anthropology, biology, political science, psychology, or sociology. It draws on all of these fields—not so much as specific disciplines but rather as areas of investigation that have dealt with the questions we raise. If there is any particular field that serves as home base, it is that of social psychology. But we do not limit ourselves to the area usually charted as the domain of social psychology—which would be too limited for the range of mysteries we are pursuing.

While not closing out the humanistic side of the social sciences, our primary intention is to explore the scientific knowledge available in those areas we examine. We conceive of science here in a rather broad way, not limiting it to the most methodologically rigorous investigations. Indeed, we build upon some ideas of writers who are more accurately characterized as philosophers than as scientists. Still, our primary thrust is toward empirical evidence. What have we found out in certain central investigations that bear upon our basic questions? What are the implications of some of the most recent findings of the behavioral sciences for the questions we raise? Such questions serve as guiding themes for this book.

This book deals with eight main mysteries: the mystery of identity, the mystery of conscience, the mystery of intelligence, the mystery of beliefs, the mystery of attraction, the mystery of aggression, the mystery of crowds, and the mystery of social order. Each of these constitutes a separate chapter. There are also introductory and concluding essays, making ten chapters in all. The book has been written so that each of the chapters (except perhaps the final one) could be read independently; that is, none requires as a background the information presented in other chapters. However, the understanding of a given chapter will be enhanced if it is read after the earlier chapters. There is a sense in which each builds on insights presented earlier—not so much to put together the particular information found for a given question as to build the perspective most profitably applied to this information. The general pattern is that the earlier chapters deal with issues most commonly treated as matters of the behavior of individuals, while the topics treated later in the book more obviously involve matters of social structure and group life.

For whom is this book written? The intended audience covers a rather broad range—from college students first being introduced to the social and behavioral sciences to advanced professionals in these fields. Admittedly, it is difficult to write a book for such a variety of readers. For the benefit of introductory students and other general readers, I have tried to write as simply as the subject matter permits. Of course, some of the ideas dealt with are not particularly simple. I have tried to lead into the more complex ideas as painlessly as possible, but I have not avoided them. I assume that most readers are motivated to learn about new ideas and new findings and not simply to search for support for generally prevailing opinions. To make the main text relatively easy to read, I have kept it free of bibliographic references and technical information. Instead, such information may be found by more advanced readers in fairly extensive notes for most chapters. These notes, keyed by number to particular paragraphs and found at the end of each chapter, serve several purposes. They provide sources to help support assertions I make in the text. They also provide further comments or information, often of a more specialized nature than the main body of text. Finally, they point out where one may go to read more on the subject being discussed. Even these notes will not satisfy many specialists for whom the topics are their own special areas of expertise; the book is too general to claim much in this direction. What I hope to provide those readers who are themselves advanced scholars is, first, some evidence that my highly summarized treatment has at least not grossly misrepresented the current state of knowledge in their field of scientific work and, second, important information about areas beyond their specialties. The subjects covered in this book, as I emphasized at the beginning of this preface, will range significantly beyond those of any single discipline.

I especially wish to thank my reviewers: Dan O'Conner, Northern Colorado University; Robert A. Ellis, University of Georgia; Clyde Franklin, The Ohio State University; Worth Summers, California State University-Sacremento; and Kathleen McKinney, Illinois State University.

Authors in the bibliography at the back of the book represent many hundreds of scholars who have had a strong influence on what is presented here. It would take too much space to give adequate acknowledgment to even the most important of these persons; I hope that what I say in my notes at least indicates who they are. I do, however, wish to make special mention of some of the organizations and persons who have made the most direct contributions to this book's production. Indiana State University generously provided me with a year's leave from administrative and teaching duties, and most of this book was written during this period. My university also provided suitable library facilities, including a quiet place to work close to the main social science and psychology holdings and special help in obtaining some works not on our library shelves. Finally, I wish to mention the special encouragement of Karen Hanson, Senior Editor, and the fine support of other editors and assistants at Allyn and Bacon in helping to shape this book into its present form.

James A. Schellenberg

Chapter 1

On Being Human

HUMAN DISTINCTIVENESS

Human nature. Two words, so easy to say, yet so rich in possible meanings. So often have they been used to try to explain some commonplace behavior that their value for more serious discussion has been compromised. Behaviors ranging widely—from collecting shark teeth to obtaining as many dollar bills as possible, from rejoicing over a victory on the basketball court to praying fervently for rain during a dry spell, from enjoying eating grub worms as a delicacy to having tea every afternoon, from practicing monogamy to avoiding its restrictions—have at some times and places been seen as so naturally human that nothing further need be said in explanation. Yet each of these actions, to some humans, would be seen as odd behavior indeed, requiring very special explanation. The cultural dimension of human behavior is so strong that what seems perfectly natural to one group appears very much otherwise to those of another tradition. Realizing this, we sometimes wonder if the phrase "human nature" can ever be used with a clear meaning.

Nevertheless, there is a sense in which humans of all kinds have characteristics in common. As one way of approaching what these characteristics might be, we shall seek to examine the ways in which humans show themselves as a distinctive species within the animal kingdom. In this section we summarize some of what has been learned on this subject, taking special note of the ways

1

humans distinguish themselves from their nearest relatives, the monkeys and apes.[1]

In terms of physical structure, there are several things that appear most clearly to set humans apart from other animals. One of these is the size of the brain, with special attention to our relatively large cerebral cortex. Another is our fully upright posture, with all other primates being more functionally quadrapeds. Other matters set apart the human form, including our eyes, our teeth, our hands, and our relatively hairless skin; but these are probably less central for defining humanity than the features of relative brain size and upright posture. These two features of human anatomy markedly distinguish us from other animals.

Given the apparent physical differences between humans and apes, it is with some surprise that we learn that humans and apes are very similar genetically. The most careful biochemical studies that have been applied to this question reveal that humans and chimpanzees have approximately 99 percent of their genetic materials in common. They are as similar to one another as are closely related species of fruit flies. This gives us a special puzzle for interpreting human nature: If we are genetically so similar to other animals, why are we not more similar to them in behavior?[2]

Two main ways that humans have been seen as distinctive in behavior are in their unique abilities for language and for using tools. It has been traditionally held that man is the only animal truly able to use symbolic speech or to develop a meaningful use of tools. These, in turn, are seen as reflections of the unique qualities of the human mind. But the confidence of assertions of human uniqueness in these areas have become more and more restrained by what has been shown in animal studies in recent decades.

As far as we can tell, none of the great apes has developed a natural language. At least, if any group has a symbolic code more complex than fairly simple social expressions of sound and gesture, it has not yet been discovered by humans. But work with individual apes has demonstrated quite clearly that they can learn the rudiments of American Sign Language, a system of symbolic gestures developed for the hearing impaired. Not only have some apes developed vocabularies of more than one hundred signs, but they have shown some ingenuity in creating new signs. Washoe, the pioneer chimp in breaking the language barrier, invented her own sign for bib; she also has put different signs together to create new concepts, as when she referred to swans as "water birds." What still remains problematic is the extent to which language structures have become fully internalized in these highly communicative apes. Although proper word order and some structures of grammar appear to be used by some of the specially trained chimps, there seem to be limits in the extent to which they can use language to reconstruct ideas in new ways.[3]

On the matter of tool usage, this ability has now been demonstrated by a wide variety of species. What is less widely found is the purposeful creation of tools. Jane Goodall's discovery in the late 1960s that wild chimpanzees may break off sticks or grass stems to poke into termite or ant holes and fish out insects was the first widely noted documentation of wild animal tool creation, but many other examples of tool manufacture have since been identified. These include behaviors not only by the great apes. A captive capuchin monkey has rolled pieces of newspaper to make a reaching tool, and wild members of the same species have peeled twigs to make them more suitable for probing for insects. Of course, such tools remain quite simple, by human standards at least. There is nothing approaching a technology (that is, a complex system of making and using tools, which may in turn be applied for a variety of purposes) among any animals in the wild, although some individual animals can learn to use parts of man's technology. The chimp Lana, for example, has proved to be quite adept in her use of a computer keyboard.[4]

What about the distinctiveness of the human mind itself? We may not be clear about just what the human mind is, but most of us strongly believe that it is somehow special. Still, as we break down our human mental processes and examine their ingredients, they more and more show their similarity to our nearest relatives in the animal kindgom. What at first seems like a sharp difference in kind comes to appear as only a difference in degree.

Consider simple sensory processes. Here humans seem to have abilities quite continuous with those of other animals. As is characteristic of primates, we give particular emphasis to vision, but our visual acuity is shown by tests to be quite similar to that of apes and old world monkeys.[5]

As another example, take perceptual processes, which organize sensory inputs. Evidence on perceptual processes is not as easy to obtain as that regarding sensation, but there is no reason to believe that there is a sharp discontinuity between human perception and that of some other animals.

Among the most interesting studies of perception are those requiring subjects to make contact first with an object in one sensory mode, then show recognition or discrimination in another mode. Such research has come to be called that of "cross-modal transfer." For example, subjects first may be given an object to touch in a box, then asked to choose which of several visually presented objects it might have been. Humans are quite adept at this, and some neurologists have suggested that this is because of a special feature of the human brain. There is a part of our brains, known as the angular gyrus, which connects with all main sensory areas of the cerebral cortex. Only humans appear to have an advanced development of this area; this has sometimes been suggested as critical for the development of human symbolic abilities generally, as well as more particular perceptual skills in cross-modal transfer. This part of the brain, by allowing the transfer of associations between different forms of sensation, facilitates a generalized experience of the objects with which we come into contact. Such is a reasonable inference about some special features of the kind of brain found in humans. But are humans the only animals able to show cross-modal transfer? Admittedly, there are some rather tricky problems in doing research with subjects that are unable to talk. Nevertheless, studies have been done with other animals that appear to overcome the communication problem. The early studies suggested that cross-modal transfer was not to be found outside the human species. But more recent research has demonstrated quite clearly that apes (mostly chimpanzees, but at least one orangutan has also been successfully tested) make discriminations indicating quite significant levels of perceptual integration. Of special interest is the fact that chimps can respond to a photographed object as if the real object had been viewed; in addition, they have discriminated between objects, previously only viewed, when subsequently they were only allowed to touch them. That this was the case even for chimps who had never before seen photographs suggests perceptual powers significantly more acute than necessary for simple cross-modal transfer.[6]

What about learning abilities, where sensation and perception come together to affect behavior at a later time? Ever since Wolfgang Köhler's studies of ape learning during World War I in the Canary Islands (where he found himself cut off from his German homeland by the war), psychologists have had a high regard for the problem-solving abilities of chimpanzees. The exploits of Sultan, one able chimp observed by Köhler, have become almost legendary, demonstrating to Köhler's satisfaction clear examples of insightful learning. Sultan performed feats such as inventing a new tool to pull bananas into his cage by fitting two sticks into each other. Since these early studies, an enormous range of research on animal learning has accumulated, most (though not all) showing clear primate superiority over other animals, as well as special skills of the great apes when compared to other primates.[7]

Among the most complex forms of learning are those involving quantitative concepts and those demonstrating the assumption of object permanence. Some animals have shown an ability to discriminate on the basis of numerical differences, but the limit reached (by chimpanzees, of course) seems to be at about six or seven. It is not clear whether or not chimps can count (as human children do in quickly mastering far more complex numerical concepts), but it is known that they have some very simple quantitative abilities.[8]

Object permanence (the ability to consider an object as continuing to exist even when it is out of sight) has been described by Swiss psychologist Jean Piaget as developing through a series of stages during the first two years of a child's life (the period of what he called "sensorimotor" intelligence). The full development of object permanence may be seen when a child continues to search for an object once it is hidden from view. Although a variety of animals (including cats) appear to have some of its elements, object permanence has been fully demonstrated only among primates.

Another concept suggested by Piaget is that of "conservation," an ability to discriminate between changes in appearance that do not change the amount of something, as compared to those in which the amount is actually changed as well. This is typically studied with the same amount of water poured into tall and shorter glasses, with young children seeing the water in a taller glass as being more than in one with a bigger base. Effective conservation for humans typically develops at about age six or seven. At least one chimpanzee, given special training by humans, has also demonstrated a satisfactory achievement of conservation ability.

What do such lines of evidence about the mental abilities of other animals say about our view of a sharp difference between human minds and those of animals? Of course, each species is different, and thus distinct in many ways, including the features of mental processes. But are humans the only animals possessing "reason," as we used to assert so confidently? Our confidence should no longer be so freely expressed. Some differences between primates and humans that once seemed absolute now appear much more to be differences in degree.

After many years of research on cognitive processes of primates, William Mason has characterized the ability for planning of an adult chimpanzee to be roughly equal to that of a human child of about five or six years of age. But Mason also points out that "the more remote the action is from present circumstances, the greater the discrepancy between ape and man." Apes, he says, "appear to be severely handicapped, as compared to man, in any situation that requires them to 'plan ahead' for more than a matter of minutes, or at most hours."[9]

This human capacity for greater foresight has its application in important differences in tool using between humans and other primates. Monkeys and apes have shown considerable dexterity in using tools—both those borrowed from humans and those developed through their own trial-and-error learning. But tool-using for nonhuman primates serves quite immediate ends. Extending their reach or helping to focus the power of their muscles are key functions of the use of sticks and stones as tools by monkeys or apes. Personal display is another common primate purpose of tools, such as to brandish a stick to indicate strength or resolve. But longer-term purposes (such as would be implied by treating tools as personal or group property) seem absent from nonhuman tool use. And, of course, nonhuman primates have nothing like a set of interrelated tools that may be used by different individuals and that continue to be available for future use. In brief, nonhuman primates may have tools, but they do no have technologies.[10]

A similar point to that made regarding tool use can be made about economic exchange. Exchange relations do occur among nonhuman primates. A you-scratch-my-back-and-I'll-scratch-yours philosophy may be applied quite literally, and extensive networks of grooming partners may develop within a monkey or ape community. Associated with these networks sometimes are very simple transfers of food. This, however, is a far cry from the systems of exchanging goods and services developed by humans. There may be exchanges among nonhuuman primates, but nothing like the economic systems of even the simplest human societies.[11]

The examples of human distinctiveness mentioned thus far— in such features as language, technology, and economic structures—all seem to have a common theme. Humans appear to possess a more structured imagination than do other species. This allows them a greater transcendence of the present instance of space and time, giving them a reality beyond the immediate physical situation. Moreover, this reality has a systematic structure that goes far beyond the needs of the moment. The structured nature of this imagination tells us something about the distinctive features of the human mind and human society.

After reviewing the distinctiveness of the human mind, we should also take note of some of the special features of human social relationships and social organization.

Looking at social behavior generally, we must be impressed by the social sophistication sometimes shown by nonhuman primates. Take, for example, the following set of observed events:

> Two young mothers sit in the shadow of an oak tree, while their children play nearby. Near the mothers is someone lying on the ground. Suddenly the children start screaming, hitting one another and pulling at each other's hair. The mothers pause uncertainly, obviously concerned about the behavior of their children. Then one of the mothers goes to the reclining figure, an older female. She pokes her several times in the ribs to awaken her, then points to the quarreling children. The older individual arises, makes one threatening step forward, and expresses loudly but briefly her displeasure. Immediately the children stop their quarreling. The old matriarch then again lies down to continue her nap.

Such instances of behavior are included among descriptions given by Frans de Waal in his fascinating book, *Chimpanzee Politics*. Just for clarity, we should make clear that the behavior being described in this instance is that of chimps, not humans. Cases such as this provide ample evidence that complex social relationships, including cunning social manipulations, may occur in nonhuman species. But of course this is still very different from the complex kinship and political systems found in even the most simple of human societies.[12]

In looking at some of the roots of human society, one fact of central importance is the relative helplessness at birth of the human infant. In many species of mammals, the newborn can walk from the first day. Among primates, however, this is not the case. Though some monkeys can walk within a week, most species require several weeks. Apes take longer than monkeys to learn to walk, though most chimps are able to walk freely by about forty-three weeks. Most humans require at least a year before they show such abilities. [13]

Physical abilities (such as shown by age for walking) demonstrate only one aspect of the dependency of young humans. Even more important are elements of social dependency—including an especially close relationship to a primary caregiver. Most monkeys can be functionally independent of their mothers by the end of the third month. Among humans, it is not easy to give a definite time for typical independence, but it is clearly measured more by years than by weeks or months.

Still more difficult to express precisely are the more emotional features of early social relationships. Here we should be especially careful in asserting a distinctive difference between humans and other primates. Harry Harlow's work documenting the effects of maternal deprivation in rhesus monkeys has made us aware of how important mothers seem to be across the primate order, and Jane Goodall has documented at least one case of a young chimpanzee in the wild whose death could be most simply expressed as the result of a broken heart following the death of its mother. Still, there appear to be at least some distinctively human aspects of emotional expression. These include the early recognition of faces and the tendency to smile when seeing a human face.[14]

A face seems to evoke smiles spontaneously in a human infant at about three months of age, which in turn evokes special interest on the part of parents. Although we cannot say that there are not counterparts to this important infant-parent relationship in other species, it is noteworthy that the smile does not have the same meaning for other species as it does for humans. Widely recognized in many primate species is the "fear-grimace" opening of the mouth to show teeth. Although occasionally displayed in dominance rituals, its main primate correlations are with flight. Even for chimpanzees, the associations of such an expression are quite different from those of humans. Thus, in a real sense, only humans smile. Also, only in humans is there close association between the expressions we know as smiling and laughter. The counterpart to laughter in other primates is seen in a relaxed, open-mouth display associated especially with playful biting. In the chimpanzee this is often accompanied by short vocalizations, which is the nearest approximation to human laughter shown by nonhuman primates. It is unlikely that these distinctive human features of smiling and laughter (including their convergence) would have developed in a species that was not intensely social, with a close mother-infant relationship a key ingredient in that sociability.[15]

The fact that the male parent is generally around for child rearing is another important ingredient in the distinctively human pattern of social life. It is not unknown in the animal kingdom for males to watch over a nest or care for the young, but among primates such care by males is rare. It is a distinctively human complex that combines a home base for the rearing of the young, a relatively permanent and usually monogamous bond between male and female (in turn associated with a relatively continuous sexual receptivity of the human female and distinctively contrasting forms of male and female physique), and involvement of the male in helping to provide care for the young. This complex of features, combined with the highly dependent and docile human infant, sets the stage for a depth of social contact that is one of the primary characteristics of the human species.

Our highly elaborate systems of social organization are also distinctively human. Other primate species have hierarchical systems within a local group and recognize close relationships, but only humans appear to have clearly identified systems of marriage and kinship. And beyond this is a network of human cooperation characterized by a division of labor unknown in other species.

Bringing together some of the characteristics previously mentioned, we begin to see how the most characteristic feature of all—human culture—might have emerged. Creatures with an especially structured imagination, who had begun using tools and language, who were intensely social in their relationships to each other, and who were elaborating wider forms of social organization—such creatures would already have developed the rudiments of what we call culture. In our next section we discuss further how human culture might have arisen.

THE HUMAN REALITY

Two million years ago inhabitants of eastern Africa were already behaving in ways that clearly set them apart from the apes. They were using large animals for food, were carrying tools with them to use on such animals, and were carrying food to be consumed at special locations. This much we know from the conditions under which bones and stones have been unearthed. We do not know for sure that these remains are signs of hunters, for the consumption of meat such as the hippopotamus (whose remains have been found at one notable site) may be more likely the result of scavaging than of hunting; but at least some organized hunting appears likely for those who showed such a well developed taste for meat. Of course, apes in the wild also sometimes eat meat, though never large animals. What is more distinctive, however, is the evidence of simple hitting and cutting instruments being moved to the site of their use; this suggests a systematic and purposeful use of tools unknown among other primates. The evidence of a variety of animals being consumed at one place is even more distinctive, for it suggests systematic food sharing and at least the beginnings of an economic and social division of labor.

Who were those who left these examples of tool carrying and food sharing? Were they humans? Such questions seem simple enough, but the answers are much more complex. Certainly none of the great apes we know today would have left such marks. Equally certain are we that the current species we call human—that is, *Homo sapiens*—was not yet in existence. We do not know for sure that there was only one species that left such evidence for us to find after two million years, for there were at least two kinds of man-apes living then. Whoever it was, their skeletal remains indicate that their brains could not have been more than half the size of humans today; nevertheless, they walked with a fully erect posture. Although we cannot be certain of a direct evolutionary line from these man-apes to humans today, it does seem reasonable to assume such a lineage and to see the evidence as marking an early way-station to human culture. It is easy to imagine these hominids combining hunting and gathering with a division of labor related to age and sex. With evidences for home bases, we may see signs of local communities and imagine the beginnings of kinship systems. Although there is no reason to infer language at this time, have we not identified a set of circumstances in which more sensitive forms of communication could provide real advantages for a group? Ultimately, could not such systems of communication, along with sharpened structures of social organization and more imaginative use of tools, develop into what we have come to know as human language and human culture?[16]

Let us now move on to about 200,000 years ago. We can more comfortably call those living then as humans, even though they would not be of our present species. The usual designation of these men and women is that of *Homo erectus*, and their remains show much greater similarity to modern humans than to previous forms. We know from associated bones and tools that these people had well developed hunting skills, made use of fire, and had well established home bases. But we have little systematic evidence of the human culture these people may have had. The most distinctive products to be found were their stone tools, and about this time a more efficient means of flaking stone tools was coming into use. Did these people have a system of language? It is easy to imagine that they had at least the beginnings of language, but we have no real evidence to support this supposition.[17]

Consider now skipping in time to only 20,000 years ago. By then the only living humans were of the species now recognized as *Homo sapiens*. Tools had become quite sophisticated, and we have every reason to believe that a distinctive human culture was present wherever humans lived—quite widely scattered throughout the planet, including Australia and perhaps (though this remains highly speculative) the American continents. One of the most impressive forms of evidence of the culture of this period is to be found in the artistic productions left in the caves where these people lived or, perhaps more commonly, used as religious centers. Although having fully human physical and cultural characteristics, people then still lived everywhere only as hunters and gatherers. Agriculture was still unknown, as were writing, city life, and the organization of societies into states—to say nothing of television, computers, and space exploration![18]

When was the dawn of human culture? From what we have sketched in the preceeding four paragraphs, we must recognize that there is no simple origin for what we have come to recognize as human culture. Within the great saga of human development as it has gradually unfolded over the past several million years, we can nevertheless recognize certain explosive changes in the way humans have organized their lives. One of these periods of major reorganization began in the eigthteenth century and is still transforming the world. Another was the earlier development of writing, and the formation of cities and states—to which we collectively apply the term of "civilization." More gradual, but still an explosion in the long framework of human prehistory, was the development of artistic creation, such as may be seen in Cro Magnon cave paintings in Western Europe. Probably even more gradual was the development of language. But, if anything like the development of the stone tools (whose remains have been found, which gives us a better record), this too would have come through a series of major transitions—not created in a single language explosion. Even before language development must have been the food-sharing revolution—again, only seen as revolutionary when compared to the millions of years of previous evolution, but no doubt an important early way-station on the road to human culture.[19]

Whatever the process of its creation, human culture has come to represent a new order of reality. No longer are we animals responding directly to a world of physical objects and other living things. We have become instead human animals, who respond much more directly to our worlds of cultural reality. Our fundamental reality has become a combination of the sensory world around us with an imaginary world within our heads. This world within our heads is a symbolic universe, encased in forms which we have forged through our communication with other human beings. This cultural world is no longer an option for us. It is a part of our natures just as surely as are the facts that we regularly sleep at night, smile or laugh when amused, and walk upright.[20]

There are, of course, a variety of realities that can be encased in our cultural forms. Consider such a superficial thing as clothing. Some human groups wear very little clothing, and others concoct quite elaborate modes of dress. Some groups (such as most nations of the Western world) appear to want it both ways, sometimes wearing very little and other times following quite specific codes for formal attire. Even when one is invited to "come as you are," there are still some forms of attire that just wouldn't be suitable; and through our experience with others—mostly through their easy acceptance or their raised eyebrows—we come to know what is suitable for what kind of occasion.

Or take a much more basic embodiment of human culture, that of language. There remain hundreds of distinct languages in use today, though the diversity has been much diminished within the past century. Each of these languages provides not only a working vocabulary for identifying objects of our experience, but also a structure for relating such objects to each other and to ourselves. Within each language is a ready-made structure for thought—for organizing our memories of the past, our perceptions of the present, and our anticipations of the future—which is used to communicate with ourselves as well as with other people.[21]

From the embryology of the nervous system, we learn that some of the cells that end up serving the eye, the lungs, or the stomach begin as undifferentiated cells. These neural crest cells migrate to different parts of what become the spinal column, and the functions they develop there depend on what other cells they encounter. In a highly analogous fashion, individual humans take on the cultural patterns of the area in which they find themselves. Initially, any of a seemingly endless range of possibilities could serve to help shape the person into a human mold. But once a particular pattern takes root, it is extremely difficult to reshape the person into another framework. Even moderate changes of environments may bring on what has become known as "culture shock"; and anyone who has labored to learn a second language as an adult knows how difficult it can be to shake the arbitrary associations encased in one's primary language.[22]

One can see in the diversity of human cultures generally, as in the diversity of languages and tools, an implication about human freedom. We humans can, and have, become many things. But this very diversity of human potentially also leads us to seek some order, to set some limits on what we may become. Our associations with others introduce us to these limits in the form of social and cultural norms. These then become a part of us as we come to realize our own special version of humanity.[23]

Peter Reynolds has recently put forth the hypothesis that evolutionary changes in those brain mechanisms associated with hallucinations are critical in differentiating humans psychologically from other primates. Whatever may be the fate of this as a scientific idea, his name for it—the hypothesis of "functional hallucination"—is an extremely vivid one for suggesting to what great measure humans may be the creators of their own realities. No longer constrained by the immediate present, the human mind can bring into reckoning many other visions of what has been or what might be. But in the company of others, humans have forged limits to this "hallucinatory" process—limits imposed by their own social groups and their cultural traditions.[24]

"In the beginning," Ruth Benedict has quoted from the musings of one Native American chief, "God gave to every people a cup, a cup of clay. And from this cup they drank their life. They all dipped in the water, but their cups were different." It would be hard to imagine a better figure of speech than this to portray both the dependence of humans on a cultural reality and the range of diversity possible for that reality.[25]

In this chapter we have outlined the characteristics of the human animal that are most distinctive; we have also shown how these characteristics might converge in the creation of human culture. In so doing, we recognize that only a small part of the mystery concerning human origins or human nature has been clarified. Much remains only partly understood, and a profound wonder about human emergence is only sharpened by the limited answers we have found so far.

NOTES

1. Other introductory discussions of the nature of human nature include books by Dubos (1968), La Barre (1954), and Montagu (1951). (All works cited in these notes are listed in detail in the Bibliography at the back of this book.)

2. A review of the evidence for genetic similarity of humans and chimpanzees is given in King and Wilson (1975).

3. General reviews of ape language ability are given by Fouts (1975) and by Rumbaugh, Savage-Rumbaugh, and Scanlon (1982). Washoe's language learning is described in detail by Gardner and Gardner (1969). Bronowski and Bellugi (1970) discuss what may be the limits, as well as impressive achievements, in ape language learning.

4. A general survey of primate tool using is given by Beck (1975). A popular account of Jane Goodall's studies of wild chimpanzees is contained in Goodall (1971). The activities of Lana, a computer-trained chimpanzee, are detailed in Rumbaugh and others (1975).

5. Primate sensory abilities are reviewed in Forbes and King (1982a, 1982b).

6. General reviews of primate perceptual abilities may be found in Riesen (1982). Work in cross-modal transfer is reviewed by Rogers and Davenport (1975).

7. Köhler's early studies are described in Köhler (1927). Primate learning abilities are reviewed generally in Forbes and King (1982c), where some studies with other animals are also reviewed. Blue jays and mink are among the animals who do very well on tests of discrimination learning set, often considered a measure of animal intelligence.

8. Evidence for the complex learning summarized here and in the following two paragraphs is reviewed by Forbes and King (1982d).

9. The quotations here regarding ape planning abilities are from Mason (1976), p. 291.

10. Beck (1975) provides a comprehensive review of primate tool using.

11. Reynolds (1981), Chapter 5, includes a thorough discussion of primate exchange systems.

12. The case presented in this paragraph is adapted (not quoted) from de Waal (1982), p. 47. It shows, among other things, the respect with which the chimp called Mama (the leading female in the colony) is treated by other associates at the zoo in Arnhem.

13. Sackett, Gunderson, and Baldwin (1982) summarize developmental patterns among primates, with pp. 155–156 providing an especially helpful table of comparisons.

14. Work with rhesus monkeys by Harry Harlow and associates is summarized in Harlow and Harlow (1966). Jane Goodall's case of Flint, a wild chimpanzee that apparently died of a broken heart after the death of his mother, is summarized by Suomi (1982), pp. 179–180. Research on the early smiling response by humans is summarized in Spitz (1965), especially in Chapter 5.

15. Van Hooff (1967) describes the "silent bared-teeth face" as the closest counterpart to human smiling and the "relaxed open-mouth face" as the closest approach to human laughter. Generally, the primate occasions for these expressions are very different from those of humans. The chimpanzees come the closest to human expressions in both of these facial displays. For example, a chimp can appear to smile freely on a motion picture screen, even though it is likely that a mild electric shock helped to produce this (for the chimp) anxious response (Reynolds, 1981, p. 89). And the chimp's short vocalizations with the relaxed open-mouth display can sometimes be elicited by tickling, which shows a clear similarity to human responses.

16. Isaac (1978) and Lewin (1984) provide further evidence about huminids living about 2 million years ago.

17. Further information about humans about 200,000 years ago can be found in Leakey (1981) or Lewin (1984).

18. Again, Leakey (1981) and Lewin (1984) are among the helpful sources for early *Homo sapiens*. Incidentally, just when humans first came to the Americas is not known with any certainty, though some evidence suggests it may have been as early as the period here described; solid evidence supports a date of at least 11,000 years ago. Certainly America was discovered many years before 1492. It may also be noted that an important discussion of the relation of human biological evolution to the emergence of culture may be found in Dobzhansky and Boesiger (1983).

19. In this paragraph it is suggested that the present computer or information revolution may be seen as a continuation of the mechanical age that began with the industrial revolution. The other "revolutions" here discussed probably are less matters of dispute than how we classify the most recent ones.

20. Of course, we can adjust to daytime sleep or revert temporarily to crawling—and likewise adjust to major shifts in our cultural realities. But these are usually seen as different from normal behavior.

21. Benjamin Whorf (1956) has described every language as "a vast pattern-system, different from others, in which are culturally ordained the forms and categories by which the personality not only communicates, but also analyzes nature, notices or neglects types of relationship and phenomena, channels his reasoning, and builds the house of his consciousness" (p. 252).

22. The example of the neural crest cells is from the description by Kagan (1984), in turn based upon Le Douarin (1982).

23. Some of the writings of Erich Fromm deal with the main point of this paragraph, especially *Escape from Freedom* (Fromm, 1941; see also Fromm, 1947).

24. The hypothesis of "functional hallucination" is developed in Reynolds (1981), especially pp. 251–252.

25. The eloquent philosophy of the Digger Indian chief was originally quoted by Benedict (1934), pp. 21–22.

Chapter 2

The Mystery of Identity

THEORETICAL REFLECTIONS

When does a person develop a sense of identity, of having a self that is both comprehensive and unique? To avoid this question, one may suppose that the self is present before birth, that the self is inherent in the arrangement of protoplasm from the moment of conception—or perhaps as an eternal soul embodied in some other living form even before conception as a fertilized cell. Still, as we look at a newborn infant, we can see no evidence of a sense of identity. Only with time do signs appear to indicate that some form of selfhood is developing.

Consider how people respond in different ways to a baby girl. She recognizes some of these differences within her first year of life; does this not imply some recognition of the self in relation to these others? And the enthusiasm for imitation in the second year—does this depend not only on the child's increasing control of her own behavior, but on some sense that this behavior is becoming distinctively hers? Certainly by the time personal pronouns are correctly used in the third year, she must have made a very clear distinction between the self and others. But there is no obvious normal indicator of the emergence of the self, no point at which, like the body, it is "born" to be part of a new reality.

If it is unclear just *when* the self comes to be, *how* a self-identity comes to be is even more of a mystery. Even if we believe that there is some pre-existing soul (or set of genes, if one prefers a more scientific mode of reference), we must still marvel at how this becomes a self-conscious individual. Of course, there is no end to the speculative answers that may be given to impose a general meaning on the process—from what may be "written in the stars" to what may be nurtured by the differential reinforcement parents give their young children for certain behaviors. Some of the special theories of psychologists and sociologists formulated to help us explain the emergence of the self should be noted.

Let us begin a brief review of social psychological conceptions of the self with the formulations made by that pioneer of American psychology, William James, in the late nineteenth century. James conceptualized the self as consisting of two main aspects. One of these is the self as knower (also called the "I" or the "pure ego"). The other is the self as known (also called the "me" or "empirical ego"). These two aspects of a functional unity are not clearly separated in our commonplace thinking. Nor are they distinct in most empirical observations we make about human behavior. Nevertheless, this duplex nature of the self seemed to James (and to many since him) to assist our psychological analysis of human identity.[1]

The self as knower (or the "I") does not need to be seen in terms of some permanent entity residing in the person. James avoided any assumption of transcendental qualities for this aspect of selfhood; indeed, this requires no permanence beyond the present moment of consciousness. The self as knower is, for James, simply the activity of consciousness; this consciousness can be directed toward anything, including oneself.

To the extent that consciousness is directed toward oneself, the self as known (or the "me") becomes active. This is observed more clearly by others than by the self as knower, for we note what an individual may say about herself as well as the way she says it. We can also note a continuity in this aspect of self from one occasion to another, for there are similarities of self reference that tend to be used repeatedly by the same individual. One's name, occupation, general abilities, and memories of the past do not shift markedly from one occasion to another. But James saw here nothing more continuous than is shown by the common realities of life. The identity thus constructed of the self for oneself is always, for James, "a loosely construed thing" similar to what "any outside observer might find in the same assemblage of facts."[2]

James divided the self as known into three constituent parts: (a) the material me, (b) the social me, and (c) the spiritual me. The material me includes the body, of course, but it also includes the physical objects that surround us. Our home and clothes thus become part of this material self. The social me consists of the reflected appraisals of others around us; it is based on "an innate propensity to get ourselves noticed, and noticed favorably, by our kind." The spiritual me refers to our reflections on our own psychological processes. Thus a woman's sense of her own attention being directed to some object, or her awareness of probing for something she was trying to remember, would be part of her spiritual me. Although there are no religious connotations in this conception of a spiritual me, James did point to the sense of certain of these feelings and desires as being more "the very core and nucleus of our self" than other kinds of self-reflections.[3]

Is the spiritual me, then, the true center of the self? In one sense, this would appear to be the case, for James says that our more active senses of self-consciousness here appear "as if they *went out to meet* all the other elements of our experience." But, in another sense, the material me can be seen as more basic than the others, for the individual can no longer exist if the needs of his body are not attended to. But James is reluctant to give a clear priority to any particular segment of the self, even for needs perceived as biologically based. For a man "is esteemed a poor creature who is unable to forgo a little meat and drink and warmth and sleep for the sake of getting on in the world" and "the social self as a whole ranks higher than the material self as a whole." Finally, the spiritual self is "supremely precious"; in its defense "a man ought to be willing to give up friends and good fame, and property, and life itself."[4]

Although James suggests that the self as known constitutes a kind of unity, he does not give a clear explanation as to why a unity should exist. He specifically avoids basing it on the biological organism. Further, in his discussion of the social self, James makes it quite clear that there can be a wide variety of elements, for *"a man has as many social selves as there are individuals who recognize him* and carry an image of him in their mind." In practical terms, this amounts to a different self for each distinct group of which we are a part. It would appear, then, that any central unity in the self as known must be in that part James called the spiritual me, perhaps reflecting in turn its closeness to the self as knower.[5]

How does the self—as knower or as known—come to be? On this question, James fails to give any systematic answer. He assumes a generally evolutionary context for the development of humans. Through past developments we have, James asserts, acquired a number of instincts, such as "the hunting, the acquisitive, the home-constructiong and tool-constructing instincts, as impulses to self-seeking of the bodily kind" or the equally basic human "desire to please and attract notice and admiration" or "our love of glory, influence and power." We do not, however, find here a clear theory of just how these tendencies were developed in the human species, or how they come to form the self within the life cycle of the individual. How the self comes to be thus remains, in the writings of William James, very much a mystery.[6]

During the first half of the twentieth century, a number of theories were put forth that did give answers to the question of how the individual self came to be. Among these answers are those of the psychoanalytic tradition (especially the psycho-sexual theories of Sigmund Freud) and those of a more cognitively based theory (such as seen in the writings of the gestalt psychologists or those of Jean Piaget). These theories will be discussed at some length later in this book. For purposes of our present discussion, however, we turn to two theorists who were more directly influenced by William James and whose work is more closely related to the issues pursued in the rest of this chapter. These two theorists are Charles H. Cooley and George H. Mead.[7]

Charles Horton Cooley was a rather withdrawn scholar who spent nearly his whole life on or near the campus of the University of Michigan in Ann Arbor. Although not a gregarious man, Cooley was a keen observer of the social life around him, and he had a graceful style of expressing himself in writing. He therefore came to write several highly influential books, and his writings gave at least one clear answer of how the human self came to be.[8]

Not a scholar known for formal research, Cooley got his data as much by watching his own children as from any other source. But his observations, first conveyed in 1902 in *Human Nature and the Social Order*, did lead to a clear conclusion about the emergence of the self. This conclusion is most simply summed up in the metaphor of the "looking-glass self." Let us quote what Cooley had to say on this subject:

> As we see our face, figure, and dress in the glass, and are interested in them because they are ours, and pleased or

otherwise with them according as they do or do not answer to what we should like them to be; so in imagination we perceive in another's mind some thought of our appearance, manners, aims, deeds, character, friends, and so on, and are variously affected by it.

Such an idea of the self has, according to Cooley, "three principal elements: the imagination of our appearance to the other person; the imagination of his judgment of that appearance; and some sort of self-feeling, such as pride or mortification." He continues:

> The thing that moves us to pride or shame is not the mere mechanical reflection of ourselves, but an imputed sentiment, the imagined effect of this reflection upon another's mind. . . . We always imagine, and in imagining share, the judgments of the other mind.

The self, in this view, is an imaginative reconstruction of the meanings of our own actions, using the perspectives of others around us.[9]

Although he cites the earlier work of William James with general approval, Cooley appears to differ in the extent to which the parts of the self are seen as unified, and he also is more clear as to the social sources of that unity. For Cooley, the self is always a social self, emerging through interaction with others. For example, the body is thought of as a part of the self only "when it comes to have social function or significance," and something so private as conscience is as much a social as an individual matter ("individual conscience and the social conscience are not separate things, but aspects of one thing, namely the moral life"). Likewise, the individual and his society always are parts of the same social process. "Our life," Cooley said, "is all one human whole, and if we are to have any real knowledge of it we must see it as such."[10]

Individuals gradually develop their sense of selfhood. "The first definite thoughts that a child associates with self-feeling," according to Cooley, "are probably those of his earliest endeavors to control visible objects—his limbs, his playthings, his bottle, and the like." But soon other persons become central parts of his world, and he attempts to extend his power into this world of people. Of special importance in this is language, for developed thought always involves language. Finally comes the full identification of the individual with various groups, especially groups such as the family that have such a primary influence on shaping his nature.[11]

In the end, though, like James before him, Cooley still had to see part of the emergence of selfhood as residing in our inherited supply of instincts. Cooley could refer to "instinctive self-feeling" as "doubtless connected in evolution with its important function in stimulating and unifying the special activities of individuals." So clearly does this instinct appear to Cooley that he credits an infant with having a self "even in the first weeks" of life. This native feeling of self, however, becomes altered as it takes on personal ideas through interaction with other people.[12]

Despite Cooley's central attention to the role of language in social life, he still did not see the learning of language as providing a necessary mechanism for the emergence of self. It remained for George H. Mead to add this as a central theme for a theory of identity.

George H. Mead, though trained in psychology, was by profession a philospher. Briefly a colleague of Cooley's at the University of Michigan, he spent most of his career as a philosopher at the University of Chicago. There he was associated with the pragmatic movement, which identified the meanings of ideas with their consequences. William James had been an initiator of this movement, and John Dewey was its most active spokesman throughout the first half of the twentieth century. Mead freely acknowledged Dewey's leadership, though on particular social psychological questions it was sometimes Mead who made the more fundamental contribution. This is especially the case with Mead's theory of the origin of the self, which he set forward in his social psychology lectures, published after his death in the book titled *Mind, Self and Society*.[13]

In Mead's view, Cooley had gone only halfway toward an adequate view of the emergence of the self. Cooley had properly shown the close interdependence of the self with other persons by describing how self judgments develop through reflected appraisals. Mead felt, however, that Cooley had been too willing to accept this as occurring within an already formed mind, not questioning how the mind itself came to be. In this Cooley still saw human society as lodged in the minds of individuals rather than as as more objective reality in the collective life of human beings.[14]

For Mead, minds as well as selves arise as social products, and they arise together in the same process. This process is part of that larger whole that is human society. Its foundation may be seen in the internalization of social gestures, or what Mead liked to call "taking the role of the other."

Animals may use social gestures, and it is in such gestures that the beginnings of human communication (and thus too the primary stuff of human society) are to be found. Charles Darwin, for example, had pointed to how initial parts of an act of one animal called forth changes in the actions of another—such as in the posturings of two dogs seeking the same bone. Darwin saw these as examples of innate emotional expression; Mead saw these as signs of something else—social interation in which each individual comes to react to early signs of the other's behavior. Though animals may do this, it is only among humans that the process becomes fraught with symbolic meaning. Somewhere in the human past, the communication of gestures became shortened, so that only the barest beginnings of an act could call forth the full response of another individual. This appeared to happen especially in the case of vocal gestures. Thus was gradually developed human language, as animal gestures came to be replaced by "significant symbols" for human social communication.

The meanings carried by significant symbols are always social in nature. A symbol, in Mead's words, "always presupposes for its significance the social process of experience and behavior in which it arises." This "social process" is primarily a matter of group life, for humans come to develop significant symbols to represent that which is common in their group experience.[15]

This, then, is the foundation Mead saw for the emergence of human selfhood. It grows out of the same conditions as does "mind"—the emergence of significant symbols out of social acts. When these symbols allow an individual to become an object to himself (which means that he has acquired meanings for his gestures similar to the meanings held by those around him), we can say that he has developed a "self."

Selfhood does not emerge all at once in the life of the individual. It tends to develop through a series of stages. First, of course, are the fundamental processes of biological adjustment which have, for humans, an especially social content. Then comes the development of a self through simple role-taking, as the individual develops a sense of his own behavior to reflect the reaction and judgments of his most significant others. But the process, for Mead, does not stop with this "looking-glass self." There is another stage in which the individual comes to reflect not only the specific judgments of others, but the entire constellation of attitudes generally held in his group. "Only insofar as he takes the attitudes of the organized social group to which he belongs," according to Mead, does the individual "develop a complete self." He has then become able to assimilate the attitudes of others into a "generalized other," to serve as the framework of the individual's self-appraisal. This generalized other, in turn, reflects the way the individual's society is organized. This organization provides the larger reality which sets the stage for the particular interactions with other people. Language, which provides a chief vehicle for both communication with others and communication within the self, includes an embodiment of many of the forms of this larger social organization.[16]

The views we have summarized for William James, Charles H. Cooley, and George H. Mead have together come to be known as "symbolic interactionism," and they provide a primary framework for the thinking of most sociologically trained social psychologists. Usually Mead is given special status as providing the final word, in that he built upon the ideas of the others but added a distinctive theory of the origin of mind which those before him had lacked. In any case, we may summarize this tradition of thinking about the nature of human identity by the following set of propositions:

1. The individual develops a sense of self through interaction with others, an interaction through which he tends to reflect the appraisals of his own behavior that he observes in other people. (It follows that only through communication with others can a sense of self develop.)

2. A fully organized self-conception depends on the use of language by organized social groups; only with such language is fully symbolic self-reference possible, and only an organized human society can develop language. (It follows that only humans will have fully developed self-conceptions, for this reflects the distinctive symbolic quality of human society.)

3. As the social environment of the individual changes, so also will his sense of self change. (If the self is anchored in social interaction with others, it follows that changed contexts of interaction should lead to changed self-conceptions. Thus the self needs to be seen as a part of an ever-changing process of social adjustment.)

It is often held that the main ideas of symbolic interactionism are not in themselves amenable to empirical test. That has been the main complaint made by psychologists about the self theories of James, Cooley and Mead—not that such ideas are implausible, only that they have such a general character as to be unsuitable for precise scientific work. It is for this reason that much of twentieth century psychology (in contrast to sociology) has given such limited recognition to Cooley and Mead. Sometimes the symbolic interactionists themselves have seemed to agree that their basic ideas need to be perceived as general truths rather than demonstrated through empirical research—Cooley himself practically asserted as much. But we do not need to leave these reflections on human selfhood on such a theoretical and nonempirical level. We may instead use them as a starting point for examining some things that empirical work has revealed about identity formation and change. By the end of this chapter, we hope to be able to say whether or not each of the three key propositions we have just summarized is primarily supported or not supported by the evidence. Not to give too much away in advance, it might not be out of line to anticipate that we will discover that at least one of these three propositions is well confirmed by the evidence, but that at least one of the other two is clearly unsatisfactory.[17]

REFLECTIONS OF ANOTHER SORT

Given the rich supply of observations of the behavior of children before mirrors, as well as Cooley's suggestive "looking-glass self" metaphor, it is surprising that systematic studies of self recognition through the use of mirrors were not done before the late 1960s. A rather simple technique was then independently developed by two investigators that could clearly indicate the presence or absence of self-recognition. Such recognition of the self as a distinctive individual reflected in the mirror could then be taken as indicating a relatively well-established sense of selfhood.

Similar mirror techniques for experimental studies of self-recognition were developed by Beulah Amsterdam and Gordon Gallup. The basic procedure involved an unnoticed brightly colored mark added to a part of the face that a subject could not see directly, then providing a mirror and observing how the subject responds to a mirror image. If the response is to move the hands directly to the spot on the face, this would be a fairly objective indicator of recognition that one's own body is being reflected in the mirror. Other forms of behavior before the mirror can be used as supplemental evidence of the kind (or absence) of self-recognition that may be taking place.

We will first note Beulah Amsterdam's work, which was done for her doctoral dissertation, with the studies of Gallup to be discussed later. Amsterdam studied eighty-eight children with ages ranging from three to twenty-four months, including two males and two females at each age level (in months). While being undressed by the mother, each child was given a spot of rouge on the side of the nose. Attention was then directed to a mirror, and the mother and an observer followed a standard procedure to assure that the child would attend to his or her own reflection. The observer took careful note of everything the child did, which later allowed a general categorization of this behavior. Most children under twelve months seemed mainly to interest themselves with the movement in the mirror, and those between six and fourteen months appeared to treat their reflection as a sociable playmate. No children under eighteen months showed clear signs of self-recognition, while most children over twenty months clearly recognized the image as their own reflection.[18]

Amsterdam has followed up this research with suggestions on how it relates to stages in child development, especially as conceived in the psychoanalytic literature. Others who have pursued similar research methods have tended to corroborate her findings. Probably the most extensive related research has been that carried out by Michael Lewis and Jeanne Brooks-Gunn, reported in their book, *Social Cognition and the Acquisition of the Self*. After using not only mirror techniques similar to those of Amsterdam, but also systematic use of videotapes and pictoral representation of the self and others, Lewis and Brooks-Gunn suggest that the beginnings of visual self-recognition may occur near the end of the first year, and that some children may show full self-recognition by as early as fifteen months—slightly younger than Amsterdam had found. Between eighteen and twenty-one months there is a large increase in self-recognition as shown by a variety of different methods. Although avoiding any interpretation in terms of definite stages of development, Lewis and Brooks-Gunn find self recognition to be well established in nearly all children beyond the second year of age. But this success in recognizing an image as that of oneself must follow a much earlier developed set of skills. Among such skills are recognizing the differences in effects of one's own actions and those of other persons (developed in the first few months of life); noting the permanence of objects, including one's own body (usually late in the first year of life); and providing for cognitive and linguistic representation of the world (primarily developed in the second year). Throughout the process of developing a sense of a distinct self, the young child is also developing a sense of differences among other persons. As these authors conclude:

> Knowledge of self and others, both being aspects of social knowledge, proceeds in parallel fashion, developing at the same time and from the same material. Moreover, this development has as its source the interaction of the young organism with others— both people and objects.

Such implications are clearly in line with most of the theoretical reflections presented in the first section of this chapter.[19]

As we mentioned earlier, Gordon Gallup has also pioneered in experimental studies of self recognition through the use of mirrors. The most interesting thing about his work is that it shows how human self-recognition may compare to that shown by other animals, since Gallup's research has been primarily with nonhuman animals.

Even in lower animals, such as goldfish or chickens, mirrors can have important effects upon behavior. Some birds show clear preferences for being near mirrors rather than in other settings, even sometimes preferring the mirror to another bird or food. In one interesting study, the mirror behavior of monkeys born in the wild was compared to that of animals born in the laboratory and reared in social isolation. It was found that the socially isolated monkeys were more interested in viewing the mirror than the sight of another monkey, while the opposite was the case with the more normally reared monkeys. However, none of the animals we have mentioned were found by Gallup to show any signs of self-recognition, even though spot-marking tests were specifically applied to monkeys of at least three different species.[20]

Does this mean that humans are the only animals that show clear signs of recognizing themselves in a mirror? Not quite, for Gallup also did a study with several chimpanzees born and raised in the wild. Tested individually, these animals first were systematically introduced to mirrors (for ten days). The mirrors, especially after the first day or two, seemed to provide a clear stimulus for responses toward their own bodies, suggesting the presence of self-recognition. This was then confirmed by anesthesizing the animals, marking them with red dye above their eyebrows, and observing their subsequent reactions (after they recovered from the anesthesia) in front of a mirror. Attention to their mirror images increased markedly, and even more dramatic was the attention paid to the place on their own bodies where the red mark had been added. These chimps clearly passed the test of self-recognition.[21]

Apparently, previous experience with mirrors was an important ingredient in producing these results, for Gallup repeated the experiment with other chimps who had not had such previous acquaintance with mirrors, and, in these cases, the dye on their own bodies was ignored. "Throughout the test," reports Gallup, "their orientation to the mirror was as though they were seeing another chimpanzee." Also, when the experiment was repeated with chimps who had been reared in social isolation, the results for self recognition were consistently negative, even when allowing for extensive previous experience with mirrors. This suggests that selfhood depends on previous experience with others, and that its demonstration through mirror experimental techniques also depends on some previous experience with seeing the self in a mirror. Normally, the previous social experience is with others of the same species; however, anecdotal evidence suggests that chimps brought up among humans also have self-conceptions—but with a distinctly human flavor. A dramatic instance of this was when Vicki, a chimp reared as a human child, without hesitation sorted her own picture into a human pile rather than classifying it as an animal.[22]

What about other apes? Not surprisingly, attempts to identify self-recognition in gibbons (apes, though not among the great apes) have not been successful. More surprising has been the lack of success in several attempts with gorillas. Given the general similarity of gorillas to both chimpanzees and humans, it might be expected that they would show similar self-recognition through experience with mirrors; however, so far all results with gorillas have proved negative.

So are chimps and humans alone in providing clear evidence of selfhood? No, for mirror recognition results similar to that for chimpanzees have also been obtained with those solitary great apes from the East Indies, orangutans. Although not studied as extensively as chimps, orangutans also show solid evidence for self–recognition. We must therefore count so far three currently living species as giving clear evidence of the attainment of a self-conscious personal identity. This refutes one common notion of human distinctiveness, showing, as Gallup has put it, that "man may not be evolution's only experiment in self-awareness."[23]

GAMES INFANTS PLAY

In Sigmund Freud's psycho-sexual theory of early development, a sense of identity is gradually developed as the "ego" becomes differentiated from the more primitive "id." However, in his theory, it is usually only after the first four years of life that a fully social self begins to emerge in the form of the "superego," with its behavioral counterparts of moral self-judgment and gender identification. In Jean Piaget's more cognitively based theory, egocentric thought is seen as predominating not only the early "sensorimotor" period (essentially the first two years) but the "preoperational" stage as well (that is, up until about the age of seven). George H. Mead was not as clear as Freud or Piaget about how his stages of development might be applied concretely to studies of child development, but he too set forth his theory in terms of stages. Children in Mead's "play" stage were only capable of taking on particular roles of others, while those in the "game" stage were able to adjust to an entire constellation of roles. It is only in the game stage that we have a fully socialized self; and while an age level for this cannot be very precisely given, it would clearly not precede the systematic use of language.

All of these stage theories have made important contributions to our understanding of early social development, and all have some empirical support to validate their distinctions between stages. But recent evidence also indicates a key problem with these theories: They all draw our attention away from very important beginnings of a social identity within the first two years of life. By characterizing early development in other terms, they all fail to recognize the extent to which the differentiation of a socialized self-concept might be developing even in the very earliest months of an infant's life.[24]

John S. Watson has been involved in a remarkable series of experiments with eight-week-old infants that show an unusual facility to initiate social games. The natural counterpart of what

Watson calls "The Game" occurs when adults approach the infant and, in Watson's words,

> They touch his nose each time he widens his eyes, or they bounce him on their knee each time he bobs his head, or they blow on his belly each time he jiggles his legs, or they make sounds after he makes a sound.

What all of these have in common is that the adult produces an act closely contingent upon some special behavior of the infant. As such a game is played repeatedly, the infant soon shows pleasurable emotion in the form of vigorous smiling and cooing.[25]

Watson and his associates developed artificial analogues of such a social situation. For example, one experiment compared infants with mobiles activated by their own pillow movements to other groups of infants. One control group had similarly placed objects that did not move, and another group had mobiles with essentially random movement. Those infants whose pillows activated mobiles clearly showed more pillow activity (which generally increased over time for the two weeks of the experiment) than did those in the other two treatment groups. What is even more noteworthy was the marked smiling and cooing activity that accompanied these pillow movements (after the first two days or so) of those who were activating mobiles. They seemed to take a real pleasure in their successful control of this part of their environment. Watson sees this as very similar to the way an infant of the same age will enjoy social play with an adult caregiver.

This association of vigorous smiling with "The Game"— whether played with a real mother or a mobile above the crib— suggests some sense of pleasure is associated with distinct actions of oneself that have recognizable consequences. Indeed, we may see in such activities very simple beginnings of self-consciousness as early as eight weeks of age.

Watson realizes that "The Game," and the pleasure infants appear to derive from it, can be seen from at least two perspectives. According to one perspective, the pleasure comes because of association with a primary caregiver. Thus infants come to enjoy this kind of playful interaction because they are attached to their caregivers. However, Watson thinks that another interpretation fits his experimental data better. The signs of pleasure at a human face tend to come later than the period used for his studies; and, besides, he obtained clear signs of pleasurable interaction without using human responses at all. He therefore suggests the hypothesis that

> "The Game" is NOT important to the infant because people play it, but rather people become important to the infant because they play "The Game."

According to this hypothesis, infants come to smile at another person in a face-to-face position (and, as studies have shown, not at a face turned some other way) because this is the position most used when adults play "The Game"—that is, when they provide episodes that confirm the infant's ability to show some mastery of the immediate environment.[26]

Whatever significant social interaction may be going on at eight weeks, we will soon see evidence that significant discriminations among other people occur within the first year. Some of these discriminations imply at least the beginnings of a consciousness of oneself as an entity.

Just as Charles Cooley got some of his main insights from observing his own children, so Michael Lewis noticed in 1962 something remarkable in the behavior of his daughter, then about eight months of age. As should be expected from the child-development literature, Felicia tended to withdraw from strangers. Such a discrimination between familiar persons and strangers is apparently easily made by persons at this age. But Lewis noticed something else: Felicia did not show this "stranger fear" toward friends of her three-year-old brother, even when meeting them for the first time. Apparently, this fear of strangers was selective; some strangers more "like me" might be more acceptable. Or at least the hypothesis was suggested that selective interaction on the basis of some beginning notion of the self might be observed even within the first year of life. Such thoughts led Lewis (unlike Cooley before him) to consider how he might submit his thinking to a systematic experimental test.[27]

In an experiment with twenty-four subjects, ages seven to nineteen months, Michael Lewis and Jeanne Brooks tested reactions to various kinds of strangers. A male adult, a female adult, and a four-year-old child were presented under standard conditions, each approaching close enough to touch the subject's hand. Finally, either the mother then approached the child in a similar way, or the child was moved to view itself closely in a mirror. The child was very carefully observed, with detailed behavior ratings made.

Interview data were also taken from the mother, and special tests were later made of the child's cognitive development.[28]

The results were quite striking in demonstrating that the child responded quite differently to another child than to an adult. Responses tended to be mildly positive toward another child, while those toward an adult stranger became increasingly negative the closer that the adult approached. In contrast, reactions toward the mother or toward the mirrored image of oneself tended to be positive—and increasingly positive as they came closer to the child. While similar patterns applied for both younger and older subjects in this study, reactions (positive toward the self or mother, and negative toward adult strangers) tended to be more strongly exhibited by those subjects over one year old. Generally, girls and boys showed similar patterns in relations to strangers, though there was some evidence that girls are more fearful of male adult strangers than are boys.

"Perhaps," say Lewis and Brooks in interpreting their most striking finding, "the positive response to the child stranger is produced because the infants find the child to be like themselves; that is, they use themselves as a referent, find the child like them, and are therefore not afraid." They see this as indicative of something of a categorical self already developed by the child. Not only is she distinguishing between herself and her mother—this is done much earlier—but she is also, by the end of the first year, beginning to view the self in terms of a more differentiated set of personal categories. These authors believe that their own work, as well as the research of others, is sufficient to demonstrate that even very young children begin to differentiate themselves and other persons on the basis of familiarity, age, and gender. Such differentiation is well underway even before a clear demonstration of self–recognition can be documented in mirror studies.[29]

The research we have cited so far in this section shows that, long before a distinct sense of self recognition is evident (which in turn is usually shortly before the end of the second year), important distinctions are made between the self and others. Pleasurable association of others with particular kinds of actions of oneself begin within the first three months; and by one year of age most infants distinguish among other people—even among other people not previously seen—on the basis of simple similarities or differences to oneself. This does not mean that a full cognition of the self has emerged, only that some of the key ingredients are there, waiting to be given systematic organization as the child's cognitive powers increase.

At times even very young children appear to show remarkable insight into the feelings of their fellows. Martin Hoffman, for example, cites the case of little Michael:

> Michael, aged 15 months, and his friend Paul were fighting over a toy and Paul started to cry. Michael appeared disturbed and let go, but Paul still cried. Michael paused, then brought his teddy bear to Paul but to no avail. Michael paused again, and then finally succeeded in stopping Paul's crying by fetching Paul's security blanket from an adjoining room.

Michael here shows not only the imagination to get a special object for his friend from another room; he also shows an ability to distinguish between Paul's motives and his own. Such cognitively differentiated empathy is probably rare in a child as young as Michael. Still, such cases suggest that an ability to take the role of the other need not wait for the egocentric stage to end at age seven or so; rather, the sense of particular others and their needs may develop side-by-side with a sense of one's own selfhood. Indeed, all the evidence we have examined in this chapter is consistent with the idea that these are not two separate processes. One develops a sense of self as one develops a sense of others. A self-concept emerges along with a sense of personal identity for others.[30]

So the games infants play with their parents and with each other begin to shape them in the direction of self-consciousness long before their talk can bear witness to the mastery of first person pronouns. Such situations of interaction with others is apparently the stuff out of which selfhood develops in children. In all children? Well, nearly all, and the process is so normal that the exceptions provide us with puzzled concern. The fact remains that there are some children who are severely autistic, who appear unable to make genuine contact with other people despite being offered every opportunity. Such cases remind us of the importance of contact with others for the normal development of the self. They also imply that certain processes of the human brain need to be present if one is to assimilate social experience into a normal form of personal identity.[31]

THE SOCIAL RECONSTRUCTION OF IDENTITY

If it is true that a sense of personal identity develops through interaction with other people, we would not expect that identity, once emerged, to remain static. After all, relationships to others do not remain unchanged. Why should not the self continue to change as one's social interaction with others changes?

Certain cases of persons we may have known, or otherwise heard about, tell us that personal identities may be reconstructed. However, we often do not realize to what extent the process is predictable or can be applied by those segments of society that are especially in the person-remaking business. We of course think of schools and religious organizations as important socializing institutions, and at times their impact can be significant in reshaping human lives. But most often such establishments promote continuity; they tend to encourage a sense of selfhood similar to that already developed. Some other establishments, however, are not as accepting of their members just the way they are.[32]

Sanford Dornbush has shown how military academies serve as agents of resocialization. He describes in detail the way the United States Coast Guard Academy "isolates cadets from the outside world, helps them to identify themselves with a new role, and thus changes their self-conception." Basic training for military forces everywhere is similarly geared to produce not only technical training in certain military skills but also a reshaping of the self so that an individual comes to look upon himself as a soldier—ready to do the often disagreeable things that soldiers are called upon to do.[33]

Even more extreme examples of the reshaping of the self through social settings can be given. Erving Goffman, for example, has traced what he calls the "moral career" of a mental patient, suggesting how the process of confinement for mental illness may itself be a key determinant of the individual's self-conception. "The self," he concludes,

> can be seen as something that resides in the arrangements prevailing in a social system for its members. The self in this sense is not a property of the person to whom it is attributed, but dwells rather in the pattern of social control that is exerted in connection with the person by himself and those around him.

Also, Bruno Bettelheim's recollections of his own experience as a political prisoner of the Nazis point out how destructive of any pre-existing sense of self such an ordeal could be. Many long-term prisoners with Bettelheim actually took on for themselves the attitudes and behaviors of their Gestapo guards, as they adjusted to the prison setting.[34]

But, of course, these are not the usual settings of most adults. In most situations there is a more diversified opportunity for the development of social identities, reflecting what the individual wants to put forth to define the self as well as what others want to accept. Such more tolerant settings for self-construction still involve socially situated identities. Expectations associated with age, occupation, and gender roles are examples of how interaction with others tends to shape the identity a person may take on and claim. Even more informally structured expectations—and sometimes especially such more informal cues—may be incorporated into one's sense of self in a given social setting.[35]

We would be remiss, however, if we left the impression that Cooley's metaphor of a looking-glass self would be as applicable to the shaping of personal identities throughout life as it is for the initial development of a sense of selfhood. There are at least four reasons why our personal identities tend over time to become progressively less responsive to signals from other people around us.[36]

First, the sense of self, once formed, becomes a filter for interpreting the reactions of others. One selectively perceives signals from other persons in terms of their congruence to one's own self-conception; and even when the perception of the views of others is not distorted, the meanings for their actions may be misinterpreted. Furthermore, the individual is not typically a passive agent in interacting with others, but the interaction is itself shaped to serve the interests of one's own sense of selfhood.[37]

A second reason why personal identities may not freely shift with changing social contexts lies in the ambiguities of social settings. Most social settings are ambiguous in the signals they give us. A full sense of selfhood is seldom conveyed by any consensus of others present. In fact, for many settings there may not even be a dominant social role that is expected to anchor a person's interaction. When this is the case, the likelihood is increased that the individual will fall back on a dominant pre-existing sense of selfhood to guide the construction of a present personal identity.[38]

A third point regarding the limits to which selves may be reshaped through interaction with others lies in the fact that the immediate situation gives only part of the interaction that an individual has available. The person has the memories of past self-other interaction in comparable situations as well. Once a reflective self-consciousness has been attained, each person carries a veritable library of memories, available for re-reading in the face of a new situation. No one else has this same body of information to draw upon, which leaves other persons less effective than oneself in trying to frame signals that might control the construction of one's present sense of identity.[39]

Finally, one's sense of selfhood is not just a product of social definition. Individuals come to know who they are by seeing for themselves what they can do. This is only partly filtered by the reactions of others; it is also seen in the more direct feedback a person may have regarding his or her actions. A person's concept of his ability for football, for instance, may be much more the result of what he learns in scrimmage than what he hears from his coach or his teammates.[40]

To return to the conceptualizations of William James presented earlier in this chapter, it may be true that a person has "as many different social selves as there are distinct *groups* of persons about whose opinion he cares." We thus develop, to some degree, a different social self for each group or social situation we enter. But, as James pointed out, the social self is only part of the self. Perhaps Charles Cooley and George Mead were too ready to promote the social self to center stage, but James was quite clear that there are also physical and private (or strictly subjective) aspects that become important parts of self-conceptions. Then there is also the self as knower, as well as the self as known; and in that active seeking out for consciousness, there are important individual differences that must have at least indirect effects upon the identity one comes to fashion. These have effects for the self in general as well as for the construction of the self in any particular social setting.[41]

Fairly strong evidence for temperamental differences that may affect styles of self-conceptualization has been given by Mark Snyder. A "self-monitoring scale" was developed by Snyder to measure the extent to which a person self-consciously reflects cues of the immediate social situation. Application of this scale to studies of twins has shown that its results correlate very closely with degrees of genetic similarity. Identical twins give practically the same results, while fraternal twins show far less similarity—though still much more than randomly sorted pairs. Such results indicate that elements of a person's style of self-conceptualization (including probably aspects of William James' "spiritual me" as well as the self as knower) may be rooted in important genetic differences.[42]

RECONSIDERATION

At the end of the first section of this chapter, we put forward three main propositions. These summarized the theoretical reflections on the nature of self reviewed to that point in our explorations. To conclude, we now reconsider these propositions, giving special attention to the empirical work reviewed since we first presented these propositions.

"The individual develops a sense of self through interaction with others, an interaction through which he tends to reflect the appraisals of his own behavior that he observes in other people." This was our first proposition, and we have seen little to suggest a need for its revision. All the evidence we have reviewed—including studies of apes as well as of young human children—supports the notion that the sense of one's own personal identity develops side-by-side with a sense of the identity of others; the two appear to be parts of the same process, which occurs only through social interaction. Our only qualification is that the "looking-glass self" metaphor may give too strong an emphasis to the reflected appraisal (or role-taking) aspects of self formation. Social interaction always combines at least three influences for self-conceptualization: (1) a social setting in which an individual may observe the physical effects of his actions, (2) a social setting in which one may internalize the evaluative reactions of other people, and (3) a social setting in which one may compare his behavior to that of others. It may well be that the second of these three influences may be most critical for an initial development of a personal identity (as Cooley and Mead assumed). However, self-conceptualizations in later life seem to be less influenced by the reflected appraisals of others than by other social forces or (especially) by one's previously developed sense of identity.

"A fully organized self-conception depends on the use of language by organized social groups, for only with such language is fully symbolic self-reference possible, and only an organized human society can develop language." This was our rather complex second proposition, emphasizing the importance of organized society and its forms of symbolic communication for the development of selfhood. Despite its reasonable sound, this proposition can no longer be considered as well supported. Man is not alone in having a capacity for selfhood (or apparently for symbolic communication either), and those great apes that have also shown a capacity for personal identity have generally done so without language and without complex forms of social organization. Also, studies of the emergence of self-recognition in children show that this does not depend on the prior use of language—even though language learning tends to follow rather closely. It therefore seems appropriate to conclude that a sense of personal identity may be greatly enriched by symbolic abilities, but an initial sense of selfhood does not require symbolic communication.[43]

"As the social environment of the individual changes, so also will his sense of self change." This was our third proposition, and we must now recognize only mixed support. It is better supported than our second proposition, but not so well as our first. The main problem is not that we cannot agree with the statement, for we have found nothing that sharply contradicts it. The problem is that it does not tell us *how much* change of the self will occur with changes in the social environment. As we have seen in our discussion of the social reconstruction of identity, there are important limits to the extent to which personal identities may change. Perhaps it would be more accurate to conclude only that as the social environment of the individual changes, so will there be *influences* toward a changed sense of self—especially when the sense of selfhood is not firmly fixed or when there are fairly great changes in the social environment.[44]

In the present chapter we have pieced together some clues regarding the mystery of identity. If we have shed some light on the subject of how we know who we are, we have also pointed to much that remains unanswered. What evolutionary processes, for example, led certain segments of the order of primates to develop habits of self-reference? What characteristics of the human brain continue to provide special support for this as a normal part of being human? And what, more precisely than we have identified, are the social conditions for significant changes in self-conceptions? We have only offered a few hints toward the answers of such questions. Much more remains unanswered than we have been able to clarify.

NOTES

1. The theory of the self of William James may be found in James (1890/1892), especially Chapter 12.

2. The quotation here is from James (1890/1892), p. 205.

3. The quotes in this paragraph are from James (1890/1892), pp. 179 and 181, respectively.

4. The first quote in this paragraph is from James (1890/1892), p. 181 (italics in original); all other quotations are from p. 191.

5. The quote is from James (1890/1892), p. 179 (italics in original).

6. All quotes in this paragraph are from James (1890/1892), p. 184.

7. Further information about Freud's theories of the self may be found in his own extensive writings or in Hall (1954) or Schellenberg (1978). A gestaltist view is found in Koffka (1924). Summaries of Piaget's theories may be found in Piaget (1977) or Voyat (1982).

8. Cooley's life and works are described in Coser (1971), pp. 304–330.

9. The quotations here may be found in Cooley (1902), pp. 184–185.

10. "Man's psychical outfit," said Cooley (1902), "is not divisible into the social and the non-social"; rather, "he is all social in a large sense, is all a part of the common human life" (p. 47). Quotations included in the main text are from Cooley (1902), pp. 183 and 377, and from Cooley (1909), p. vii (the opening words of his Preface).

11. The quote early in this paragraph is from Cooley (1902), p. 177. On the subject of language, Cooley further said that because language has been "developed by the race through personal intercourse and imparted to the individual in the same way," it "can never be dissociated from personal intercourse in the mind; and since higher thought involves language, it is always a kind of imaginary conversation" (pp. 91–92). The subject of group identification is discussed at length in Cooley (1909), where the concept of the "primary group" (referring to those face-to-face groups with primary influence in shaping the individual and also primary in the organization of the social order) is presented.

12. The quotes here are from Cooley (1902), pp. 177 and 178, respectively.

13. Mead's main contribution to a theory of identity is to be found in Mead (1934). General descriptions of Mead's life and thought may be found in Coser (1971), pp. 332–355, and Schellenberg (1978), pp. 38–62.

14. Such ideas are most clearly presented in Mead (1930).

15. The quote is from Mead (1934), p. 89.

16. The quotation in this paragraph is from Mead (1934), p. 155.

17. That Cooley was more concerned with "sympathetic introspection" (as his method has sometimes been called) than experimental research is well illustrated by this comment, after his general discussion of primary groups: "If this view does not recommend itself to common-sense I do not know that elaboration will be of much avail" (Cooley, 1909, p. 30).

18. This research is described in Amsterdam (1972). Her analysis of how this relates to stages of early development are also found there, as well as in Amsterdam and Levitt (1980).

19. The quotation here is from Lewis and Brooks-Gunn (1979), p. 241. On the subject of stages in the development of self-recognition, these authors say that they "do not support a stage concept; rather, we prefer to think of self-recognition as a continuous process, a slow transformation and addition of new skills into a growing repertoire of behaviors we call self–recognition" (p. 219).

20. This research is described in Gallup (1975).

21. This work is also described in Gallup (1970) and Gallup (1977).

22. The quote in this paragraph is from Gallup (1977), p. 333. Further information in this paragraph is based on Gallup (1983), with the case of Vicki recounted on p. 486.

23. Recent reviews of self recognition (or the lack thereof) in the great apes are found in Gallup (1982) and Gallup (1983). The final quote in this section is from Gallup (1977), p. 333.

24. Stage theories of child development are discussed in many textbooks. For example, Biehler and Hudson (1986) give a detailed review of the theories of both Freud and Piaget.

25. The quotation here is from Watson (1972), p. 324. It is also worth noting that when adults play such games with an infant, they usually present themselves in a direct face-to-face manner.

26. This hypothesis about "The Game" is quoted from Watson (1972), p. 338. Earlier research dealing with infant reactions to faces is discussed in Spitz (1965).

27. The description of the initiation of this line of research is included in the Preface of Lewis and Brooks-Gunn (1979), pp. vii–viii.

28. This research, including its results, is presented in Lewis and Brooks (1974).

29. The quotation is from Lewis and Brooks (1974), p. 219. Further discussion of the significance of such research is given in Lewis and Brooks-Gunn (1979), especially Chapter 9.

30. The charming case of little Michael is presented by Hoffman (1975), p. 612.

31. Exactly what brain functions are involved in autism (or at least in forms of autism) is not clearly known. However, there is at least strong evidence that severely autistic persons do differ in important neurological ways from most other human beings (Courchesne and others, 1988).

32. Some religious sects do attempt (often with success) to restructure the lives of their new members. However, this is not characteristic of most mainline groups. Even those Protestant churches with a strong evangelistic emphasis tend to be quite modest in their social expectations associated with the theological turning point of being "born again." Also, some special schools may have a heavy resocialization function, but this is hardly characteristic of most public education.

33. The quote is from Dornbush (1955), p. 321. The movie *An Officer and a Gentleman* gives a dramatic, if idealized, illustration of the possible effects of military training for the self-conception. The discussion of Dyer (1985) is also applicable, especially Chapter 5 (titled "Anybody's Son Will Do").

34. Goffman's comment about the socially constructed self of a mental patient may be found in Goffman (1959a), p. 141. An insightful analysis of concentration camp experiences may be found in Bettelheim (1943).

35. Rich insight about informal influences upon self construction and presentation is found in Goffman (1959b).

36. To the specific points discussed here could perhaps be added a general decline in human plasticity with age. However, we should note that we may learn to be especially sensitive to certain kinds of influences, so that our behaviors may become more responsive to cues from others even while our personal identities may remain quite stable.

37. Greenwald (1980) goes so far as to characterize the self-protective measures as bearing witness to a "totalitarian ego." He sees the ego as an organization of knowledge "characterized by cognitive biases strikingly analogous to totalitarian information-control strategies" that "function to preserve organization in cognitive structures" (p. 603). Swann (1985) also reviews evidence for the active role of the self in seeking to confirm its sense of identity.

38. Also, times change; and the extent to which a self is anchored in a relatively stable social structure varies greatly from time to time and from place to place. With rapid personal and social change, the self may become more of a process of continual adjustment than a fixed structure anchored in a basic social reality. For evidence and analysis of this possibility, see Zurcher (1977).

39. Of course, memories are highly selective; so memories of past interaction may differ from what actually happened. But this just further illustrates the extent to which the individual may provide his own self-constructed material for a present sense of identity.

40. Solid evidence to support the football example is given by Felson (1981a, 1981b). Further evidence for the limited role that socially reflected appraisals may play in personal identities is reviewed by Shrauger and Schoeneman (1979) and by Gecas and Schwalbe (1983).

41. The early quote in this paragraph is from James (1892), p. 179 (italics in original). With regard to the self as knower and as subjectively experienced, Rosenberg (1979) provides evidence that children become more internally self-reflective with age. The self-conceptions of young children are rooted more in their physical natures and in stable social definitions than is the case with older children, who tend to become more introspective. Rosenberg suggests that this change may itself be a product of a child's increased skills of communication, which may be turned inward in self-reflective thought, as well as outward in a more sensitive reading of the thoughts and feelings of other people.

42. See Snyder (1987), especially Chapter 10.

43. The position implied here is that simple thinking and self-conscious reflection may occur without language, but that an ability for such thinking (as well as a social process to give substance to self-conceptions) is a prerequisite for selfhood. This position is more in harmony with Furth (1966) than Mead (1934). Interestingly, even Benjamin Whorf—usually considered as something of a linguistic determinist—can be cited in support of this position. Says Whorf (1956, p. 239): "My own studies suggest, to me, that language, for all its kingly role, is in some sense a superficial embroidery upon deeper processes of consciousness, which are necessary before any communication, signaling, or symbolism whatsoever can occur, and which also can, at a pinch, effect communication (though not true AGREEMENT) without language's and without symbolism's aid."

44. Our discussion of this issue provides only the barest introduction to the extensive literature of social influences upon self-conceptualization. Much more is known than our brief summary has been able to indicate. Further reviews of this literature are included in Baumeister (1986), Gergen (1971), Gordon and Gergen (1968), Mischel (1977), Rosenberg (1979), and Wylie (1961, 1974, 1979).

Chapter 3

The Mystery of Conscience

In the present chapter we seek to unravel one central element among those serving to bind the individual so closely into the social fabric. This is the inner sense of right and wrong, most commonly referred to as conscience.

For any society, most social control is self-control. The socialization process works to produce a person who generally seeks what is necessary to live as a proper member of society. As one psychologist has expressed it, the child "acquires that character which makes him want to do what he has to do" to live in society. This happens in two main ways: (1) by building into social institutions various sets of incentives, so that persons are generally rewarded for socially constructive behavior and punished for other kinds of actions; and (2) by building into the individual an inner sense of what is right and wrong, so that he will be comfortable and self-satisfied when doing what his society considers good and uneasy about doing what is considered wrong—even when no one else is present. We will for present purposes leave aside discussion of the first of these two aspects of socialization. The second is the subject of this chapter.[1]

SIGMUND FREUD'S MYTH

How do we account for our most basic notions of morality? Why have humans developed such numerous moral prohibitions and taboos? And what forces impel us to feel guilty about breaking these standards of propriety?[2]

Sigmund Freud once told a story that implied answers to these questions. Freud borrowed from Charles Darwin the assumption of a primal horde. This meant for Freud that in the early dawn of development, human social organization was built around bands of females and children dominated in each case by a powerful old male. The old man kept all the females for himself, and the younger rivals—sons and all—were driven off. Such a band is the setting for Freud's story.

One day, so the story goes, the brothers joined forces and killed their father. "Of course," says Freud, "these cannibalistic savages ate their victim"; thus "they accomplished their identification with him" and sought to gain "a part of his strength." But they also had more positive sentiments toward their father, now deceased, and they sought some means whereby he could be considered to live on. His most immediate rebirth was in their own guilty consciences over what they had done. Also, they created taboos to continue the old man's prohibitions. "What the father's presence had formerly prevented, they themselves now prohibitied"; they outlawed killing "the father substitute, the totem" and denied themselves sexual access to the women. Thus were created the two basic prohibitions of primitive society—against murder and incest. Thus also was created the original form of human religion, totemism.[3]

This is, of course, an outrageous story, and it may amuse us that Freud took seriously the notion that something of this sort might have actually happened way back in the mists of time. But questions of historical details aside, what main ideas can we derive from this story? Let us list them in the form of three propositions that all repeat a central Freudian theme:

1. The original form of human religion, totemism, emerged out of the ambivalence of sons toward fathers.

2. Primitive morality reflected at its core this same ambivalence, and the guilty consciences developed as a result.

3. Morality ever since has been supported by the same forms of ambivalence and feelings of guilt.

Let us examine these ideas further to consider what merit they have. Along with several other scholars of his time, Freud assumed that all religions emerged out of totemism, a form of primitive religion in which a natural object (usually a particular species of animal) was revered as a representative of the clan or tribe. Freud also believed that totemism everywhere included not only an identification of the family, tribe, or clan with an animal symbol but also a recognition of this animal as the group's ancestor; and there were always rituals for participating in the spiritual power of the totem, and taboos against killing this animal except for the special ceremony of the totemic feast. Assuming such features to be universal experiences of early man, Freud sought their roots in a common human theme. The theme he pointed to was the rivalry of sons with fathers. Everywhere sons have resented the power and privilege of their fathers, and how much more must this have been the case when the human family was based (or at least as Freud imagined it was based) more simply on the brute strength of dominant males. But sons have also always admired their fathers and thus felt guilty about their acts of rebellion. In totemism we have the collective expression of this guilt projected toward an animal that symbolizes paternity. The moral taboos against murder and incest are a part of the same complex, developed to express respect for these parental spirits, for whose sake sex and aggression must be controlled.

Freud had a magnificently generalizing mind. He put many pieces together to come up with a bold theory into which they all fit. But, alas, many of the assumptions he made about totemism were premature. We now know that totemism is not always accompanied by taboos in regard to the totemic animals, that a totemic feast is not always present, and that not all totemic groups claim descent from the totem. Furthermore, there is no longer the general assumption that totemism was universal, or even that it was specifically religious.[4]

With our later anthropological knowledge of the varieties of totemic forms, part of what Freud attempted to explain has evaporated. So let us pass from the specific subject of totemism to the more general subject of primitive morality.

Freud's general explanation for the taboos against sex and aggression may still apply—that they arise out of inhibitions of actions toward parents. More specifically, Freud saw morality in primitive society as emerging out of the following patterns of what he considered to be basic human facts:

1. Young boys are sexually attracted to their mothers.

2. Therefore, they feel hostility and envy toward their fathers.

3. Since they cannot defeat their fathers to win their mothers, they suppress their hostility—at least so far as conscious feelings are concerned.

4. As a result of the same defeated aspirations, they suppress sexual desires—at least toward the mother and others closely associated with her.

This pattern became tagged by Freud as the "Oedipus complex," reminding us of the tragic fate in Greek drama of Oedipus, who unwittingly married his own mother. But what is the evidence for the universality of such a complex? Do we really have any evidence that it applies to societies other than the late-Victorian Europe that Freud observed?

It is hard to test ideas of the Oedipus complex directly in different cultures because there is marked cultural variation in the expression of such themes as father-son rivalry. Certainly such rivalry should not be expected to be the same in societies where the father is the chief disciplinarian as in societies where the father has little power. But such variation in cultural roles may nevertheless provide a means of testing the validity of the basic ideas of the Oedipus complex. If cultures that create conditions for greater father-son rivalry are also the same cultures with more sexual inhibitions, one could conclude that there is general support for the Oedipus complex.

William N. Stephens is an anthropologist who has made cross-cultural analyses of precisely such phenomena. For example, he tested the predictions that societies with long postpartum sex taboos (such as prohibition of sex relations between husband and wife for at least a year after the birth of a child), presumably a condition that produces father-son rivalry, will also be societies with other features suggestive of Oedipal themes (such as severe brother-sister avoidance, extensive menstrual taboos, and generalized sex anxiety). After a comparative study of such variables in one hundred cultures, Stephens concluded that the cross-cultural evidence supports the basic assumptions of an Oedipal complex.[5]

It is one thing to find supporting evidence for an early rivalry between sons and fathers being followed by certain inhibitions; however, it is quite another thing to use this as a general foundation for explaining the moral systems of primitive man. Consider, for example, patterns of incest avoidance. Incest avoidance is not only one of the basic forms of morality in Freudian theory, but it also happens to be one of the few themes found in all forms of human culture. All societies have incest taboos, though what is defined as incest may vary somewhat from society to society. How adequate is the Freudian explanation that these are residues of the basic resolution of the Oedipal problem (that is, by the son's repression of sexuality toward the mother, or a daughter's repression of sexuality toward the father)?[6]

After a thorough study of incest patterns in 250 cultures, George P. Murdock concludes that some common features do show a significant harmony with Freudian ideas. Freud's theory, he believes, helps to explain the peculiar emotional quality of incest taboos, the universal occurrence of incest avoidance within the nuclear family, the diminished intensity of taboos outside the nuclear family, and the occurrence of violations in spite of the taboos. But Murdock believes that Freud's psychological theories must be supplemented by sociological considerations for a full understanding of incest. Incest taboos serve group needs as well as psychic purposes. Such taboos provide one means of limiting conflict within the family group. They also avoid the genetic deterioration and cultural stagnation that would be likely to occur if family groups were not forced to go beyond themselves for mates. Presumably, therefore, those societies with weak or absent incest taboos were not successful enough to survive until anthropologists could arrive on the scene to study them.[7]

Let us now proceed from the subject of primitive morality to discuss more fully what was earlier presented as a third proposition of Freud's interpretation of morality, namely that feelings of guilt and ambivalence have continued as the key supports for morality ever since the days of primitive society. In brief, Freud's view was that adult morality is built around a sense of guilt, and that this guilt is in turn the product of the Oedipal situation. When the family structure provides inevitable defeat for early aggressive and sexual urges, the child develops the capacity to suppress these impulses. The agency of such suppression is the superego, that internalization of the demands and prohibitions of society; itbecomes built into the personality to guard against misbehavior. When the impulses of that most primitive part of the personality, the id, bring their temptations, the response of guilt from the superego tends to inhibit such behavior.

It is hard to make a direct empirical test of this picture of the dynamics of individual morality. If true, however, several predictions may be made that can be tested. One is that persons who feel the most guilt (that is, who have the strongest superegos) tend to be those who show the least misbehavior. As Freud once expressed this point:

> The more virtuous a man is, the more severe and distrustful will be the conscience, so that ultimately it is precisely those people who have carried saintliness furthest who reproach themselves with the worst sinfulness.

For, according to Freud, although misbehavior may activate a sense of guilt, much more does the potential for guilt suppress such behavior.[8]

A second prediction implied by Freud's theories is that persons who have most successfully identified with the parent of the same sex will be those with the strongest consciences. It is, in other words, those who have most fully resolved the conflict of the Oedipal situation (through identification with the parent of the same sex) who should have the most effective consciences.

A third expectation of Freud's theory of conscience that should be amenable to some kind of empirical test is that a strong conscience should provide for a high consistency in behavior. Since the superego is a major feature of personality developed at an early age, it should give continuity to a person's acts such that the degree of morality in different situations should be highly consistent.

Is there scientific evidence regarding such predictions? Yes, a number of research studies have dealt with such questions. Does the evidence support Freud? Here the answer cannot be a simple yes or no. Nevertheless, there is at least some positive support for our first two predictions—that persons with a stronger sense of guilt are less likely than others to violate moral standards, and that these persons also tend to be those who have most successfully identified with the parent of the same sex. Far less evidence is available to support the third prediction of a high degree of consistency in moral behavior. Indeed, one of the most common findings in empirical studies of moral behavior is that of great situational variation, which tends to limit sharply the role of the personality patterns Freud had in mind.[9]

SUPEREGO OR EGO?

Personality, in the theory Freud formulated in his later years, has three main parts: the id, the ego, and the superego. Both the ego and the superego reflect our adjustment to others in society. The ego is the first subsystem to become differentiated from the more primitive id, and this new system primarily involves our testing of reality. The superego, more unconscious in its origin and operation, reflects a more strongly ingrained, and largely automatic, sense of moral judgment. We, following Freud, have so far sought our clues for the emergence of conscience in the superego. While this search has yielded some success, our understanding of the mystery of conscience is still unsatisfactory. Would it help if we considered the more self-conscious aspects of the self in the foundations of our morality as well? Could it be that morality is more an expression of the ego than it is of the superego?

Of course, our realistic adjustment to the social world around us begins before we attain a clear sense of selfhood. Certain acts of the infant receive social reinforcement, while others do not. The approval of adults is an important part of the normal setting for reinforcement, and gradually the child will come to choose those actions associated with such approval.

The effects of simple conditioning (and not-so-simple combinations of what psychologists call classical and operant conditioning) begin early in infancy, and they continue to operate throughout the human life cycle. They constitute an important influence on what we learn to do, what we learn about how others react to what we do, and how we learn to categorize what we do (including use of categories such as "right" and "wrong"). But something more complex also typically comes to be involved during the second year of life. This is the development of an individual's sense of identity, a self-conception. This provides a new organization for the human experience of reality, including the reality of moral standards.

It is surely more than a coincidence that the first clear signs of the awareness of moral standards emerge in the child at almost precisely the same age as do those of a self-concept. Children appear to recognize that a broken toy is not right, and they seek help from a parent to fix it. They also recognize that certain behavior is not considered right, looking for a parental response if they find themselves doing it. Are such signs of the consciousness of standards reflections of the same rapidly expanding intelligence as is the development of a sense of self? Or is selfhood itself a major determinant of these early signs of moral standards?

However the question just posed may be answered for the second year of a child's life, there is little doubt that soon thereafter the self-concept has itself become a key player in the child's moral drama. Morally charged terms—good and bad, pretty and ugly, clean and dirty—become applied to features and actions of the self. Moral standards clearly come very early to have a strong point of reference in the self, whatever may be their existence beyond.

As a young girl becomes aware of herself as an entity, so also she becomes aware of the personhood of others. An ability to sense what others are thinking and feeling facilitates at least three important kinds of moral learning for the child:

1. she sees the behavior of others as representing a possible model for her own behavior;

2. she can observe the consequences for others of their behavior and feel some empathy; and

3. she learns more clearly what in her own behavior is approved and what is not.

Although the first two of these processes are most associated with the "social learning theory" of such psychologists as Albert Bandura, all three of these are strongly observational and interactional in nature. And all three add important content to a child's sense of morality.[10]

With the development of language comes a verbalization of moral judgment. Categories of good and bad or right and wrong appear to come as easily as those of sound, shape, or color. This is because the child is fully a member of a moral universe as soon as she is able to talk in sentences. Not only does she take on the moral universe she finds in other persons, but she has already applied it to her own behavior—apparently even before she had words to speak about it.

A number of psychologists have identified a series of stages that they consider characteristic of moral learning and development. These include Jean Piaget, who wrote a book on the subject in 1932. This work, *The Moral Judgment of the Child*, was written before Piaget had devised his full theory of cognitive development, so there is some confusion about how the moral stages he describes in this book relate to his later cognitive stages (though there is a rather natural correlation). Piaget treats three different subjects as areas for the study of moral judgment: (a) an awareness of rules in games (or "rules of the game," especially studied in children playing marbles); (b) tendencies to universalize moral rules (or what Piaget called "moral realism," which later gives way to more relativistic modes of judgment); and (c) conceptions of what is fair or just. Each of these areas is seen as having a slightly different series of stages, based on the empirical work of Piaget and his associates in closely questioning the Swiss children they observed.[11]

Although Piaget does not give us a stage theory that applies to moral judgment in general, the main direction of development in the children he observed (mostly ranging in ages from six to twelve years) was fairly clear. He expressed this as a progression from a morality of "heteronomy" and constraint to one of "autonomy" and cooperation. The younger children show a morality based on acceptance of rules as given by others, with the rules having a kind of absolute quality. The older children show a morality based on rules that embody the mutual cooperation that people work out in their relations with each other. Such rules are more relative, more based on the particular social situation and the mutual agreement with which persons come to regard it. While general cognitive development was seen as an important influence for this change in moral judgment, Piaget appears to place even more emphasis upon the quality of social relationships of children at different ages. The children at the early ages had social lives that were primarily organized by adult authority. By late pre-adolescence the peer group had become increasingly important, and this was reflected in the greater importance given to themes of independence and mutual cooperation as criteria for moral judgment.

About thirty years ago Lawrence Kohlberg formulated what has become probably the best known theory of moral development. Kohlberg was heavily influenced by both Piaget's early work on moral judgment and his later more general formulations of cognitive development. However, Kohlberg was also concerned that Piaget's work had little to say about persons beyond early adolescence. Kohlberg's initial research was with boys from ten to sixteen years of age, and he became convinced that adolescence was often a critically important period for changes in moral judgment. The stages Kohlberg formulated allowed for important changes during this period, with the implication that the pattern of moral judgment would be fully mature and relatively fixed by the end of adolescence.[12]

Kohlberg has identified six stages as being characteristic of the natural progression of moral judgment. These in turn can be classified into three levels: (a) premoral, (b) a morality of conventional role conformity, and (c) a morality of self-accepted moral principles. Each of these levels in turn has two stages. These stages may be identified as follows:

1. premoral stage based primarily on punishment and obedience;

2. premoral stage of naive instrumental hedonism;

3. conventional stage based on having good relations with other people and winning their approval;

4. conventional stage based on maintenance of the social order;

5. stage of principled morality based on mutual rights and democratically accepted law; and

6. stage of principled morality based on universal ethical principles.

These stages primarily represent ways of structuring thought about moral issues. Although Kohlberg saw these as correlated with qualities of behavior in moral situations, it is quite clear that the central subject here is moral thought, not moral behavior.[13]

Kohlberg does not try to give particular ages for these stages. Although there is an association with chronological age, individuals vary a great deal as to when they actually enter a new stage. In fact, the majority of American adults apparently never get beyond Stages 3 and 4. Movement from one stage to another clearly is associated with a general growth in intelligence and reasoning ability; but it is also dependent on the quality of social relationshps and the way an individual sees himself within these relationships. Despite this social relativity, Kohlberg claims a universality and invariance for these stages. They are universal in that they appear to describe the sequence of development for all societies to which they have so far been applied. Also, they appear to be invariant in their sequence. Once a person attains one stage, he does not revert again to the general orientation of a lower stage (though some characteristics of lower-stage thinking may remain mixed with elements of a higher stage). The progression, Kohlberg claims, is always in the same order, without jumping over any stages in the sequence.

To illustrate how these stages may apply to a concrete issue, let us consider the case of a man whose wife is likely to die. She can only be saved by use of a very expensive drug, which the family cannot afford. If the druggist will not give away the drug, might the man, under these special circumstances, be justified in stealing the drug? A person at Stage 1 might say no, the man shouldn't steal the drug because he might be put in jail; or perhaps yes, he should steal the drug to avoid trouble in the family. At Stage 2 one might suggest that even if the man is caught for stealing, he might reduce his sentence by offering to give the drug back—or that even after a jail sentence, he might still have his wife. On the other hand, if he is likely to get caught, maybe he had better not try. At Stage 3 the concern may be what others will think of him—either for letting his wife die or for getting arrested for the theft. At Stage 4 the consideration is the guilt the man might feel over either having let his wife die or having broken the law—in either case going against the general expectation of society. At Stage 5 the issue is more one's own self-respect in doing what is best under the given circumstances. Finally, at Stage 6 the issue is still self-respect, but now it is self-respect for living up to one's highest ideals.[14]

Kohlberg's work has been criticized on a wide variety of substantive and methodological grounds. We will mention here only three issues. First, there is some question about the validity of the particular stages that have been identified. Second, there are questions about some of the value judgments implied by the work. Third, there is the issue of the extent to which such work relates to actual behavior. Let us consider each of these issues briefly.[15]

Kohlberg freely admits that his stages are not sharply distinct but rather are distinguished by the relative predominance of certain ways of thinking. Still, he claims that the order of these stages is universal; they are applicable to all forms of human society. Furthermore, he holds that the sequence of development always follows this order. Both of these claims have been questioned. The methodological problems of clearly assigning a given individual to a particular stage and the task of combining the limited (but growing) cross-cultural evidence conspire to make it extremely difficult to provide confirmation that these particular stages are universally applicable. Especially subject to question are the two stages of the highest (postconventional or principled) level, due both to the limited number of cases to be found and to the question of a clear distinction between these two stages. In Kohlberg's defense, however, it should be pointed out that the preponderance of evidence now available is consistent with seeing the stages as an ordered set that apply across different societies.

Aside from their descriptive validity, are not Kohnberg's stages described in such a way as to present a general bias? Certain kinds of thinking are suggested to be more "mature" than others, thus downgrading the less intellectualized frameworks characterizing the earlier stages. Is there a confusion here between intellectual fluency in using abstract conceptions and a genuine maturity in moral judgment? Also, might this same confusion also carry a possible gender bias—tending to favor male-preferred styles of abstraction to those styles of social involvement more associated with the moral judgments of women? The question of a possible bias becomes most clear when Kohlberg's work is applied to programs of moral education, as it frequently has been. This gives opportunity to question the implicit criteria of moral maturity. It also raises the issue of Kohlberg's attention to general frameworks for ethical decision making at the expense of any particular normative content. Many people, in contrast to Kohlberg, feel that moral education should instill adherence to particular norms, and not just try to elevate general frameworks of thought.[16]

Finally, the question must be raised as to whether Kohlberg's stages of moral judgment really are reflective of significant differences in behavior. Are we seeing real moral development here, expressed in qualitative differences in actual behavior, or are we only seeing a growing ability to frame intellectual rationalizations about behavior? At this point, it is difficult to anwer such a question, for few of those who have sought to apply Kohlberg's theory of moral development have looked very much at actual behavior.

Kohlberg has expressed the position that "moral development has a cognitive core." For him this means that normal human development includes a growth in rationality, and that this involves both how people make moral choices and how they reflect on issues regarding such choices. Moral development, for Kohlberg, is "a result of an increasing ability to perceive social reality or to organize and integrate social experience." This increasing ability is essentially cognitive, and it rests on the kind of foundations Piaget had so carefully explored in his research on cognitive development. But it also rests on the realities of social life, as experienced by the individual. Kohlberg has said:

The main experiential determinants of moral development seem to be amount and variety of social experience, the opportunity to take a number of roles and to encounter other perspectives. Thus middle-class and popular children progress farther and faster than do lower-class children and social isolates. Similarly, development is slower in the semiliterate village cultures that have been studied. Being able, through wide practice, to take another's viewpoint, to "put yourself in his place" is the source of the principled sense of equality and reciprocity.[17]

In emphasizing the self-conscious and cognitive aspects of moral development, Kohlberg has clearly aligned his work with those who see morality more in terms of the ego than the superego. Major consistencies in moral conduct are seen as reflecting decision-making capacities rather than either unconscious emotional reactions (as Freud would have emphasized) or automatically learned bahavior patterns (as some learning theorists would emphasize). Furthermore, Kohlberg has given empirical evidence for the kinds of frameworks that come to be used in such decision making, including how these structures for moral thinking tend to change as the individual matures.

Whatever may be the relation of Kohlberg's structures of moral thought to the way people may actually behave—the linkage that seems most unsettled in the work of Kohlberg and his associates—it is no small task to have elucidated some of the main structures of moral thinking. Whether or not the human animal is consistently a rational being, humans surely are rationalizing animals. And as we become adults, we become more preoccupied with questions of the consistency of our thoughts. These include issues concerning the consistency of our beliefs with each other and of our beliefs with our behavior. Kohlberg at the very least helps us to understand some of the frameworks within which we search for such consistency.

WHISPERS OF DIVINITY

In pursuing the mystery of conscience, we have so far mainly conceived of our subject in psychological terms. True, it was understood to be within a broader context of socialization, but not much has been said about the nature of the society that gives the context for socialization. Nor have we said much about the particular aspects of society—especially religious aspects—that are usually seen as having a special relation to the development of conscience.

The most generous attitude that science can take toward religious claims for specially revealed truths is that of skeptical silence. But the reality that humans hold religious beliefs and engage in religious practices can hardly be ignored by the sciences of human behavior. Nor should we neglect the religious context in which fundamental issues of morality are often posed. Even those who make no particular claims for being religious often invoke religiously colored ideas when they reflect on their fundamental notions of morality.[18]

We may view religion broadly as those beliefs and practices designed to deal with whatever is considered sacred, with the sacred in turn viewed as those special ideas and events that give an extraordinary dimension of meaning to otherwise mundane activities. Myths about supernatural events and associated rituals typically play a central role in religious traditions. What may not be so obvious is that these myths and rituals are usually also richly symbolic of fundamental ideas about human morality. For example, the Christian traditions concerning Christmas and Easter are rich in themes of the supreme value of humanity despite a common tendency toward sin; also central is the theme of self-sacrifice, which even secularized mythologies such as Santa Claus or the Easter Bunny find it necessary to reflect at least vaguely.

Not all religious traditions have been so closely linked to moral concerns as are those religions most prevalent in the world today. In the simplest societies studied by anthropologists, moral questions are often only incidentally tied to religious beliefs and practices. However, as societies became more complex, recurring moral issues tended to become matters for supernatural sanction; and the new religions that developed in the wake of major civilizations tended to treat moral questions in a central way. The major religious traditions that spread from the eastern rim of the Mediterranean Sea in the last three thousand years—primarily Judaism, Christianity, and Islam—have had a most intense concern for moral questions. The God of these traditions represents not only a universalization of the divine in a radically monotheistic form, but also promotes a universalization of ethical principles. In the case of such religions, the voice of God within the believer becomes more generalized in guiding individual behavior, thus adding a special intensity to what we have come to know as conscience.

Sigmund Freud was of course aware of the strong moral concern of such religions as Judaism and Christianity. But he tended to see these primarily as projections from the psyches of individuals, reflecting the central internal conflicts children must experience in their early families. Religious beliefs too were seen as psychological projections—relics of less enlightened ages given continued nourishment by the neurotic nature of typical relationships within the family. As we have seen, Freud's insights are of some value in helping us understand the dynamics of conscience. But his psychological bias was so strong that he failed to recognize the importance of some broader social forces at work.

A nice counterpoint to Freud in this regard is provided by the French sociologist, Emile Durkheim. At the same time that Freud was studying the latest reports regarding Australian aborigines, so was Durkheim. He, like Freud, saw here a close correspondence between basic religious and ethical phenomena. Also, like Freud, he overemphasized the extent to which Australian totemism could be seen as a prototype of early religion. Both used totemism as a vehicle for illustrating what they saw as a central truth about the tie between religion and morality. For Freud this central truth was that religious beliefs and moral taboos have their foundations in psychic experiences within families. For Durkheim, it was that the larger society has a reality that cannot be reduced to the experience of individuals.

As Durkheim saw it, "a society is not made up merely of the mass of individuals who comprise it, the ground which they occupy, the things which they use and the movements which they perform." All these are ways of referring to a society, but its central reality is still something more. This something more is the idea society forms of itself. These "collective representations" of society, as Durkheim prefers to call them, are especially apparent in religious beliefs and practices. Society itself, he holds, is the origin for the sense of the sacred, but it becomes expressed more concretely in myths and rituals. Closely intertwined with religious mythology and ritual are the ethical ideals and moral taboos that uphold the fundamental structure of society.[19]

"Nearly all the great social institutions," said Durkheim, "have been born in religion." Religious forces have had this central role because religion is the purest way a society expresses its self-representation. "If religion has given birth to all that is essential in society, it is because the idea of society is the soul of religion."

Durkheim adds: "Religious forces are therefore human forces, moral forces." It is our consciousness of being a part of a social order that is the central fact for human existence, and from this beginning we proceed to create the various ramifications of human social institutions—from the family to our largest political entites and most universal religions.[20]

Durkheim was probably as one-sided in his interpretation of moral and religious phenomena as was Freud. Though pushing their interpretations in opposite directions, both yielded important insights into the nature of human conscience. From Freud we learn something of the intensity of certain negative injunctions from deep within—especially those that direct us toward the control of sex and aggression. From Durkheim we learn something of the positive prosocial values that are so deeply entwined in our moral sense; and we see why these are so often tied to religious symbolism.[21]

Durkheim's great insight was that society's representation of itself plays a central role in private consciousness as well as in public activities. Once we see at least partial truth in this insight, a wide variety of social phenomena take on new significance.

First and foremost, we come to see that society always has a moral structure. Our central human nature requires a social universe, and that universe has a central structure that must be upheld. We begin to assimilate this structure in our earliest moral learnings. We treat it as a part of objective reality. As Peter Berger has pointed out,

> This world encompasses the biography of the individual, which unfolds as a series of events *within* that world. Indeed, the individual's own biography is objectively real only insofar as it may be comprehended within the significant structures of the social world.

In this way the social institutions of the world into which we are born come to have their own imperatives for the private selves which we form.[22]

Going back into human prehistory with such a perspective, we may see in the emergence of localized human communities something more than a convenient coming together for the exchange of goods and services. As Lewis Mumford has pointed out in *The City in History*, "the first germ of the city" is the ceremonial meeting place. Says Mumford:

In the earliest gathering about a grave or a painted symbol, a great stone or a sacred grove, one has the beginning of a succession of civil institutions that range from the temple to the astronomical observatory, from the theater to the university.

We also see in these ceremonial beginnings the signs of a consciousness heavily involved in symbols of the common life.[23]

In the modern world a Durkheimian view prepares us to see many religious overtones in public life that otherwise would be inexplicable. The reverence with which avowed atheists (at least until recently) have honored Lenin's tomb in Moscow, the ceremonial respect with which the monarchy is still greeted in the United Kingdom, and the celebration with which Americans commemorate their federal Constitution or build a monument to their first President—all these are signs of religious sentiments being directed toward national political institutions. And a national anthem or flag can for many people stir sacred feelings that are very deeply rooted in a sense of personal identity.

A quite different arena for Durkheimian analysis is in our everyday face-to-face interaction. Durkheim viewed the soul as the individualized form of the sacred character (or "mana") of society. Erving Goffman believes that such an insight serves as a suitable foundation for looking at ritualized aspects of everyday social life, including the common ways that individuals greet each other. He has reviewed patterns people use to present themselves to others, noting especially the deference and demeanor expressed. He concludes that "the self is in part a ceremonial thing, a sacred object which must be treated with ritual care and in turn must be presented in a proper light to others." A ritual of self-presentation must follow definite social rules and, furthermore, is always the joint product of more than one individual. Says Goffman:

> While it may be true that the individual has a unique self all his own, evidence of this possession is thoroughly a product of joint ceremonial labor, the part expressed through the individual's demeanor being no more significant than the part conveyed by others through their deferential behavior toward him.[24]

But Durkheim's insights also have their limitations for understanding fully the foundations of human morality. We have already examined some of the other considerations that should be applied. With Freud we have seen the importance of repressed wishes within the nuclear family as an important force in human morality; and with Piaget and Kohlberg we have seen how forces of social and cognitive development may give structure to moral thinking. These represent the more psychological side of our moral universe. Going in the other direction, beyond the individual, we may also wonder if there is not something even beyond society that provides a wider grounding for our sense of morality. Might there not be something biologically given in the nature of the species that supports a fundamental moral consciousness?

Given the immense range in various societies of human values and ideals, as well as the great differences of specific taboos, it may seem audacious to consider a moral sense as in some way biologically given. Certainly if there is a biological propensity for moral judgment, it must be quite open in the kinds of content toward which it can be directed. Still, is it any more preposterous to suppose that we might have an innate propensity for moral judgment than to suppose (as leading linguists are now suggesting) that we have an innate capacity for grammar?

Few psychologists have observed the beginnings of moral judgment in children as closely as has Jerome Kagan. It is therefore of interest to note the conclusions of this psychologist after considering the biological basis of morality. Kagan clearly recognizes great differences in the early socialization experiences of children and the great variety of human values that may be promoted by adults in modern society. Still, he says:

> Although the surface virtues children develop will be relative to the cultural demands they encounter, we can count on the appearance of empathy and an appreciation of right and wrong in all children before the third birthday. . . . Although humans do not seem to be specially programmed for a particular profile of moral missions, they are prepared to invent and believe in some moral mission.[25]

In other words, there appears to be *something* biologically given to humans generally that serves as the foundation of moral development.

If we assume that a moral sense is in some way rooted in the biological nature of humans, a problem immediately arises: by what evolutionary process might we assume that it could have arisen? This problem is made more acute by the assumption that natural selection involves a competitive struggle favoring the survival of self-centered over altruistic motivations. Genes, we are told, are "selfish"; their very survival is fostered by animals who seek their own survival at the expense of others of their own species, if need be, and who try to maximize the number of their progeny. These are the imperatives of natural selection. Where is there room here for a socially directed sense of morality?

Perhaps an illustration will help make clear the issue at hand. Let us imagine that two young men are swimming in a lake of considerable depth. While one is resting temporarily on the shore, the other disappears under the surface of the water and does not reappear. Now comes the question for the man on the shore: Does he dive into the water to try to save the other fellow—even at some risk to his own life? This would appear to be the "good" thing to do, but would it be a biologically sound course to follow?[26]

Looked at most simply, in terms of the immediate survival interests of the man on the shore, there is no reason for him to jump into the water. This would only reduce (maybe not greatly, but still significantly) his own chances for survival. Let the other guy try to take care of himself; "I must look out for Number One."

But a more sophisticated biological analysis would reveal that it is not the individual organism but its genes that carry the basis of biological success. We therefore need to consider how helping the drowning man might enhance the survivability of one's own genes. If the man in the water is a brother or other close relative, that might be reason enough. The survival of another individual's genes that are largely shared by oneself would be a way of extending one's own genetic survival. This might be worth some personal risk. Some biologically based moral sense to aid kinfolk might therefore be expected. Even if the other man is not related, but is a very close friend, "reciprocal altruism" might provide a justification for coming to his aid. Doing good for those who are apt to be able to return the favor would make good biological sense.

Yet anyone who observes a fellow swimmer sink from view, and who remains on shore without acting to help this other person at all, is very likely to have a sinking feeling in the pit of his own stomach. This feeling does not just represent anxiety over the possibility of drowning, but concern that he has not done the right thing—that an important moral obligation has been missed. He will, in a word, feel guilty.

Humans do have a wider sense of moral obligation than any other animal species. This reflects not only our intelligence, but something more as well. The easiest way to conceive of this "something more" is as the product of social and cultural evolution.

We live in societies that have come to demand more in the way of moral obligation than would be required for biological survival. With this comes a possible basis for conflict between biological needs and social requirements—with the social requirements often taking the upper hand. That, at any rate, is a brief outline of the conclusions of some who have thought deeply about these issues.[27]

If there is a genetically programmed biological basis for the human sense of morality, it is a rather surprising development to find in the animal kindgom. But, of course, humans are surprising animals in a lot of ways. If in the future we find better empirical evidence than is now available to support an innate basis for morality, we might expect that it will turn out to be closely tied to the biological roots of our self-identity and of our peculiar propensity for language.[28]

"AND A LITTLE CHILD SHALL LEAD THEM"

In trying to communicate his vision of universal peace, an ancient prophet sought for images to emphasize the radical transformation of the apparently natural order that would be required. We thus have in the book of Isaiah a rather remarkable passage that ends with the words, "And a little child shall lead them."[29]

We must be a bit puzzled about what the prophet may be saying. Certainly we do not ordinarily expect political leadership from little children; neither do we ordinarily look to our children for moral leadership. After all, important cognitive development associated with mature moral judgment continues at least through adolescence, as Lawrence Kohlberg and others have shown. Even young adults have limited experience in the social responsibilities that are such an important part of adult morality.

Despite all this, it is sometimes remarkable to discover how well developed the moral sense of a young child may be. Just as a child in the late preschool years has internalized an amazing supply of linguistic rules that he is able to apply in ordinary speech (even though the sophistications of written language may be still to come), so also a child at that age has an unusual wealth of moral sensitivities (even though some of them are not yet well integrated with complex social institutions). At times we may be surprised, if we but take the time to notice, how well integrated the moral judgment and behavior of a child may be.

Robert Coles has provided an instructive example of a child's moral capacity in his report of the the case of Ruby Bridges. Ruby, at six years of age, was one of a small number of black first graders who took part in court-ordered desegregation for the public schools of New Orleans, Louisiana, in the early 1960s. The court had demanded at least a token enrollment of black children in previously all-white schools, starting with the first grade for the first year. This was implemented despite the resistance of state authorities and the opposition of the great majority of the white citizens of New Orleans. A white boycott of schools with black children was initially quite successful; and to encourage that boycott, a howling mob gathered around school entrances to shout their displeasure at any student, white or black, who came to school. Under these circumstances, it was necessary for federal marshals to accompany each of the black first-graders coming to school, and Ruby Bridges was one of those receiving such an escort.[30]

Shortly after Ruby came to the attention of Robert Coles, one of the teachers at her school recorded these observations:

> I was standing in the classroom, looking out the window, and I saw Ruby coming down the street, with the federal marshals on both sides of her. The crowd was there, shouting, as usual. A woman spat at Ruby but missed; Ruby smiled at her. A man shook his fist at her; Ruby smiled at him. Then she walked up the stairs, and she stopped and turned and smiled one more time! You know what she told one of the marshals? She told him she prays for those people, the ones in that mob, every night before she goes to sleep!

At first Coles assumed that this little girl must be psychologically disturbed. He began looking for other symptoms of the inner turmoil she must be experiencing. But he found few signs of any deep internal strain. Instead he noticed how the child was simply trying to live each day as best as she knew how. He also noted her surrounding sources of support. When he asked Ruby about how she reacted to the crowd at her schoolhouse gate, she said:

> They keep coming and saying the bad words, but my momma says they'll get tired after a while and then they'll stop coming. They'll stay home. The minister came to our house and he said the same thing and not to worry, and I don't. The minister said God is watching and He won't forget, because He never does. The minister says if I forgive the people, and smile at them and pray for them, God will keep a good eye on everything and He'll be our protection.

As Coles questioned Ruby more closely about her prayers for those who spat at her, she said simply, "Yes, I do pray for them." When he pushed further on this matter, Ruby replied, "I go to church every Sunday, and we're told to pray for everyone, even the bad people, and so I do."

No doubt Ruby Bridges was still immature in some of her moral conceptions. She had not taken any college courses in ethics, nor had she moved very far in Kohlberg's stages of moral development. Her theology was quite simple, as we might expect from a six-year-old child. And the socioeconomic position of her parents—of sharecropper background, only recently moved to the city—could clearly be classified as "disadvantaged." Despite all this, how many adults can claim a higher level of moral behavior than that which Ruby was able to show as a first-grader?

Ruby's mother, though herself unschooled, had some interesting comments about moral judgment. "There are a lot of people who always worry about whether they're doing right or doing wrong," she said. Then, she added, there are others who "just put their lives on the line for what's right, and they may not be the ones who talk a lot or argue a lot or worry a lot; they just *do* a lot."

Several years later Ruby herself looked back at her experience in her first year in school:

> I knew I was just Ruby trying to go to school, and worrying that I couldn't be helping my momma with the kids younger than me, like I did on the weekends and in the summer. But I guess I also knew I was the Ruby who had to do it—go into that school and stay there, no matter what those people said, standing outside. And besides, the minister reminded me that God chooses us to do His will, and so I had to be His Ruby, if that's what He wanted. And then that white lady wrote and told me she was going to stop shouting at me, because she'd decided I wasn't bad, even if *integration* was bad, then my momma said I'd become "her Ruby," that lady's, just as she said in her letter, and I was glad; and I was glad I got all the nice letters from people who said I was standing up for them, and I was walking for them, and they were thinking of me, and they were with me, and I was their Ruby, they said.[31]

Human morality is a rich combination of ingredients. It includes sets of obligations and prohibitions that are associated with a deeply ingrained sense of right and wrong, derived ultimately from early childhood experiences. It also includes a more reasoned sense of moral judgment, which is generally associated with cognitive development, and a positive identification with society, its people, and its social institutions. This is partly represented in explicitly religious forms and partly seen in other ritualized elements of our life with others. It may also include a genetic predisposition to develop a moral sense, though this is quite speculative, given the limits of our present knowledge. But all of these ingredients of morality must be exercised in behavior with other people in our concrete day-to-day situations. Most of the time we take little note of these embodiments of conscience in ourselves or in others. Occasionally, though, we are put to special tests which may bring out either the best or the worst in us. Ruby Bridges faced such a special test as she began the first grade of her public school education. That she, at age six, dealt with her situation both creatively and responsibly makes us more fully aware of just how strong and deeply rooted is the human potential for morality.

NOTES

1. The psychologist quoted in this paragraph is Erich Fromm (1947), p. 60. His concept of "social character" is also discussed in Fromm (1941), especially pp. 277–299.

2. This section follows very closely the earlier discussion of the author in Schellenberg (1974), Chapter 23.

3. Our source for "Totem and Taboo" is Freud (1913/1938), with quotations from pp. 915–916 and 917.

4. As anthropologist Alexander Goldenweiser (1931) has pointed out in his review of totemism, "the intensity of the religious *attitude* toward the totem is scarcely ever pronounced" and "totemism, in *no* instance, constitutes the whole or even the center of the religious aspect of a tribal culture" (p. 374).

5. Our source here is Stephens (1962).

6. Strictly speaking, in Freudian theory the Oedipal complex refers to early conflicts of boys, and an Electra complex represents parallel (but slightly different) problems for girls. As we follow the story for males, we should be aware that Freud saw a roughly similar process for females.

7. This classic analysis of incest taboos is found in Murdock (1949). Such psychological and sociological theories as we have mentioned still do not explain well the patterns of incest avoidance beyond the nuclear family. For this, one must take account of the particular configurations of different cultures. This does not mean that there are not cross-cultural regularities in such patterns, but rather that such patterns have to be seen within the logic of other cultural relationships. For example, some societies extend incest taboos beyond the nuclear family primarily to cover relatives

on the mother's side of the family. With very few exceptions, these turn out to be societies with matrilineal kinship groups. Other societies extend incest taboos primarily to cover the paternal side of the family, and almost all of these are societies with patrilineal kinship groups. Also, Murdock points to some evidence that suggests that the distance to which incest taboos are extended among relatives may be primarily a function of the time that has elapsed since the establishment of the kinship group.

8. The quotation here is from Freud (1930/1962), pp. 72–73.

9. Support for our first two predictions may be found in MacKinnon (1938) and in Sears, Rau, and Alpert (1965). A classic study documenting the high degree of situational variation in moral behavior was reported by Hartshorne and May (1928), though a later reanalysis of their data by Burton (1963) suggests that at least a moderate degree of personal consistency is also involved.

10. For Bandura's social learning theory, see Bandura (1977) or Bandura (1986).

11. A widely available edition of Piaget's pioneering work is Piaget (1932/1948).

12. Sources for Kohlberg's work include Kohlberg (1964, 1972, 1980, and 1984).

13. Our listing of Kohlberg's stages does not follow his precise wording in any one source, but it does represent the basic progression he described. At one point Kohlberg (1978) considered dropping the sixth stage, largely on the grounds that so few persons appeared to reach it; however, most later presentations of the theory have continued to use this stage.

14. Note that how a person reasons is more important than the answer given. Our illustration here is based on a rather free adaptation of material in Kohlberg (1964) and Kohlberg (1980), especially pp. 96–98 of the latter source. Given the rarity of stage 6 responses, we should note what Kohlberg gives as an example of reasoning at this level. From a sixteen-year-old comes this answer for the rare drug dilemma: "By the law of society he was wrong but by the law of nature and of God the druggist was wrong and the husband was justified. Human life is above financial gain. Regardless of who is dying, if it was a total stranger, man has a duty to save him from dying" (Kohlberg, 1964, p. 401).

15. Strong methodological criticisms of Kohlberg's work may be found in Kurtines and Grief (1974). More balanced assessments of the full range of Kohlberg's work may be found in Modgil and Modgil (1985). Other discussions may be found in Graham (1972), Rich (1985), and Rosen (1980).

16. The work of Gilligan (1982) is especially important in suggesting that Kohlberg tended to omit in his highest stages attention to genuine care for others and sensitivity to their feelings. These, she claims, are results of ignoring the distinctively feminine voice in matters of moral judgment, a

voice as compelling in mature moral judgment (for both men and women) as is the more autonomous and principled reflection on rights and duties that characterizes Kohlberg's highest stages.

17. The quotations in this paragraph are from Kohlberg (1980), p. 38, and (the last two) from Kohlberg (1972), p. 15.

18. Note, for example, the way Walter Lippmann ends his *Preface to Morals* with an appeal to the "religion of the spirit" (Lippmann, 1929).

19. Our primary source here is Durkheim (1915). The quotation above is from p. 422. An important later work that follows the Durkheimian position is that of Swanson (1960).

20. The quotations in this paragraph are from Durkheim (1915), pp. 418–419. In a footnote, Durkheim (p. 419) acknowledges that one area of social life—economic activity—may not have direct religious ties. But even here he points to important indirect associations between economic and religious values.

21. Is religious symbolism inevitable here? Perhaps not. Although Adam Smith included God in a general background sort of way, his book *The Theory of Moral Sentiments* (first published in 1759, and as worthy of careful attention as his later economic writings) gave the central role in moral judgment to what he calls the "impartial spectator" (Smith, 1759/1976). This was essentially an internalization of the individual's experience with other persons; it need have no specifically religious connotations. Others who essentially fall in Smith's tradition occasionally use religious terms for referring to the same basic phenomenon. Note, for example, the following from Charles H. Cooley (1927), p. 252: "I may call it conscience, I may call it the contending movements of life coming to decision in my brain, I may call it a deep self, I may call it the voice of God—all comes to much the same thing. It is authoritative, it is in a high sense necessary; I must listen and obey on pain of disintegration, decay and despair."

22. We are indebted to Peter Berger not only for the quotation in this paragraph—from Berger (1967), p. 13—but also for many other insights included in this section.

23. Our quotations are from Mumford (1961), pp. 10 and 9, respectively.

24. The paper cited here is that of Goffman (1956). Quotations are from pp. 497 and 493, respectively.

25. Our quotation here is from Kagan (1984), pp. 152–53. In the very thoughtful chapter in which Kagen comes to this conclusion, he shows a strong sense of the social relativity of most human values. Even within the broad pattern of Western civilization, different values and their associated moral perspectives tend to vary greatly with time and place. He says, for example (p. 120): "Each of the four virtues of fifth-century Athens— courage, justice, wisdom, and restraint—had a special actualization in Athenian life that would be difficult to similate in nineteenth-century

Boston, where the comparable virtues might have been called: loyalty to personal convictions, charity toward the poor, insight into one's intentions, and moderation of ambition." A somewhat different view of the social relativity of moral ideals has been stated by Mumford (1951), p. 164: "Within the great circle of the historic civilizations the main directions of morality have been well set: to follow customs and frame laws that regulate social relations, in order to make conduct predictable, instead of wholly erratic and self-willed; to respect symbols and conserve values; to refrain from murder, violence, and theft; to respect organized and sanctioned forms of sexual relationship; to nurture the young and stand by them as long as they are helpless; to tell the truth and to refrain from falsehood. . . . This basic morality is in fact common to all human society: what distinguishes civilization is a heightened consciousness of the occasions for moral choice and a positive effort to extend the benefits of the moral code outside the community where it originated."

26. This example has been suggested by Jencks (1979).

27. A particularly important discussion of this issue is found in Campbell (1975). See also Jencks (1979).

28. Might not the foundations of moral consciousness extend more widely than the human species? This question is of course even more speculative than the biological issue we have raised. Religious views tend to appeal to the heavens—or to other cosmic forces—for an ultimate justification regarding matters of morality. We must recognize most of this as a projection outward from our human concerns. Peter Berger put the matter succinctly when he referred to religion as "the audacious attempt to conceive of the entire universe as being humanly significant" (Berger, 1967, p. 28). Still, can we afford *not* to cast our moral network more widely than our own species, given our current concerns over the environmental degradation of planet Earth? Might not such a wider basis for an ethic—the "reverence for life" of Albert Schweitzer (1969) comes to mind as an example—be as relevant to current realities as one more reflective of a Darwinian past.

29. Our source here is Isaiah, Chapter 11, Verse 6.

30. The primary source for material in this section has been Coles (1986). Quotations in the following paragraphs regarding or from Ruby Bridges are, respectively, from pp. 22-23, 24, 22, and 9 of that source. At one point (p. 29) Coles himself makes this comment: "Moral life is not to be confused with tests meant to measure certain kinds of abstract (moral) thinking, or with tests that give people a chance to offer hypothetical responses to made-up scenarios. We never quite know what will happen in this life; nor do we know how an event will connect with ourselves. It is no secret that we all contend with moral inconsistencies, contradictions—the disparate elements that each of us tries, day in and day out, to forge into a particular life. Meanwhile, there is the world around us, with various social and political and economic issues, the sweep of history even, which

together offer us possibilities or, sadly, take them away, deny them." See also the following note.

31. *The Moral Lives of Children* by Robert Coles. Copyright © 1986 by Robert Coles. Used by permission from the Atlantic Monthly Press.

Chapter 4

The Mystery of Intelligence

THE IQ PHENOMENON

In 1904 the French Minister of Public Instruction appointed a commission to look into the problem of educating retarded children. This commission decided to establish special schools for such children, but they also decided that no child should be sent to these schools unnecessarily. They sought an examination that could show which children would be unlikely to profit from attending regular schools. But what sort of an examination should this be? It was only natural that the commission would turn for help to the leading figure in French psychology at the time, Alfred Binet.

Binet was a professor at the Sorbonne, where he had in 1889 established the first psychological laboratory in France. A man of wide learning, he also had already done some careful studies of the early mental development of children (with rather disappointing results for the then-current doctrine regarding the importance of brain size for mental ability). Binet had practical concerns regarding the issues with which the commission was wrestling. His concerns were partly with what might be the effects of such testing if it were not done effectively. "The interests of the children," he said, "demand greater circumspection" than an arbitrary and capricious assignment. Furthermore, "it will never be to one's credit to have attended a special school. We should at least spare from this mark those who do not deserve it." And, finally, there was the scientific concern, expressed by Binet as a desire to put into practice "the precision and the exactitude of science every time one can." So Binet accepted the challenge, and the result was the 1905 Binet scale for measuring the mental ability of French children.

It is noteworthy to quote what Binet himself had to say about the purposes of his original instrument, given the great controversy that has been engendered by the subsequent use of such tests. As he then wrote:

> Our goal, when a child is placed in our presence, is to make a measurement of his intellectual capacities, in order to learn whether he is normal or is retarded. To this end we must study his present state, and that state only. We need concern ourselves neither with his past nor with his future; in consequence, we will neglect the etiology, and specifically we will not make a distinction between acquired and congenital feeble-mindedness; even more emphatically, we will set aside all considerations of pathological anatomy which might explain his intellectual deficit. So much for the past. Concerning the future, the same abstention; we seek not at all to establish or prepare a prognosis, and we leave unanswered the question of knowing whether his retardation is curable or not, ameliorable or not.

Binet's initial scale consisted of thirty items or tests, each measuring a particular aspect of mental functioning—ranging from visual coordination to defining abstract concepts. These were arranged by order of difficulty, and an average level of performance for each age level was tentatively identified. The number of tests for which a child was successful yielded a score, which could be interpreted as a measure of general mental ability.[1]

Binet produced a major revision of the scale in 1908 (in collaboration with Theodore Simon, who had also been involved in creating the initial instrument). The revised tests were graded more clearly by age level, allowing the total score to be interpreted in comparison to age norms. Thus was born the concept of "mental age." After another revision in 1911, a German psychologist, Wilhelm Stern, suggested a procedure whereby an individual's score would be *divided* by that most characteristic of his age level. The result could be called an "intelligence quotient," or what we have come to know as "IQ."

America proved to be an especially fertile ground for the promotion of intelligence testing. With its broad system of public education came concerns about the quality of that education, including attention to the placement of students to make best use of their levels of ability. There were also widespread fears concerning the possible deterioration of the American population in the face of a massive immigration of peoples considered by some to be of inferior stock. An especially active proponent of Binet's tests in America was H. H. Goddard, who had far less doubt than Binet that they measured a unitary quality, that this quality could be called intelligence, and that intelligence was a simple function of genetic inheritance. Goddard used such tests of intelligence not only in the placement of children at his own school for the feeble-minded in New Jersey, but also in the promotion of social reform measures. Among his preferred projects for social reform were legislation to restrict immigration (his studies appeared to prove that most recent immigrants had very low levels of intelligence) and laws that mandated the sterilization of persons with especially low measured intelligence (again, to help protect the genetic pool from deterioration). Another important figure in American intelligence research was Lewis M. Terman, whose careful 1916 and 1937 revisions of the Binet tests (known as the "Stanford-Binet," named after the university where Terman taught as a psychology professor as well as to honor Binet's pioneering work) made them for many years the model to which all other intelligence tests were compared. Terman, like Goddard, assumed that high test scores reflected innate intelligence, though he was less impressed than others with the theoretical significance of what the Stanford-Binet measured.[2]

By the time of World War I, the American movement for intelligence testing was such that, shortly after entry of the United States into the war, almost two million men were given *Army Alpha*, an adaptation of an IQ test allowing administration to many individuals at one time. Draftees were given either this test or *Army Beta* (a form intended for use with persons who could not read and write English) to help place them within the armed services. In World War II more than twice as many men were given another intelligence test, the *Army General Classification Test*, to assist in their placement. Such widespread and official use of intelligence testing bears witness to the high regard people in America had for the significance of IQ scores.

Was this high regard for IQ measures misplaced? Many people have come to think so, especially in the last half of the twentieth century. This is due partly to changes in the general framework of public opinion. Equally important are the more scientific contributions that have led to a questioning of the validity of any simple or single measure of intelligence.

As new nationality and racial groups have generally moved toward greater integration into American society (let us not pretend that the process has been easy, only that the general movement of the twentieth century has been in that direction), it is harder to assume that they represent lower levels of natural intelligence than those of Anglo-Saxon stock. As Americans spend more of their years (and their dollars) in educational institutions, they come to see their own intelligence, and that of their peers, as more and more a product of what may be learned. And the more they have come into contact—either directly, or through the mass media—with persons who have learning disabilities, the less easy is it to conclude that a simple fact like an IQ score can be predictive of what such persons either can or will do. All of these influences have led to a public opinion in America much less receptive to widespread IQ testing, or at least more inclined to be critical about what an IQ result might mean. Meanwhile, in most other parts of the world, IQ testing never quite reached the vogue that it had attained in the United States. There was therefore less of a noticeable change in public opinion than was the case in America, as we entered the final decades of the twentieth century.[3]

Side-by-side with the influences of public opinion upon the current IQ debate have been more academic and scientific influences. These include questions about the consistency of IQ results, the possibilities of cultural bias in test construction, the explanation of individual differences in results, and the implications of results for the conceptualization of intelligence.

Studies of repeated IQ tests given to the same individuals often show ranges in scores of more than 10 percent, with changes of 30 or more points (based on an assumed average of 100) not uncommon. Compared to most measures used in behavioral science research, this should not be surprising. But compared to the aura of precision with which intelligence testing has been associated, such differences in results are disturbing. They suggest either that the reliability of the tests is rather modest or that the intelligence of individuals itself shows considerable variation from time to time. Indeed, both of these may be factors, and it is an extremely difficult task to sort out their separate effects.

Even more troublesome is the issue of cultural bias in test construction. In Binet's original tests, there was no attempt to measure something that was free from cultural background or school learning. But as the tests were later revised, there was more of an effort to present them as measuring pure intelligence, which could be abstracted out of one's cultural background. The tests, it was often and too easily said, measured capacity, not achievement. True, there was an attempt to get beyond the most obvious kinds of cultural learning in items selected for the tests, but any careful review of the contents of any IQ instrument can produce numerous examples of items where cultural learning could have a significant effect on what answers might be given. This is not a major problem when IQ tests are used within a population that is quite homogeneous culturally. But when applied to more heterogeneous populations, one should not be surprised if the tests show quite significant group differences. Nor should it be surprising that culturally dominant groups will tend to show higher measures of IQ than others. That this has indeed been the case need not imply any intellectual inferiority for those of other subcultures, only that the intellectual achievements measured by the tests are more common in the more dominant cultural groups.

Hand-in-hand with the rise in the use of IQ testing was the assumption that the tests measured innate intelligence. But this could no longer be so easily asserted as cases of significant IQ change were reported. It then became a major research effort to assess just how much of the differences in test scores can generally be attributed to differences in heredity and how much to identifiable environmental differences. The statistical issues in this effort become quite complex, and we need not pursue them here. We only need to point to a few of the most obvious features:

1. We can make IQ comparisons of identical versus fraternal twins, of parents with biological children and with adopted children, and of other cases where we can assume a certain degree of genetic similarity. These give us evidence on the question of the hereditary base of measured IQ.

2. Formulas can be derived to give estimates of the amount of variation in IQ scores in a particular population that is associated with other known variables (including similarities in heredity). These serve to explain general variation in scores in a particular population for a particular kind of test; they do not explain the differences between any particular individuals.

3. Such formulas have given us estimates of the "heritability" of IQ in particular populations. These results generally support

heredity as a stronger factor in IQ differences than variations in environmental factors.

Despite a large number of studies devoted to assess the heritabilty of IQ, researchers still offer a wide range of estimates for this. Not the least of the problems with this line of research is the fact that some of the strongest data for the inheritance of IQ—reported by the distinguished British psychologist, Cyril Burt—has since been judged by many to have been fraudulent.[4]

Perhaps even more serious than doubts about what causes differences in IQ scores are doubts about just what the scores themselves represent. IQ tests were first developed to serve a practical purpose. They never have been clearly tied to a satisfactory theory of intelligence. Factor analytic studies of what is being measured as intelligence by IQ tests have not, on the whole, been reassuring. Charles Spearman, who pioneered in techniques of factor analysis, believed he had identified a central underlying factor, which he assumed was genetically based. However, other forms of factor analysis did not support the existence of such a general factor. Using special techniques to base his factors on actual clusters of results, L. L. Thurstone discovered what he considered to be seven primary mental abilities: verbal comprehension, word fluency, numerical computation, spatial visualization, associative memory, perceptual speed, and reasoning. The debate has gone on for many years as to whether or not some general factor of intelligence is being measured by the IQ tests, or whether what is measured is only the general average of a variety of more specific abilities.[5]

At the heart of the issue is a question: Just what is intelligence, anyway? The IQ tests seek to abstract a particular quality (or set of qualities) from the way individuals deal with problems of a particular sort, namely those requiring abstract reasoning abilities. But what about other kinds of problem solving? May not other kinds of abilities also be regarded as forms of intelligence, even though they may not be readily measured by IQ tests?

A broader approach to the study of intelligence is illustrated by the work of Howard Gardner, who has suggested that we approach the question of mental ability in terms of a series of "intelligences" rather than as functions of a single intellectual dimension. Most forms of human adjustment—in school learning, for example, or in pursuing a career—require skills of several of these intelligences; but, suggests Gardner, the biological foundations of these abilities might be quite distinct. Somewhat tentatively (leaving the door very much open for revision in the light of further findings), Gardner posits the following seven main intelligences: linguistic intelligence, musical intelligence, logical-mathematical intelligence, spatial intelligence, bodily kinesthetic intelligence, interpersonal intelligence, and intrapersonal intelligence.[6]

Whatever may be the conclusions that psychologists of the future draw about the proper measurement of human intelligence (or intelligences), one point that deserves emphasis now is that intelligence always must be observed in some kind of human *behavior*. Furthermore, it is a quality of that behavior, rather than something that is inherent in the individual, that most properly deserves to be called "intelligent." This suggests that intelligence is a quality of behavior that fosters effective problem solving. To the extent that IQ tests reflect the kind of problem solving associated with effective adjustment to ordinary life situations, it may be reasonable to refer to this as intelligence. To the extent that the tests reflect something correlated only with other IQ tests, we should question the relevance of their scores for helping us understand the mystery of human intelligence.[7]

Of course, there are other approaches to studying intelligent behavior besides that most associated with IQ testing. A developmental approach is examined in our next section, with still other approaches to be treated later in this chapter.

THE DEVELOPMENT OF INTELLIGENCE

After Binet's death in 1911, his work was continued by his associates, especially Theodore Simon. Simon, seeking to standardize for French children a new intelligence test from England, turned to a young scholar from Switzerland for assistance. This bright young man, who already had a doctorate in biology, was studying psychology and philosophy at the Sorbonne. Professor Simon arranged for the use of Binet's laboratory in a Paris school for this young man's work. Thus began the systematic research by Jean Piaget on the development of intelligence in children.

Piaget later recalled that he "started the work without much enthusiasm," but that his attitude soon changed. "There I was my own master, with a whole school at my disposition—unhoped-for working conditions." Although recognizing the diagnostic value of the tests he was standardizing, Piaget became more interested in trying to find the reasons for wrong answers than simply in obtaining scores for the tests. He therefore initiated, as he later described it, "conversations patterned after psychiatric questioning, with the aim of discovering something about the reasoning process underlying their right, but especially their wrong answers." He was surprised to find that very simple reasoning tasks "presented for normal children up to the age of eleven or twelve difficulties unsuspected by the adult." He pursued these questions with great energy, trying to identify how children at different ages tend to reason about simple cause-and-effect relations. "At last," he said, "I had found my field of research."[8]

After two years of this work in Paris, Piaget returned to Switzerland, where he continued his work at Geneva. He later reported making the following plans at this time:

> I would devote two or three years more to the study of child thought, then return to the origins of mental life, that is, the emergence of intelligence during the first two years. After having thus gained objectively and inductively a knowledge about the elementary structures of intelligence, I would be in the position to attack the problem of thought in general and to construct a psychological and biological epistemology.

This progression of work quite clearly summarizes Piaget's subsequent career, except that the time anticipated for the initial study of children's thought extended considerably beyond two or three years. And the dozens of books that he wrote have had an impact far greater than he could have imagined when he began his work.[9]

The research procedures of Piaget and his associates have been simple, but effective. They include careful observation of children in their natural settings, direct questioning of a child to discover how particular inferences and conclusions are made, and specific experimental test situations to discover what problem-solving methods a child may use in dealing with the situation. Avoiding complex statistical analysis, Piaget placed the emphasis upon the study of particular individuals, always noting the subject's age level when an observation was made. The underlying purpose was to understand how the thought processes of the child are organized.[10]

Let us take a simple example of Piaget's observations of one of his own daughters at one year and three months of age. Jacqueline happened to drop a stick outside her playpen, seeing it roll on the floor. Then, observed Piaget: "As soon as I bring the stick toward her, Jacqueline grasps it and repeats the experiment. She raises it slightly, then lets it fall so that it may roll. The same thing happens ten times." Then Piaget places a cloth on the floor to keep the stick from rolling. Jacqueline again lets the stick fall, but when she sees that it does not roll, she puts her hands through the bars of the playpen it give it a little push. After repeating this two or three times, she gives up.[11]

Now most people would simply say that this child is playing with a stick. But for Piaget, what is important is the way she plays. She is not pursuing some direct effect of the stick for her own body, as earlier grasping or hitting might have indicated. Her attention is rather upon some external effect—how the stick rolls on the floor. Furthermore, she is systematically seeking to bring about this reaction, not just observing it as a chance event. She even seems to be observing a relation between how high she holds the stick and how much it rolls. All of this indicates a rather advanced level of infant intelligence; however, the world is still an infant's world of direct sensory experience. It is still an infant playing with a stick of wood. But this is not just the repetition of a past response, nor even fitting a new object into an established framework of behavior; rather, we see here what Piaget calls the "discovery of new means through active experimentation."[12]

Perhaps the most important contribution of Piaget's work has been his painstaking documentation that a child's view of the world is not the same as an adult's. He further showed precisely how the child's world appears to be organized, and how this characteristic form of cognitive organization changes as the child grows older. Furthermore, such changes do not come simply by degree, but occur through a series of reorganizations, yielding Piaget's famous stages of cognitive development.

Piaget identified three main stages of cognitive development. The first is the sensorimotor stage, from birth to about eighteen to twenty-four months of age. The infant, in physical interaction with the world, then develops his first ideas about the meaning of objects around him. The second is that of concrete operations, which continues until about age nine or ten. This begins as language takes over as the dominant framework for the child's conceptualizations. However, language is used primarily to assist in adjusting to a world of concrete reality. The formal-operational stage is the third main stage, beginning with late pre-adolescence and continuing until adulthood. In this stage the individual is able to deal with ideas abstractly; he is no longer tied in his thinking to a world of concrete experience.[13]

More important than the identification of specific stages is the recognition of how a child's manner of conceptualization changes. Take, for example, the conceptualization of space. An infant at one year may be seated at a circular table, on which three cups are placed upside down. An object is placed under one of the cups, and she is shown which one. She then proceeds to find it under the right cup. But change the baby's location, and she will change the cup selected—choosing in physical relation to herself rather than in relation to the table. But shortly after this age the child begins to conceptualize space more in its own terms, being able to see physical relationships in the environment—discovered through means such as shown when Piaget's daughter dropped a stick outside her playpen. She will then be able to pick up the correct cup in our experiment, regardless of her own placement at the table. With the development of language, however, some of the gains made during the sensorimotor period begin to be lost. From about age our to age seven language is used to organize only the physical world that is immediately related to the child. We quote one psychologist of child development:

> Children between four and seven have the same egocentric concept of space at a verbal level as is seen in the motor behavior of one-year-olds. In the classic experiment demonstrating this, a child is seated before a three-dimensional model of a landscape. He is shown a series of pictures of the landscape and asked to pick out the picture that represents the view he sees. Children four to seven years old can choose correctly. The child is then asked to pick out the picture that represents the panorama seen by the experimenter sitting at right angles to the child. Without exception, children in the early phase of the concrete operations stage will choose the view seen by themselves, an egocentrism formally identical with that shown in the sensorimotor period.

Later, of course, children come to recognize how others who are located differently in space will have different views. And much later will come the more abstract concepts with which spatial relationships may be conceived in geometry or physical science.[14]

Piaget gave not only a description of how the conceptualizations of children change; he also formulated a theory of why this happens. His theory is fundamentally a biological one. All living organisms must organize their reactions to their environments.

Human cognitive organizations are just another—albeit especially sensitive—form of this, and human intelligence is the distinctive form that this takes in our species. Within each individual, at whatever stage of cognitive development, there is a self-regulating mechanism that provides an internal structure for experience and action. To this mechanism Piaget applies the term "equilibration"; it provides for the coordination of both internal and external forces in the adaptation of the human organism to its surroundings. It includes a way of representing the environment within the individual, and a way of organizing one's actions. With age and new experience, this system becomes progressively differentiated. However, there are points at which it fails to organize effectively all the elements that are then significant parts of experience. When such a point is reached, the individual may develop a new mode of organization, leading to the main stages and substages of cognitive organization that Piaget has identified. At different stages of development, the form of this organization—or "equilibration"—is different; however, it always provides an organized adaptation to the world in which one lives.[15]

Intelligence, in Piaget's view, is not some special quality that different individuals have to different degrees. It is a quality we all have, just as we all have more specific ways of perceiving the world and satisfying our needs for food or oxygen. Of course, this intelligence will be qualitatively different for different individuals, especially when we compare individuals of different age levels. But the main emphasis in Piaget's work—in marked contrast to that in the IQ measurement field—is to underline the basic similarity of the potential for intelligent behavior of humans generally. Practically all humans move through the same basic stages of cognitive development, thus sharing essentially parallel (if always individualized) forms of intelligence. But do not some persons progress through the stages at a more rapid rate than others? Yes, but so what? Why should we be so concerned if a child begins talking three months before or three months after most of her peers? The miracle of speech occurs in either case, and with it a new mode of organizing experience. Different degrees of speech fluency may be of some interest, but these mostly reflect the opportunities and pressures to speak—not the fundamental internal organizations of experience that are the root of intelligence.[16]

On the nature vs. nurther issue, Piaget clearly disappoints the strong proponents in both camps. From one point of view, it all seems a matter of natural biological endowment for humans to organize their worlds the way that they do. In support of this is the close relation between age levels and stages of cognitive development. But from another view, all is the result of environment. Only as one adapts to the environment do systems of equilibration emerge, and the content of experience is totally that of one's environment. "The adaptation of intelligence in the course of the construction of its own structure," said Piaget, clearly taking a middle ground on the issue at hand, "depends as much on progressive internal coordinations as on information acquired through experience." Cognitions develop neither as "a simple copy of external objects nor of a mere unfolding of structures performed inside" but rather as "a set of structures progressively constructued by continuous interaction between the subject and the external world."[17]

Piaget's work can be criticized on a number of grounds. Some researchers have questioned the particular age levels given for stages of development, and many have doubted that the stages are as clearly marked as Piaget indicates. Some would fault him on methodological grounds—such as the absence of controlled experimental designs or his limited statistical data. And other leading scholars frequently differ from Piaget on particular issues of interpretation; an example of this can be seen in our next section. However, despite such criticisms, Piaget's work remains as the source of the most widely cited descriptive and theoretical materials concerned with the subject of the development of intelligence in human beings.[18]

Despite the obvious achievements of Jean Piaget, the hows and whys of cognitive development remain as open to further study as ever. We still know little about how the intelligence of a person such as Albert Einstein (or Jean Piaget) may be qualitatively different from that of most Swiss adolescents. And stepping back just a bit from that level of intellectual maturity, why should humans ever have developed formal operational thought in the first place? One contemporary psychologist, T. G. R. Bower, has made these comments on the question:

> The real mystery of the formal period, both phylogenetically and ontogenetically, is why humans take the step from a mind that is limited to coping with the perceptible properties of the world to one that invents entities and conjures up explanations for those perceptible properties. That step, to angels or atoms, is the most mysterious evolutionary step mankind has taken.[19]

AFTER THE BEGINNING WAS THE WORD

A symbolic world begins to dominate the consciousness of children near their second birthday. Piaget marked this as the beginning of a new major stage of cognitive organization. Words may now be used to represent the environment and to organize responses to other people. With this use of words, a new mode of adjustment—a symbolic mode—becomes possible. We no longer deal only with things or people as immediate physical entities, but more directly with our internal representations of them; these in turn are encoded in the language forms we learn from our parents.

Despite his recognition of the importance of language, Piaget was quite clear that this new medium did not itself create any fundamentally new cognitive structures. Thinking existed first, in his view; its expression in language is a secondary manifestation of the cognitive powers already developed. That persons born deaf appear to develop their own organized forms of intelligence with little help from language is evidence that supports Piaget's view. It is also of importance to note that children will organize their actions in relation to physical objects (apparently without language) in some ways quite parallel to the way they organize ideas into words.[20]

It may well be true that when a child learns to speak he is applying already developed cognitive skills. But it is also true that the communicative skills involved in speaking reflect a long history of their own, tracing back to the earliest levels of cognitive development. Contrary to what Piaget suggested, we now know that infants begin to imitate their mothers during the very first weeks of their lives, and that they are able to discriminate rather subtle differences in speech sounds by the age of six weeks. That this does not at first result in any more organized speech than babbling should not close our eyes to the extent of communicative contact the infant is able to form during the first few months. And this communicative contact grows rather naturally as the child matures and expands in learning.[21]

A number of children whose early language has been systematically observed (usually by their own scientifically inclined parents) have helped us considerably in understanding how language is learned. We select one of these cases, that of Nigel Halliday, to help us illustrate this most critical process of learning. Nigel's father, M. A. K. Halliday, a professor of linguistics, has given us an especially useful account of his son's initiation into the English language. We will draw on this account at some length.[22]

Let us describe, in summary form, the progression of Nigel's language learning over a period of approximately twelve months:

A. At nine months Nigel has five regular elements for communication. Three of these are physical expressions or gestures. For example, he grasps an object firmly to say, in effect, "I want that;" a light touch indicates "I don't want that," and a firm touch of a person or object means something like "do that again." Only two expressions are made with sounds. Using similar sounds (with neither having any relationship to adult speech), Nigel can say something like either "look" (usually directed to something moving) or "let's be together."

B. At one year Nigel has twenty-one regular elements. All of these are now vocal, the gestures having been replaced by sounds. With few exceptions (such as a "d" sound in relationship to "dog" and an "n" sound in relationship to his sister Anna), these show little resemblance to any adult words. These elements appear to include such general meanings as "give me that," "nice to see you," "that's nice," and "look, that's interesting." More specific expressions include sounds for "I want my bird toy," and "I'm sleepy"; there are also different expressions to distinguish "do that again" from "do that right now."

C. By one year and three months Nigel has thirty-two elements of speech. Most of the meanings of three months ago are still present, though many of the sounds have shifted slightly. There is only a modest increase in similarity to adult words. The main change is the greater diversification in meanings. There are now different sounds for dog, cat, and birds. Two individuals (his father and his sister) are now each associated with a special personal expression. Also, still finer distinctions of meaning are possible, such as between "yes, I want what you just offered" and a more general "yes, I want that." There are also beginning to be some imaginative elements, including a high-sung sound that seems to represent a bit of music and a distinction between "let's pretend to go to sleep" and "I'm sleepy."

D. By one and a half years Nigel has begun to show a rather remarkable change. Many of his approximately 145 elements are now similar to adult words, and he imitatively repeats the words he hears adults using. Indeed, the rapid proliferation of new elements out of adult speech makes any count of those existing at any one time only an approximation. Even more significantly, the elements show some shifts in meaning, depending on interactional context. All use of language, however, is still limited to utterances of a single element.[23]

E. By twenty-one months of age, Nigel has increased his repertory of elements (mostly now approaching adult forms) so greatly that it is no longer possible to count them in any meaningful way. Furthermore, he has begun to show orderly systems of combining elements. On the first day that he clearly combined two elements into one utterance, he followed quickly with others; by the end of the following day a three-word combination ("more meat please") had been given. Two other clear speech patterns emerged at about the same time: (1) he adapted his speech readily to a dialogue format and (2) he made a sharp intonation distinction between two main groups of utterances. In regard to the first point, within a period of two weeks Nigel developed his dialogue skills so rapidly that, at the end of that brief period, he could function with appropriate verbal differentiation to (a) answer a question, (b) respond to a command, (c) respond to a statement, or (d) respond to a response. He even could initiate dialogue—though only by asking "what's that?" On the matter of intonation, Nigel had from the beginning included tonal qualities in differentiating his elements of speech. By this time, however, he had also made a general distinction between utterances that demanded a response from some other person (which were consistently rising in tone) to most other utterances (which tended to fall in tone).

When in all this, we may ask, is it most appropriate to say that Nigel had learned language? This is not an easy question to answer. Only just before the age of eighteen months had Nigel's speech begun to approximate the sounds of adults with any regularity, and it was shortly after then that he began to put words together into a single utterance. This might lead us to suggest that the levels we have identified as D and E mark the beginning of language. But what about the earlier levels—do these not also show language?

Professor Halliday's own answer is that Nigel is beginning to use a language at level A, and that this is the language he continues to use exclusively for more than six months. But this is his own language, the language he creates himself to mark some of his meanings in the world. It is not English. It is not the language of his parents—except insofar as they come to understand it in special relationship to their son. This language serves as a device for Nigel's increasingly effective communication with those around him, and it helps him to mark some of his most important daily events. It assists in his beginning to learn his culture, at least in its most concrete manifestations. Halliday calls this the first phase of language learning.

The second phase involves a transition to a new language—in this case, to the English language. In our descriptive summary for Nigel, levels A through C represent the first phase, while the second (transitional) phase is shown by D and E. After this point, we have Nigel fully involved as a speaker of the English language. This third phase is fully underway by his second birthday, though full mastery will continue to be a challenge for years to come.

How do we explain this remarkable set of transitions that end with effective use of one's native language? Can we explain this change in terms applicable to any other kind of learning, or is some special explanation necessary?

A great deal of the behavior of children in learning language can be understood in terms of the differential reinforcement by those around them. Parents behave in such a way that some sounds of their children will be used more than others, and reactions of parents help to determine appropriate occasions for particular sounds. Further, some attempts to copy adult sounds will yield more successful results than others. Gradually, according to this explanation, the child develops the ability to use sounds in roughly the same way as adults. He learns to mean similar things with his words and to put his words together in similar patterns. All this seems a rather formidable achievement to be explained in terms of elementary processes of learning (such as trial-and-error learning, response reinforcement, and generalization). It appears totally implausible unless we make several further assumptions. One assumption is that the very young child is an unusually social animal, that some effort at communication is almost second nature from the first few weeks. A second assumption is that learning takes place not only in terms of specific responses, but also in terms of patterns of such responses. That is, the child is reinforced for showing certain patterns of sounds as well as for making particular sounds. This suggests as well a third assumption: The child gradually develops an increasingly comprehensive pattern for his behavior. Certain forms of patterning, especially those given recognition in his particular verbal community, become more successful, and these become a part of his standard repertory for communication.[24]

Even with these added assumptions, learning theory may not appear adequate to account for the acquisition of language. What is particularly difficult to explain is the rather sudden appearance of structured speech (note that Nigel was using a three-word sentence only the day after he first combined two words, and that his "more meat please" was already patterned quite closely to adult English). Furthermore, once a child begins combining words, he is soon quite adept at making new verbal creations (many of which he could never have heard before) on the basis of rather complex rules of syntax. To explain this, some linguists feel that there must be a special capacity of the human brain for language formulation. Noam Chomsky has called this a "language acquisition device," suggesting that it must be an innately preprogrammed capacity of the human species especially evident in the deeper common structures that lie behind the surface differences in human languages.[25]

So are we to explain language acquisition primarily in learning theory terms, or is a specific innate biological capacity for language necessary? It would be rash for us to suggest a simple resolution for this debate, which continues in the field of psycholinguistics. However, it is not necessary to refute the claims of either side in order to take a third position—that whatever model might best fit the most fundamental explanation for language acquisition, the process must also be seen in a context of very active social relationships. Jerome Bruner is among those who take this third position. Language acquisition, he says, "begins when mother and infant create a predictable format of interaction that can serve as a microcosm for communicating and for constituting a shared reality." Perhaps, suggests Bruner, there may be some special predisposing capacities for language, such as what Chomsky refers to as the "language acquisition device." But these, he says, "could not function without the aid given by an adult," who enters with the child "into a transactional format." This format of interaction provides what might be called a "language acquisition support system" that "makes it possible for the infant to enter the linguistic community—and, at the same time, the culture to which the language gives access."[26]

Nigel's father gives an interpretation of his son's language learning which is quite consistent with Bruner's perspective. Professor Halliday emphasizes his son's active and creative pursuit of meanings as well as the importance of the surrounding social relationships. Nigel's language is analyzed in terms of its basic functions or uses; Halliday sees seven main ways that a child might use language:

1. the I-want use (or the instrumental function);

2. the do-as-I-tell-you use (or the regulatory function);

3. the me-and-you use (or the interactional function);

4. the here-I-come use (or the personal function);

5. the tell-me-why use (or the heuristic function);

6. the let's-pretend use (or the imaginative function); and

7. the I've-got-something-to-tell-you use (or the informative function).

Halliday classified all of Nigel's expressions in terms of these seven functions. He had expected the instrumental function to predominate at the beginning, but that is not what he found. Instead, he found the first four functions (instrumental, regulatory, interactional, and personal) all active in the early expressions. These four were the only functions evident within Nigel's first year. Early in the second year (level C in our earlier description) came indications of the imaginative and heuristic functions (though Halliday could not be as clear about when heuristic functions began as he was with the other functions). The informative function did not clearly appear until after Nigel had mastered the technique of combining words into a single utterance.

Nigel's early expressions were quite easy for his father to identify in terms of function. Later this became more difficult. At about nineteen months a critical transition occurred, marked both by a flowering of new expressions and their structural combination. Until then Nigel's system of communication seemed to have only sounds and their meanings (in terms of a particular content for each regular sound). At this point, a new order of meaning appears, a meaning that at least vaguely reflects language as a structured system. Words thus enter as things that can be manipulated to mean various other things, and they can be put together to create new meanings. A child then learns to talk with a new energy, as Nigel's case shows. And in this process grammar—that is, a structure for ordering the elements of communication—is born. Halliday sees this structure as allowing for meanings serving different functions to be encoded together, which adds enormously to what a person can communicate. "Grammar," in brief, "makes it possible to mean more than one thing at a time."[27]

Halliday also finds it important to note that Nigel's learning to use grammar and dialogue occur at the same time. He does not consider this to be a coincidence. In dialogue we learn to associate with others in terms of temporary social roles. These begin as roles of speaker and person spoken to, but they soon expand into more varied roles—such as those of questioner, fact reporter, opinion giver, or persuader. Such roles in dialogue are important both as a channel for communication and as a model for understanding social interaction more generally. Although linguistic in nature, dialogue exemplifies the basic forms of role making and role taking that can apply to more complex social structures.[28]

Perhaps at this point we can do no better than to quote some of Halliday's own comments about the close association of the learning of grammar and the learning of dialogue. These comments also give an appropriate conclusion for our discussion of how a child learns language:

> It is as if up to a certain point the child was working his own way through the history of the human race, creating a language for himself to serve those needs which exist independently of language and which are an essential feature of human life at all times and in all cultures. Then comes a point when he abandons the phylogenetic trail and, as it were, settles for the language that he hears around him, taking over in one immense stride its two fundamental properties as a system: one, its organization on three levels, with a lexicogrammatical level of wording intermediate between the meaning and the sounding, a level which generates structures which enable him to mean more than one thing at a time; and two, its ability to function as an independent means of human interaction, as a form of social intercourse which generates its own set of roles and role relationships, whose meaning is defined solely by the communication process that language brings about.[29]

THE KNOWLEDGEABLE COMMUNITY

In the closing quote of the preceding section, Halliday suggests that the language learning of a child may reproduce, in broad strokes, the development of language in the species. We should be careful about making inferences concerning how language first came to be on the basis of how it is learned by an individual. Unfortunately, we have no good evidence about the origin of language. The tools of past hominids do not say very much about what might have been their users' capacities for speech, and their bones are similarly silent. Historical linguistics may help us work backward to estimate times of divergence for present languages from a common linguistic stock, but these vanish into uncertainty when we go back more than about 15,000 years. Though sometimes implying a common origin of most presently existing languages, such studies still cannot confirm that this was the case.[30]

In view of the circumstantial nature of the evidence available, it is not unreasonable that we look at the language learning of a child to suggest some notions about the emergence of language for the species. If so, we may derive at least the following hypotheses:

1. A fairly high degree of social intelligence was developed before language systems emerged. This included simple cultural forms and some standard means of oral communication.

2. Language systems emerged in a relatively short period of time, when viewed from the perspective of the full story of human evolution.

3. Side-by-side with the development of language systems was a diversification of social structure into more complex forms.

These hypotheses do not appear to be contradicted by any currently available evidence about either the biological nature of man or the unearthed records of human prehistory. After one of the most authoritative reviews of available evidence, Philip Lieberman makes the following conclusions:

> After a long static period lasting until the *erectus* stage of hominid evolution, the specialized supralaryngeal anatomy for human speech developed in one lineage. The fossil record is consistent with the hypothesis of gradual, mosaic evolution of the species-specific skeletal structure of the skull and of the supralaryngeal

vocal tract of modern *Homo sapiens* in the course of the last 250,000 years.

The late stages of human evolution may have involved the evolution of rapid, encoded human speech that follows, in part, from the species-specific human supralaryngeal vocal tract. Rapid human speech may not have been present in some recent hominid lines like the classic Neanderthals. Rapid information transfer that allows people to exchange information within the limits of memory span may have yielded a qualitatively different form of information transfer that resulted in "collective insight."[31]

Whatever may be the details of the beginnings of human language, this new system of communication created a fundamental change for the nature of human intelligence. Intelligence was no longer limited to what one person could gain through his own individual endowment and experience. He could now draw upon the experiences of others. His ability to solve problems could therefore be based on their learning as well as his own. He had embarked on a new venture of, in Professor Lieberman's choice phrase, "collective insight."

Many thousands of years later, the means to obtain this collective insight were greatly enhanced by the development of writing. Records of experience could now be kept in a more reliable and more permanent form. This made possible an even greater wealth of the experience of others that an individual could draw upon.

If by human intelligence we mean effective problem-solving behavior that makes use of our higher cognitive functions, surely we must recognize that this intelligence is a highly social matter. It is not social only because we tend to use it in social contexts. Rather, it is social in a more fundamental sense, in that it draws on the combined experience of human beings, not just on that of the individual who is the focus of action. And this has been the case ever since humans became language-oriented animals.[32]

Did the use of language gradually evolve to allow increasingly abstract formulations? If so, was this primarily a matter of social and cultural evolution? Or were some genetic elements of brain function—"hard-wired" features—involved? Or might the shift to a more abstract world have been a rather sudden one, an "imaginative revolution," so to speak? If so, what external conditions and/or genetic mutations might be involved?

That such questions remain basically unanswered indicates just how deeply mysterious is the evolution of intelligence in the human species. We can be quite certain that the foremost human social invention of all—language—provided the foundation. But somewhere between the emergence of spoken language (even in an explicitly symbolic form, probably more than 70,000 years ago) and the emergence of written language (only a few thousand years ago) came an expansion in the powers of human imagination that is amazing to contemplate. Such monuments as Stonehenge in southern England bear witness to the acuity of astronomical insights (as well as to transportation and construction skills) of a people who must be considered preliterate and therefore prehistoric. Artistic creations left by Cro Magnon man in the caves of western Europe are earlier records of this flowering of the human imagination. Stone tools also show significantly increased variety, beginning about 40,000 years ago. Such scattered evidences are a frustratingly meager record of the enormous increase in human intelligence and imagination that preceded what we call civilization. In the absence of evidence of any particular breakthrough, we tend to see this as a gradual process—largely cultural, but also possibly involving some neurological changes. An archeologist of human prehistory has summed up this progression as follows:

> Probably more and more of all behaviour, often but not always including tool-making behaviour, involved complex rule systems. In the realm of communication, this presumably consisted of more elaborate syntax and extended vocabulary; in the realm of social relations, perhaps increasing numbers of defined categories, obligations and prescriptions; in the realm of subsistence, increasing bodies of communicable know-how.

Such advances could accumulate because they added, in balance, to the effective functioning of existing human communities. Any genetic changes that supported them apparently were favorable to those groups in which they occurred. Thus was the way prepared for what we have come to call the dawn of civilization.[33]

Early civilizations tended to be highly autocratic affairs. Power was held by a relatively small group, and the most important forms of knowledge were also reserved for a select few. Ritual knowledge and written records were the province of the priesthood and the governmental hierarchy. Over the centuries, however, the knowledge base of societies became broadened. Practical intelligence became more prized, and scholarly knowledge became more widely dispersed. Finally, within the last five centuries there has been a veritable explosion in the expansion of human knowledge.

This explosion has had two main features: (1) the wide sharing of the knowledge base among the population at large, and (2) the increasing emphasis upon scientific work for refining the knowledge base.

The printing press provided an important impetus for the democratization of knowledge, though social factors favoring a less hierarchically ordered society were already at work by the time Johann Gutenberg presented his invention in the mid-fifteenth century. The societal expansion of the knowledge base continued with the growth of literacy in modern societies. Free public education and free public libraries are leading twentieth century features of this progression, and these are now found in nearly all parts of the world.

The last five hundred years also has been an age of science. Scientific knowledge has increased remarkably in both volume and precision, often (though not always) at the expense of more traditional forms of knowledge. Science is both a method of investigation and a product of such research. As a method, its emphasis is upon ever more precise empirical refinement. One scientist reports new findings to his subject-matter constituency, and they then use his work for further investigation. The product is codified, though always temporarily and provisionally, in journal articles and textbooks. Whatever is the consensus in the community of scientists in a particular field at a particular time is treated as part of the knowledge base.

Knowledge in the modern world has become a widely shared product. It is also often a highly organized endeavor that requires a wide network of human cooperation. For example, the launching of a new space vehicle to explore phenomena beyond our planet may involve the work of many thousands of people. And when the site for a new supercollider for high energy physics experiments was established by the United States government in the fall of 1988, the prospect for an increased employment of 2,500 people came with it. Even the reporting of very specific information often involves highly complex human organizations—such as mass-circulation newspapers and magazines or television networks.[34]

In such a world as this, intelligence also becomes socialized. Intelligence is less and less a strictly individual affair; more and more it becomes an ability, cultivated through education, to be able to plug into the shared knowledge base of the society. Our intelligence thus becomes more a property of the community than of the individual. It resides more in libraries and laboratories (and in the interaction that takes place between minds in such settings) than in individual minds. There is, of course, no point in making this an either-or argument, belittling the mind of the human individual in the process. The mental capacity of the human individual—almost any individual—is a truly wonderful thing. But so also is the capacity of the knowledgeable community—initially produced through a largely mysterious process, but clearly an ultimate legacy of human language.

NOTES

1. A good source on the history of intelligence measurement is Tuddenham (1963). The quotations from Binet in this and the previous paragraph are taken from this source, all from p. 483.

2. Goddard had said that "the chief determiner of human conduct is a unitary mental process we call intelligence" and that the "mental level for each individual is determined by the kind of chromosomes that come together with the union of the germ cells" (quoted by Tuddenham, 1963, p. 491). Terman's views were more moderate, considering his own Stanford-Binet instrument as more practically useful than theoretically important. He said: "I am fully aware that my researches have not contributed very greatly to the theory of mental measurement" (quoted by Tuddenham, 1963, p. 494). However, Terman felt confident enough to assert that "the children of successful and cultured parents test higher than children from wretched and ignorant homes for the simple reason that their heredity is better" (quoted by Gould, 1981, p. 183).

3. Great Britain is perhaps an exception to what is stated here. Ever since Francis Galton (1822–1911) there has been a strong interest there in measuring intellectual capacity and in using such measures as indices of good genetic backgrounds. This tradition continues today under the leadership of psychologists such as Hans Eysenck.

4. Herrnstein (1973) reports that "most experts estimate that I.Q. has a heritability between .7 and .85" (p. 185). Jensen (1972) gives an estimate of $h2$ (or heritability) at .77, which he further estimates as .81 after correcting for test unreliability. But this, he points out, is an average value "about which there is some dispersion of values, depending on such variables as the particular tests used, the population sampled, and sampling error" (p. 127). It also should be pointed out that Jensen's data included the since-discredited studies of Cyril Burt. Jencks (1972), in attempting to estimate heritability of IQ scores among Americans, says: "Our best guess is that genotype explains about 45 percent of the variance in IQ scores, that environment explains about 35 percent, and that the correlation between genotype and environment explains the remaining 20 percent" (p. 315).

The sad case of Sir Cyril Burt is told most fully in Hearnshaw (1979); the story is told more briefly in Gould (1981).

5. For the factor analytic work of Spearman and Thurstone, see Spearman (1923, 1927) and Thurstone (1935). Summaries of their work may be found in Tuddenham (1963) and Gould (1981). An interesting recent survey of expert opinion among psychologists (Snyderman and Rothman, 1987) shows a continued diversity of views on just exactly what is being measured by IQ tests; however, in general, "experts hold positive attitudes about the validity and usefulness of intelligence and aptitude testing" (p. 137).

6. Howard Gardner's theory of "intelligences" is presented in Gardner (1976).

7. Jencks (1972) gives evidence to support a much greater relationship between IQ scores and academic success than between such scores and occupational success. Even educational achievement is only modestly related to such test results; Jencks estimates that "IQ genotype per se explains between 2 and 9 percent of the variation in eventual educational attainment" (p. 145). He concludes that "factors influencing educational attainment are overwhelmingly social, not biological" (p. 146). A useful essay on the nature of intelligence is that of Chein (1945), who emphasizes that intelligence is an attribute of behavior, not an attribute of a person.

8. All quotations in this paragraph are from Piaget (1952a), pp. 244–245.

9. Piaget (1896–1980) remained an active scholar until his death. The quotation in this paragraph is from Piaget (1952a), p. 246.

10. We have characterized here the research with children for which Piaget is best known. Of course, some of his work goes beyond such a simple description. For example, in 1929 he reported important biological contributions for the study of mollusks, continuing a special interest begun at a very early age.

11. This case is described in Piaget (1952b), p. 272.

12. See Piaget (1952b). The final quote is from p. 267.

13. In our listing of stages we have especially followed Bower (1979). In some descriptions by others the middle stage of development is divided into an earlier "preoperational" and a later "concrete operations" stage. See, for example, Biehler and Hudson (1986), who also give a clear description of substages within the sensorimotor period.

14. The quotation here is from Bower (1979), pp. 133–134.

15. Much fuller expositions of Piaget's theory may be found in Furth (1969), Piaget (1970), and Piaget (1971), among other sources. Piaget refers to the internal representation of environmental data as *assimilation*, with systematic actions upon the environment called *accommodation*. Adaptation is the combined result of assimilation and accommodation, organized by processes of equilibration.

16. Some scholars have suggested that most persons in some societies never achieve fully the mastery of either concrete or formal operations. For example, an early study of Australian aborigines concluded that they may be genetically incapable of mastering basic conservation tasks which mark development within the stage of concrete operations, but later research has shown this not to be the case (Bower, 1979, pp. 180–184). Closer to home for most readers, a majority of American college freshmen apparently fail to show fully formal operational thought when faced with Piagetian tests, considerably less than the proportions Piaget implied for European young people. Bower (pp. 216–218) suggests that this may be because they have not been trained to apply formal thinking in such contexts; they "may have thought formally about everything in the world *except* the sort of material they were accustomed to seeing in school" (p. 217). In concluding, Bower says: "No racial group, no matter how reproductively isolated, has been shown to lack any of the concepts described by Piaget. Yet the specific concepts normally viewed as correct in Western culture will remain completely absent in the absence of the requisite environmental information" (p. 219).

17. The quotations are from Piaget (1970), p. 703. See also Furth (1969), especially pp. 220–239, and Bower (1979), especially pp. 175–177 and 218–221.

18. Other perspectives on the cognitive development of children may be found in Biehler and Hudson (1986), Bruner and others (1966), Connolly and Bruner (1973), Field and others (1982), Kagen (1984), and Lewis (1983).

19. This concluding quotation is from Bower (1979), p. 218.

20. Piaget is sometimes difficult to understand precisely, but probably his most specific statement on the relationship of language to thought is the following: "In short, a verbal transmission that gives adequate information relative to operational structures is only assimilated at levels where these structures have already been elaborated on the plane of actions or of operations as interiorized actions. If language favors this interiorization it certainly does not create nor transmit ready-made these structures in an exclusively linguistic way" (in Furth, 1969, p. 127). For studies with deaf persons, see Furth (1966). Bower (1979), pp. 241–244, reviews the work of Patricia Greenfield in nonlanguage areas that supports the idea that processes of language acquisition reflect more general processes of cognitive development.

21. Some of these very early developments are discussed by Bower (1979), especially pp. 228–229.

22. Our source here is Halliday (1975). The subsequent summary by age levels is our own, based on Halliday's much more detailed account and complete listing of elements.

23. These rapid additions of new elements include a large number that have special personal reference. We would expect that Nigel would pass a mirror test for self-recognition (such as was described in Chapter 2)

at about this time. If so, it is interesting to note how closely abilities for dialogue and word combinations are to follow. It would be extremely significant to have data that could compare a large number of children on relative times for emergence of self-recognition, multiple-word utterances, and dialogue use.

24. The best known case for interpreting human language behavior in learning theory terms is given by Skinner (1957). Another useful work out of a similar tradition is that of Mowrer (1960).

25. For a fuller statement of this view, see Chomsky (1972).

26. The quotations here are all from Bruner (1983), pp. 18–19.

27. The quotation here is from Halliday (1975), p. 48.

28. Some years ago, Roger Brown (1965) pointed to some close parallels between language and social structure: "Social roles, such as male and female, guest and host, doctor and patient, as well as morpheme classes, such as article, noun, and verb, are defined in terms of the privileges and obligations of interaction enjoyed by their members. There are parallels also between the higher levels of linguistic structure and higher levels of social structure. The immediate constituents of a well-formed social event are as psychologically real as the immediate constituents of a well-formed sentence. A marriage ceremony, for instance, has such first level constituents as the procession, the vows, the reception, and the departure of the honeymooners. On a lower level of analysis the ceremony involves such roles as bride, groom, minister, and father-of-the-bride. The ultimate constituents are, of course, persons occupying the roles on a given occasion. The parallels between linguistic structure and social structure are not superficial. It seems likely that the two sorts of structure will turn out to be learned in the same way" (pp. 303–304).

29. This final quotation of this section is from Halliday (1975), p. 32.

30. Recently reported work in historical linguistics has suggested that most languages of Europe and Asia may have had a common origin (sometimes called "Nostratic") about 15,000 years ago, and that American Indian languages had a common origin ("Amerind") about 11,000 years ago (Lewin, 1988).

31. This quotation is from Lieberman (1984), p. 333. Lieberman does not believe it necessary to posit a specific genetic basis for language. He views the general cognitive and memory functions of the brain as involved, but he also suggests that speech for humans "like other vocal, gestural, electric, and other communication systems of other species, appears to involve specialized, localized neural transducers" (p. 333). Although Lieberman emphasizes the unique biological developments that make human speech production possible, there have also been auditory specializations for speech reception. Recent evidence indicates that the brain has special ways of identifying phonetic patterns that are quite different from the way most sounds are heard (see, for example, Liberman and Mattingly, 1989).

32. This is of course not a new idea. George H. Mead and John Dewey were among those who have made this a central point for their philosophies. Dewey (1922), for example, has said: "Our intelligence is bound up, so far as its materials are concerned, with the community life of which we are a part" (p. 314).

33. The archeologist quoted is Glynn Isaac, in turn quoted in Leakey (1981), pp. 135–136. The earlier reference to the origin of symbolic speech "probably more than 70,000 years ago" is a rather arbitrary figure, based on a separation of Australian groups over 40,000 years ago and a much earlier separation of African and non-African lines. See Cavalli-Sforza and others (1988) for related evidence.

34. Taylor (1968), pp. 168–169, describes how tens of thousands of persons were involved in the launching and tracking of the Gemini 3 flight of Virgil Grissom and John Young in 1965. The employment estimate for the supercollider decision in the fall of 1988 (for which a site near Dallas, Texas, was chosen) is from the *U.S. News and World Report* for November 21, 1988, p. 18.

Chapter 5

The Mystery of Beliefs

TALES OF TWO SLAUGHTERS

In 1854, British, French, and Turkish forces had invaded the Crimean peninsula in southern Russia and were advancing toward the major naval base of Sevastopol. Although ultimately successful in their objective, the allied forces had great difficulties during this campaign. Indeed, the Crimean War, as this campaign came to be known in Western Europe, was surrounded by considerable controversy—concerning both the way its battles were conducted and the ultimate war aims of the allies. Checking the ambitions of Russian expansion was the generally understood purpose; but the reasons for the extended campaign against Sevastopol could well be questioned as to its value in that quest.

Be that as it may, in September a naval blockade of Sevastopol was begun, and ground forces were moving from a British base at Balaklava toward Sevastopol. Then, on October 25, the Russians counterattacked, seizing a number of fortified positions among the outer defenses of Balaklava. At this point, the Russian advance was checked by determined oppositon, and the Russians prepared to retreat from their most forward positions. Lord Raglan, who commanded the British forces, was impatient to put further pressure on the Russians. He encouraged the commander of his cavalry units to press forward; however, they, awaiting infantry support, delayed. One brigade of cavalry that was sure to be involved was commanded by Lord Cardigan; this light brigade had seen no action at all so far that day. Without any special orders to attack, Cardigan had remained in a defensive posture, despite the fact that an intense battle had raged nearby. But this inactivity was to change very soon.

Lord Raglan, viewing the scene from a high location, noticed the Russians preparing to remove some of the allied guns from recently captured locations near where the British cavalry forces were. He sent an order for his cavalry to "advance rapidly to the front and prevent the enemy from carrying off the guns." His aide, who carried this written message, further insisted that "Lord Raglan orders that the cavalry should attack immediately." The overall cavalry commander questioned the order. "Attack what?" he wondered. The only guns he could see consisted of a well-defended battery at the head of a long valley, with Russian forces on all sides. The aide waved generally toward the enemy, saying, "There my Lord is the enemy, there are the guns."

Immediately the order was transmitted to Cardigan to advance toward the only battery of guns they could see. Cardigan too questioned the order. "Permit me to observe that we are advancing against a battery with guns and riflemen on our flanks," he later recalled saying. But he was told simply that "It is the Commander-in-Chief's order." So Cardigan issued his own order to start the advance, and he personally led the assult.

Thus began the attack that has been immortalized by Alfred Lord Tennyson's poem, "The Charge of the Light Brigade." Riding up a long valley, with enemy guns on either side, Cardigan's men kept their tight discipline despite devastating losses. They overran the enemy's batteries and engaged Russian cavalry forces before returning the way they had come. Nearly half of the 673 men involved were killed or wounded in the charge, which lasted all of about twenty minutes.

The charge by Cardigan's cavalry had no significant effect upon how forces were arrayed at the end of the day's battle, and its impact upon the war as a whole was nil. Still, it remains the most celebrated single engagement of the Crimean War. Ennobled by Tennyson's poetry, these horsemen remain the courageous "six hundred" who rode "into the valley of death" to "do or die"—and "not to reason why." The final lines of his poem make clear Tennyson's own romantic view of these events:

When can their glory fade?
O the wild charge they made!
　All the world wonder'd.
Honour the charge they made!
　Honour the Light Brigade,
Noble six hundred!

Even the enemy was moved to admire "these valiant lunatics," as a Russian field commander's report called them. But perhaps the most apt comment came from a French general who witnessed the charge: "It is magnificent, but it is not war."[1]

Let us move now to a more recent event. The time: November, 1978. The place: Jonestown, in Guyana, South America. A United States Congressman from California, Leo Ryan, was leading a group of visitors to investigate whether or not some of the residents of Jonestown (mostly from California) were being forced to stay there against their will by Jim Jones, their leader. Jones was a controversial religious leader who had gathered a devoted group of followers around him. When his People's Temple faced problems in California, he led a large group and established a self-sufficient colony (which came to be known as Jonestown) in the jungles of Guyana.

Several members of the colony had decided to return to the United States with Congressman Ryan's party. They were planning to board planes at a nearby airstrip, where rifle fire suddenly erupted and cut down most of Ryan's group, immediately killing the Congressman and four others. Later it appeared that this was a hastily improvised attack by followers of Jones. The original plan was apparently that one of Jones's most faithful followers would board Ryan's plane at the airport (in the guise of a defector), later taking it over at gunpoint and causing it to crash. However, this individual got on the wrong plane at the airstrip, so there had to be an adjustment in the plans. The attack was then made by a small group of men who had just driven up from Jonestown.

Whatever the original plan may have been, Jim Jones realized that he and his colony were in serious trouble as soon as reports came back from the airstrip. His response was to gather his followers around to announce that now was to be the ultimate test of their faith. Several times before the group had prepared for a ritual mass suicide—"White Night," Jones had called it. Now it was to be put into practice. As an eyewitness account was later summarized:

> Jones continued his wild exhortations, explaining that Jonestown
> would soon be surrounded by enemy forces, that the only dignity
> for those who had come this far was death. The potion was ready
> now and a young mother approached the vat and watched as the
> doctor took a syringe filled with grape-flavored cyanide and
> squirted it down the throat of her young child.

Thus began the process of administering poison to the faithful
followers of Jim Jones. They lined up for their turn at the vat, then
joined together in small groups to await the end a few minutes
later. The decomposing bodies of Jones and more than nine
hundred of his followers were found two days later when Guyana
authorities and newsmen inspected the site. Only a scattered few of
the Jonestown residents were not included among the dead.[2]

The world was horrified by these events in Guyana. *Time* and
Newsweek both made them a cover story, using such phrases as
"hellish nightmare" and "a tragedy that strained all
comprehension." There was sudden interest in a wide range of
religious cults and their influence on their followers, as well as
special interest in the personal pathology of the Reverend Jim
Jones.[3]

The reaction to the Jonestown massacre was very different
from that which greeted the news of Cardigan's charge in the
Crimean War. We will return to this point later. For now, however,
it might be useful to point to some basic similarities between these
two cases.

First, both cases illustrate the extent to which persons may
become devoted to a particular belief system. In one case, the belief
system involved devotion to country and to the military system
that was organized to pursue national interests. In the other, it was
a belief in a religious system, as well as in the personal leadership
of Jim Jones. In both cases we see evidence of a large number of
persons ready to put their lives on the line in support of a particular
set of beliefs into which they had been indoctrinated.

Second, both cases show the importance of authority beliefs
within a belief system. In a military system it is important that
soldiers not question the basic war aims of their nation's leaders,
and that they follow faithfully whatever their field commander
may order. In a religious system, central tenets of the faith are not
to be doubted, and local leaders are often seen as special

interpreters of the will of God. In both of these cases, most of us would agree, there was a misuse of authority that needlessly imperiled and destroyed many lives. Still, such cases demonstrate the extent of human commitment that may be made to belief systems and the central role of authority beliefs within many such systems.

A third feature that these cases have in common is the anchorage of a system of beliefs in a particular form of human organization. It was not only the military leadership of Lord Cardigan that was involved in the charge of his light brigade; the brigade itself had a central part in the loyalties of these soldiers. Their beliefs about fighting were embedded in this particular fighting group, and they (or at least the survivors) could take special pride in a well-executed battlefield performance. At Jonestown the leadership of Jim Jones was critical, but so also was the devotion of his followers to the community as a whole. When its solidarity was called into question by the Congressman's visit and by the defectors who chose to leave with him, there was a strong need to close ranks in demonstrating their devotion. Their self-sacrifice became the chief means of this demonstration.

Given the basic similarities in these two cases, why is it that our immediate tendency is to view them from such different perspectives? Why do we enshrine the noble actions of one, and detest the miserable and insane acts of the other? The difference probably has something to do with what have become mainstream values and beliefs of Western civilization. Devotion to the nation-state has become a central value, and beliefs about its structure and authority are to be uncritically accepted—especially in military contexts. How could we fight wars if this were not the case? On the other hand, religious values are to be celebrated most usually in private spheres. Despite the origins of Christianity and its central imagery of the cross, self-sacrifice (in most of the Western world, at least) is expected to be celebrated more in sentimental acts and ritualized displays than in actions of political and economic significance. Thus, the Jonestown catastrophe goes down as an inglorious and pathetic result of a bizarre cult; while the light brigade's charge is seen as a glorious example of human courage.

Still, both of these cases are alike in reminding us that human beliefs sometimes can have drastic consequences. We can therefore use them to raise some fundamental questions about the nature of human belief systems.

THE ORGANIZATION OF BELIEFS

Beliefs about the world around us emerge from a most intricate human nervous system. We are only beginning to understand how the brain works; and even as we learn more and more, we continue to be amazed at the capacity for memory and for coordination of sensation and action that are the routine products of the human brain. It is only when something is not working as we expect—such as a case of impairment in some sensory or memory capacity—that we come to realize how much we take for granted in the smooth functioning of this vast neural network.[4]

Beliefs are of course based on the functioning of human brains, but they are also based on two other kinds of reality: the objective reality of the physical world around us, and the social reality of the world we take on as members of a human community.

All mammals are heavily invested in perceptual systems, used for testing reality in order to organize reactions to it. Among primates, including humans, the visual system seems to have a special emphasis. Exploring and understanding the visual world thus seems to be as central a part of our nature as is eating or sleeping. There is a substantial foundation for the common phrase that "seeing is believing."[5]

But beliefs flow from social perception as well as from direct visual encounters. Indeed, our visual and social worlds are so intertwined that it is not usually possible to distinguish clearly between them. The clearest example of this can be seen (note the visual metaphor!) in our use of language. Language is preeminently a system of social communication, but it also becomes a way of cataloging and organizing our impressions of the physical world. And behind the language—in its vocabulary and structure—is the accumulated experience of our particular segment of human society.[6]

A belief, as we use the term in the present chapter, is an assertion about reality to which an individual may give conscious assent.

To say that a belief is an assertion is to say that beliefs are of a potentially linguistic form. This is not to say that the belief is always expressed in the same way, or that it is even clearly expressed at all—only that it is expressible. Despite the common phrase that "seeing is believing," we are now suggesting that there may be some value in excluding our most immediate perceptions from what we call beliefs. Only when there is some degree of reflection that may be expressed verbally do we speak of a belief. In this sense, "saying" as well as "seeing" is necessary for believing.

But are there not some beliefs a person may hold of which he is not aware? Although we could conceive of such a possibility, it would be extremely difficult for us to analyze such unconscious beliefs. As a practical measure, we leave them aside. Beliefs thus become, by our definition, matters of consciousness—or at least what can, upon reflection, become conscious. At any one time, of course, we are conscious of only a few of our beliefs, but many more become conscious as they become relevant to whatever receives our attention.

Of course, it is possible for a person to assert a belief he does not consciously hold or to hold a belief he does not assert. Such possibilities of human omission and deception make the scientific study of beliefs an especially difficult business. We are usually warranted in assuming that people believe what they say they believe, but we must also be alert to evidence that indicates when this may not be the case. In addition, we examine what people do as well as what they say as a means of assessing what their beliefs really are.

Beliefs, then, are images of reality that we may talk about (a) with some awareness of the meaning of our assertions, and (b) with the expectation that these images will not be contradicted by later experience.

The number of beliefs we may have is without limit, though at any one moment only a few will appear relevant. The rest are inactive, waiting to be brought forth when the occasion demands. Which beliefs are active depends upon what may be receiving our attention at any given time.

Beliefs are organized around the objects of our attention. We develop and apply beliefs about those things—physical things, places, persons, and ideas—that are repeated objects of our attention. Social psychologists express this point when discussing what they call "attitudes." An attitude is a relatively enduring orientation toward some object of experience. Attitudes are further analyzed as having three components: (1) cognitions, (2) feelings, and (3) action tendencies. Beliefs are the cognitive aspect of an attitude. Positive or negative feelings may be associated with an object, constituting what may also be called the affective component of an attitude. Finally, habits of response developed in past experiences are also associated with the objects of our attitudes. Although it is convenient to study attitudes in terms of this tripartite division, it is also important to recognize that these three components are never fully distinct. We have different beliefs about a person we find attractive than about one who repels us, and our beliefs in turn may affect the degree of attraction we feel. Habitual behaviors in a particular setting (such as attending church regularly and bowing frequently in prayer) have an important impact on beliefs (especially religious beliefs, in this case); just as, on the other hand, beliefs predispose a person toward certain action tendencies (religious nonbelievers being unlikely to attend church, for example).[7]

Attitudes are further organized by the social forces that frame the objects of attitudes. We do not simply attend to matters at random, but our attention follows a social scheduling. Our lives are encased in families, organizations, and larger communities that create the settings in which we must frame our experiences. Our roles in these various social frameworks largely determine what we attend to at any one point in time; in addition, they make certain beliefs, feelings, and behaviors more likely than others.

Beliefs are thus organized by the social worlds in which we live. They are parts of our enduring attitudes toward the things with which we must deal in our everyday lives. There is, however, one object of our attention that is central for nearly all our experience, and our attitudes toward this object have a potential for affecting attitudes toward almost anything else. This is the self. The sense of identity serves as a central anchor for our system of attitudes, and beliefs about the self color beliefs about almost everything else.

"We believe, first and foremost," Bertrand Russell once asserted, "what makes us feel that we are fine fellows." Certainly it is not difficult to find evidence of ego enhancement at work in human belief systems. We try to build our own self–respect by believing good things about ourselves, our groups, our nation, and our species. Always? No, of course not. Sometimes we enjoy a joke even when it is on ourselves; sometimes we deplore the actions of our group or our nation; and there are even occasions when we feel a bit ashamed of the record of our species. But such cases are notable as exceptions to the powerfully self-serving function of our most cherished beliefs. We seek to appear in a favorable light to others, but it is ourselves that we most wish to impress. So we generally develop beliefs that are effective in assuring this self-esteem.[8]

But we are not just ego-enhancing animals. We are also reality-seeking and socially conforming animals, and our beliefs show the imprint of all of these tendencies. To imagine one example, despite the self-serving excuses he may try to muster, a motorist who drives into a parked car must deal with the reality of being responsible for a very stupid action. Social conformity can help here. He knows the rules of the road—"and, officer, I always try to drive safely." But this time he was momentarily distracted—the sun was in his eyes, or he swerved a little too much to avoid another car. As a good member of society, he is willing to see that his insurance company covers any damages. And, with a final act of faith that pushes back reality-seeking in favor of ego-enhancement, he asserts, "It won't happen again!"

OF GRASSHOPPERS, FLUORIDE, AND BOOZE

Behaviors of eating and drinking may be seen as illustrations of many of the features of belief systems briefly mentioned in the previous section.

What may be defined as proper food varies considerably from society to society and from time to time. In some circles a vegetarian diet is preferred; in other times and places meat may be considered tasty—so long as it is not from swine (or, for others, from horses or dogs). Or perhaps beef may be acceptable any day except Friday, which was reserved for fish until recently by many in the Western world. Grubworms that were considered delicious to the original natives of Australia might, if eaten, cause more recently arrived Australians to vomit. And a certain red vegetable (or is it a fruit?) that is now almost universally found in American salads was not so many decades ago considered poisonous. Such are the taboos, preferences, and other beliefs that are often associated with food choices.

Even the most universally held food taboo—against the eating of human flesh—may for certain peoples on certain occasions be ignored. But perhaps not exactly "ignored," for ceremonies of cannibalism typically place very special emphasis on the supernatural qualities that such eating may involve, which makes this food nothing like just another beefsteak.

Beliefs about foods have sometimes been the subject of experiments conducted by social scientists. None of these have been so bold as to ask people to consider eating human flesh, but one set of experiments, sometimes considered a bit daring, did involve the eating of grasshoppers—and with some extremely interesting results.

In the original experiment, American army reservists were invited to eat fried grasshoppers. There were several different experimental conditions, but for all there was a general introduction emphasizing that soldiers might have to eat unusual foods to survive in emergency circumstances. They were then presented with plates on which rested the well-fried little beasts.

Were the grasshoppers eaten? Yes; under the conditions we have just described, they usually were. (In a later replication with R.O.T.C. students, the proportion was only about half.) But what about the beliefs the reservists had of grasshoppers as food? Data from questionnaires presented both before and after the eating ordeal showed a general increase in the acceptability of grasshoppers. After eating, these men tended to rate the grasshoppers more highly as a possible food. Not that they were ready to have them regularly for dinner—only that they passed the test of being a possible source of food.

All that we have said so far about the grasshopper-eating experiment was pretty much taken for granted by the experimenters. Their actual point of interest was in something more: How might persons in different treatment groups differ in how they evaluated their experience? In particular, what effect would it have if the grasshoppers were presented by an attractive communicator, rather than by one who would be seen more negatively? There was also a control group, where the leader made a more neutral presentation.

Our first guess might be that grasshopper eating induced by a positive communicator would produce more positive beliefs about grasshoppers as food. But such a guess would not take into account dissonance theory. Dissonance theory, as formulated by Leon Festinger and others, lead to somewhat different predictions. We focus here on those who actually eat the grasshoppers. Those who are led by a positive communicator might see themselves as eating the grasshoppers partly to please their leader. They therefore have less need to see themselves as having eaten a generally acceptable food than would be the case with a more negative communicator. When a more nasty guy induces them to eat the things, the grasshoppers should be given more positive evaluations as food.

This at least is what dissonance theory predicts—and what in fact the experimental results tended to support.[9]

What does this imply more generally about belief systems? It implies that we tend to favor those beliefs that have a strong linkage with the self and with what we find ourselves doing. If we eat something because of a reasonable inducement (such as to please an attractive fellow who asks us to do so, or because we are paid a large amount of money to do so) there is no big reason to change our minds about bad tasting food. On the other hand, when there is less good reason to do something and we do it anyway (such as in the case of being asked by a disagreeable chap to eat some fried grasshoppers), the eating must reflect something of our own volition, thus being a more genuine expression of the self. If we freely choose to eat something, it must be a suitable food ("a bit like shrimp, wouldn't you say?"). All this would be a general expression of the search for self-justification, consistent with Bertrand Russell's maxim that we tend to believe "what makes us feel that we are fine fellows."[10]

If food is often the subject of strong beliefs, so is what we may drink. Even the idea of drinking pure water may for some communities be a matter fraught with controversy. There is, first of all, the question of just what constitutes good drinking water. Hardly any communities have such a pure source of water that it can go untreated, and many people have different ideas about what should be tolerated in the process of water treatment.[11]

Fluoridation of a water supply has often been a heated issue for a community. Medical opinion generally sees a modest addition of fluoride (of about one part per million) one of the least expensive public health measures that may be taken by a community desiring good teeth for its citizens. There is indeed good evidence that fluoride reduces dental cares. But there is also evidence that too much fluoride could be medically harmful; indeed, in a few communities the natural level of fluorides is enough to badly color their citizens' teeth. Such evidence leads many persons to see fluoride as a potential contaminant best kept out of drinking water. And so the issue is drawn—the medical establishment and the community leaders usually favoring fluoridation, some other segments (concerned with what "they" may do to "us" in messing with the water) bitterly opposed, and a good number of others vaguely uncomfortable about the level of controversy (many of whom would therefore vote against fluoridation if there should be a referendum on the issue).[12]

Moving from questions of the general water supply to liquids people choose to drink on their own, we find even greater controversy possible. Alcoholic beverages pose a frequent focus for differences of opinion. Some religions proscribe alcohol altogether, while others prescribe it for their rituals. The United States, with its past experiment in national prohibition, is an especially interesting country in which to examine different beliefs about alcohol.

In America's colonial period, alcoholic beverages were generally accepted. As one of the Puritan divines expressed the common view, "Drink is in itself a creature of God, and to be received with thankfulness." However, after the establishment of the United States, there was an increased taste for hard liquor (especially whiskey) and a growing concern about its misuse. This concern developed into the temperance movement, and that movement gradually changed into a movement for prohibition. Led by the Anti-saloon League, the forces of prohibition were finally successful on the national level, and the United States was officially "dry" for the period from 1919 to 1933. Although generally viewed as a failed experiment nationally, prohibition continued to be practiced in some states and in many American localities. Even where prohibition is not at issue, controversies about regulating the sale and consumption of alcoholic beverages can be a matter of significant local disagreement.[13]

During the nineteenth century, alcohol apparently took on a highly personal value for a great number of Americans. For many, its use became a badge of individual freedom and masculinity. For others, it was a sign of moral turpitude, opposing the virtues of thrift, hard work, perseverance, and a prudent consideration of others. Such associations remain during these final decades of the twentieth century, though the years since national prohibition have seen a shift from concern with alcohol as such to a concern for alcoholics and alcoholism—or "from abusive substance to substance abuse," in the words one sociologist has used to summarize this trend.[14]

Alcohol was also often a matter of group identity. For many, it was part of a gentleman's world, with drinking styles marking those who had really "made it" socially. For others, abstinence from alcohol was a part of the role of being a good Baptist or Methodist. For still others, avoiding alcohol was not particularly a religious matter, but it marked the superior virtues of the middle-class elements of small-town and rural America—in contrast to what they considered the unseemly behavior of immigrant groups and persons of uncertain character who congregated in large urban centers.[15]

Beliefs about alcohol could be highly controversial when a referendum on the subject of prohibition was being decided. This was evident from a social psychological study done in Oklahoma in 1959, the year that state finally decided to permit the sale of alcoholic beverages. The referendum on this issue provided a convenient opportunity for research into the dynamics of beliefs. This study focused on the effects of one's own position upon the way related beliefs might be evaluated. Persons identified their own position on the referendum, and then were asked to assess the truth of a number of statements that had some relation to alcohol. Examples of such statements follow:

"Practically all crime results from the use of alcohol."
"Some mental cases result from too much drinking."
"According to the Bible, moderate drinking is all right."
"Many automobile accidents occur because of drunken driving."
"Mild drinking at social events encourages good fellowship."
"Prostitution wouldn't exist if it weren't for liquor."

What the investigators found was that the evaluation of such beliefs was strongly related to the position of the evaluator. Persons supporting the "dry" cause tended to agree with those beliefs they recognized as supporting their side and to disagree with other statements. With the "wets" it was just the opposite: They saw statements that they felt supported a vote for repeal as true, and they disagreed with those belief statements that seemed to move in the other direction. This reflected the intensity of the referendum debate, so that even apparently factual statements were highly suspect if viewed as part of the propaganda of the other side. When a struggle is on, this study seems to suggest, relevant beliefs become seen as statements of the struggle. A purely factual evaluation of such beliefs becomes, for most people, a very difficult endeavor.[16]

Although Kansas had abandoned statewide prohibition before Oklahoma, many Kansas communities used local option provisions of their law to continue a ban on the sale of alcoholic beverages. A sociologist who studied one such community was struck by the apparent unanimity of opinion on the subject. Everyone seemed to agree that drinking was immoral and that the local ban on alcoholic beverages was a very proper measure. At least in public, there was no dispute about such beliefs. In private, though, it was a different story. Many members of the community, including some of its leaders, did, in private, drink. This led one citizen to observe that in their town "they vote dry and drink wet."

Charles Warriner, the sociologist who studied this community, believed that such behavior was not as inconsistent as might appear at first glance. There were, of course, many in the community who abstained from alcohol as a matter of principle, and these people generally also felt the community was best served by a ban on any local sale of beer or wine. But what about those who would bring in a case of beer from a nearby city, consume it in their own homes, and carefully dispose of their "empties"? Did they not disagree with the local ban? Some did, although only privately, and some did not. Among the supporters of the local ban were those who felt that, while some people (such as themselves) could drink moderately, it was still best to keep the temptation away from those who might misuse alcohol. Those who privately opposed the ban also were reticent to make a public challenge. As one expressed it:

> Sure, I go along with that nonsense. It isn't worth fighting about.
> If you got up and said that there wasn't anything wrong with
> drinking a glass of beer now and then, you'd just get into a hell of
> an argument.

What Warriner concluded from his study was that there were two levels of morality in this town, and that both were real. One was the personal level, and here citizens of the town were divided. The other was on the public level, and here the division disappeared. It was part of the "official morality" that this was to be a dry town. It was an important part of the town's identity; and because this was so, one just didn't talk about beer or wine as a natural thing to drink. Being a solid citizen of the community required public disapproval of drinking. And so such beliefs were publicly expressed, even by those who drank in private. Indeed, even as drinking in private increased, so did the urgency for public disapproval of drinking. As one local resident observed:

> This has always been a dry town, but we never talked about how
> dry it was until some people started to think that drinking was
> okay. Before that we just took it for granted that people thought
> drinking was wrong.[17]

Studies such as this remind us that beliefs function on more than one level of social reality. To understand beliefs, and the way that they are expressed, we must be sensitive to more than the personal level. We must look as well to wider social levels—to the group, organization, or community. Only within this broader context is it understandable that a member of Lord Cardigan's cavalry brigade on October 25, 1854, might have held such beliefs as the following:

> We must all do as we are ordered. I shall ride with all the skill that I know how. I shall try to ignore the sounds of enemy guns, or the cries of those falling around me. I shall seek to meet the enemy and engage him in personal encounter. This all must be done— even if I die.

Or on the evening of November 18, 1978, we might imagine a resident of Jonestown with such beliefs as the following:

> This is our supreme test. It gives us a chance to show how fully we mean our faith. After all we've been through, there's no turning back now. We've always followed our Leader, and now he is saying, "It is time to die with dignity." I can hear His Voice over the loudspeaker. Only He can know the full meaning of it all—and how we are now put to the supreme test by our enemies. I don't want to die—but I really have no choice. . . .

WHEN BELIEFS FAIL

Beliefs may sometimes fail. When we say that they may fail, we mean not so much that other people think a belief is wrong (such failure is often easy to demonstrate). Rather, we mean that because of certain experiences, the individual himself may come to reconsider the belief. Such reconsideration is the subject of this final section of our discussion of beliefs.

Some of the most famous studies of social psychologists have involved casting doubt on a strongly held belief. One such study was reported by Solomon Asch about forty years ago. The basic experiment was quite simple. Subjects, present in groups, were asked to report their perceptions about the length of lines displayed before them. They were shown one line, then asked to judge which of three other lines most nearly matched it in length. The task at first appeared easy, but subjects soon faced problems in making such judgments. Indeed, they experienced considerable distress. The key problem was that their judgments did not always agree with those around them.

Asch had arranged for everyone in the group, except for the lone real subject, to agree in their answers, planned in advance. These confederates were well coached to make their answers seem genuine. Sometimes they gave correct answers; but on a preselected set of items they came forth confidently announcing their judgments as something different from what the eyes of the real subject would be telling him to reveal. It was arranged so that most of them would answer first. Then would come the turn of the subject.

When the others report the same judgment as that made by the subject, there is no problem. The fact that the others agree helps to confirm what is clearly his own judgment anyway. That's the way the exercise starts. Then comes the time the others all report a judgment different from that of the real subject. Comments Asch:

> Although the task calls for independent judgments, virtually no one looks upon the estimates of the group with indifference or as irrelevant. Each. . . notes immediately the convergence of the group responses, his divergence from them, and the contradiction between these.

The subject is confused. He has two sets of beliefs that are in conflict. One of these concerns his own ability to make simple perceptual judgments. The other concerns his faith that others, like himself, are reporting their judgments accurately. And there is no reason for him to believe that the judgments of the others—especially when unanimously expressed—are any less reliable than his own.

There were a number of variations of this experiment (such as group size, whether or not there was only one real subject, the presence of a confederate who broke with the majority, and so on). We need not go into the quantitative results for such variations, showing the extent of yielding to majority pressure. However, it should be reported that most subjects showed some yielding toward the majority opinion, allowing the study to be widely cited in textbooks as showing the strong impact of group conformity on the behavior of individuals. On the other hand, it is also possible to use results of this study to show resistance to group pressures, for, even in the face of a unanimous majority, most subjects stuck to their own judgments most of the time. Our present interest is neither to emphasize the yielding or the independence of subjects, but rather to recognize their very real dilemma, however resolved. They depended on their own eyes to tell them what was true, but they also depended on the agreement of other people. To find these two sources of beliefs in conflict created a real problem—what should the individual believe? Some subjects actually came to doubt their own perceptions, believing in the judgments made by others. Others believed their own judgments were correct but felt it safest to report agreement with the majority. Still others remained independent throughout. Even those who seemed most sure of themselves during the experiment often admitted, after the experiment was over, to have had some doubts. As one of them said, "Despite everything, there was a lurking fear. . . I might be wrong, and a fear of exposing myself as inferior in some way."[18]

Even more unsettling for subjects than Asch's experiment was a study done some years later by Stanley Milgram. Milgram's experiment involved not only a conflict about how to interpret reality, but also a conflict about actions toward another person.

In Milgram's basic procedure, two subjects came to a psychological laboratory to take part in an experiment in "memory and learning." Apparently at random, one of them was assigned the role of "teacher," and the other became the "learner." The learner was then taken into another room and strapped into an electrical apparatus. The job of the teacher was to present to the learner, over an intercom, a series of paired associations, then test him on what he had learned. Since this was described as a study of the effects of punishment on learning, wrong answers were to be followed by an electrical shock to the learner, with the shock increasing in severity with each wrong answer.

Now all this was rigged so that a confederate of the experimenter would become the "learner." It was also planned that the learner would give many incorrect answers, soon being completely unable to answer correctly. The real subject as "teacher" would then have the responsibility of sending increasingly severe electric shocks. If he hesitated, the experimenter urged him to continue to send the shocks. Soon the shocks approached potentially lethal levels of over 300 volts, but still the experimenter insisted that the teacher proceed as previously instructed. The shock machine was of course a fake, but the cries coming from the adjoining room seemed real enough.

At this point subjects are faced with a severe conflict in their system of beliefs. They have one set of beliefs about the nature of the experiment, which concerns the effects of punishment on learning and memory. The experimenter seems confidently in charge and is insisting that the experiment be continued. One's role in the experiment requires turning up the shock generator to send increasing levels of shock for wrong answers. But there is also another set of beliefs holding that it is wrong to hurt other people. That other poor fellow—who, except for a slight twist of fate, could be oneself—was obviously hurting. Why he would be so stupid in his answers was a mystery, but maybe it had something do do with the effects of punishment upon learning—which, after all, was what the experiment was all about. And, in any case, the job of the teacher is to carry on. The experimenter keeps insisting on this, and he, of course, is in charge. . . .

How long will subjects continue to turn up the shock machine and send shocks to the poor fellow in the next room? That is the critical measure in Milgram's experiment; for it was really a study of the obedience of the "teacher" rather than anything about the "learner." Those most shocked were the readers of the reports of this study, for over half of Milgram's subjects were reported as continuing to send shocks as long as they were prodded to do so by the experimenter—all the way beyond "Danger: Severe Shock" to "XXX"!

No one given a brief description of the experiment could expect such a high level of obedience, but there it was in Milgram's results. This study inspired a lot of soul-searching about our particular proneness to follow orders and our general readiness to inflict suffering on others. There was also more than an incidental concern about the ethics of such experimentation. Certainly there is no doubt that it caused severe distress for many subjects. We have, for example, the following observations of one subject:

> I observed a mature and initially poised businessman enter the laboratory smiling and confident. Within 20 minutes he was reduced to a twitching, stuttering wreck, who was rapidly approaching a point of nervous collapse. . . . At one point he pushed his fist into his forehead and muttered: "Oh God, let's stop it." And yet he continued to respond to every word of the experimenter, and obeyed to the end.

Whether or not causing such personal discomfort is acceptable ethically, it certainly helps us to recognize how naturally we accept the authority of others in a given situation.[19]

If the Asch experiment points out how commonly we depend on seeking confirmation from others for our own judgments, that of Milgram instructs us in how far we may act on judgments authoritatively supported by others. Our everyday beliefs rest heavily on the authority of others. The news of the day is given by the authority of newspapers and television sources, broader generalizations about the natural world are given by the authority of science, and meanings of words are given by the authority of a dictionary. Is it not true that nearly all credible beliefs rest in part upon an element of authority? Of course, we usually expect this authority to be benign, or at least neutral. In the case of Milgram's experiment, it exceeded its proper role—leaving subjects hesitant about just what they should do in this unusual situation.

In both the Asch and Milgram studies, the strain for an individual's orderly system of beliefs comes primarily from external sources. In two other studies that we will mention, it comes much more from within the ongoing system of personal beliefs. In both these cases, though, some external events served to pose special challenges to personal belief systems.

There may be many reasons why persons may seek to give up one identity to seek an altogether new identity. In three cases studied by Milton Rokeach, a confusion of sexual identity appeared to provide a common thread, though there were also many important individual differences. All three of the men studied developed delusional systems and came to be hospitalized as paranoid schizophrenics. There was a further common thread for all three cases—each man took for himself the new identity of Jesus Christ.

Rokeach believed that it might be therapeutic for these three mental patients to be confronted with one another. He therefore arranged that all three be transferred to Ward D-23 of Ypsilanti State Hospital, Ypsilanti, Michigan, assigned to adjacent beds, and given similar work in the laundry room. Furthermore, he arranged that they would be brought together for regular group sessions for an extended period of time and observed closely throughout their daily activities.

One of the most basic sets of beliefs a person may have concerns a sense of identity. As such, it is an anchor for most other beliefs about the self, and a general framework for behavior. One's sense of identity is something that is not easily or lightly changed. Even if it should be transformed, it is apt to become fixed in its new pattern. Hardly any other beliefs are as resistant to change. But it is also a basic belief that no two persons have the same self. Therefore, if one is truly the reincarnation of Jesus Christ, the claims of another for the same status must be false. Thus, might not the confrontation of three Jesus Christs prove therapeutic for them all—leading all of them to reconsider their central delusional systems?

If Rokeach had hoped that his research project would produce a drastic change in his three Christs, he was disappointed. When brought together, they obviously disagreed, especially in regard to their own personal theologies. They learned, however, how to avoid such issues and still get along reasonably well with each other in necessary daily activities (people do learn not to discuss religion when it proves especially divisive). They basically tried to avoid or deny the confrontation; when this was not possible, they sought to understand the others as mistaken in their beliefs. One of the three—younger and with a stronger strain toward intellectual consistency than the others—did appear to give up many of his Christological claims, though only to take on equally delusional beliefs as substitutes. Once one is supported by a delusional belief system that is immune to the objections of other people, it apparently is not easy to return to the role of being an ordinary human being.[20]

In the Asch and Milgram studies, we saw how much ordinary beliefs about the world around us are supported by what others are saying and doing. In Rokeach's study we are reminded that this is not always the case, even for beliefs of central importance. Of course, we also are reminded that such nonconformity carries with it the high price of constantly disturbed relationships with others.[21]

There is another possibility—that one might be a part of a group that shares a deviant set of beliefs. Within the group there can be strong social support, making the fact that not everyone else agrees to be of secondary importance. Such a situation is found in many religious groups, especially in small and closely knit groups of religious believers.

One such group was led by Mrs. Marian Keech, a housewife living in the suburbs of a midwestern American city. She had received messages from outer space that she transmitted through her handwriting as she received them. A small group had gathered around her, and, in a nearby city, another group of like-minded souls was led by a Dr. Armstrong and his wife. These Seekers, as they came to be called, believed that the end of the world was coming soon, but that salvation would be provided for true believers by intelligent creatures from outer space. Indeed, Mrs. Keech had received messages from these Guardians, including especially one named Sananda (who was said to be Jesus Christ, reformulated for an age of flying saucers). Sananda, through Mrs. Keech, revealed a precise date for the coming catyclism: December 21 of that same year. Immediately Mrs. Keech and Dr. Armstrong went public with their news, and their prophecy was briefly a matter of national news reports. Soon a small band of believers had gathered around them, preparing for their imminent salvation to be provided by spacemen arriving in flying saucers.

On the final evening of December 21, there were fifteen members of the group gathered in the Keech living room to await their liberation. Interestingly, this number did not include Mrs. Keech's husband, who retired early for the night; but it did include several social science observers who had infiltrated into the group, pretending to be believers. The group eagerly awaited the appointed hour of midnight with detailed instructions on how they were to receive their visitors. Midnight came, and passed, and no special visitors arrived. Soon the message came that there had been a slight delay, but that a profound miracle was still about to occur. However, as the minutes passed into hours, there clearly was a problem. Had these believers done something wrong? Had they misunderstood the date? Had they interpreted the messages too literally? Finally, at 4:45 A.M., Mrs. Keech received a new message. It said, in part:

> Not since the beginning of time upon this Earth has there been such a force of Good and light as now floods this room and that which has been loosed within this room now floods the entire Earth.

The implication of this message was that the faith shown by this little group was now to be the salvation for a much wider world. They had met, and passed, their test.

"The whole atmosphere of the group changed abruptly," we are told by the observers present. The most immediate effect was to seek out newspaper reporters with their news of worldwide redemption. Within two hours all the local newspapers and major national wire services had been called to tell the Good News.

For the next few days the Seekers tried frantically to convince others of the validity of their beliefs. They sought maximum publicity, including news of their anticipation that there would be a special visit from outer space brings on Christmas Eve. On that evening the group faithfully gathered on the sidewalk in front of the Keech home and began to sing Christmas carols. Also gathered were about two hundred onlookers, some of whom sought to make sport of the occasion. Neighbors soon flooded the police with complaints about the unruly behavior, and on December 26 a warrant with specific charges against Mrs. Keech and Dr. Armstrong was filed. Rapidly the group dispersed, and the police did not pursue their case. Mrs. Keech went into hiding in Arizona, while the Armstrongs sold their home, to be able to more effectively spread the message of the Guardians to the world at large.

Although the Seekers did not continue as an organized group, their story is instructive as a case study of a clearly disconfirmed group belief. They had committed themselves to a belief in a worldwide disaster and their overcalculation from the cataclysm going so status to predict a precise date. When the event did not occur, did the members give up their beliefs? Only one adherent left the group that fateful night; the others emerged from the occasion with renewed faith and a new explanation. A critical factor was apparently the social support they gave each other that night. They yearned to continue with their beliefs, and together they found a rationalization that would allow them to do so—with increased fervor, for at least a brief period.[?]

Most beliefs, we have seen, are not so much simple matters of fact. They are indeed partly factual—ways of summing up the evidence of our senses, but they are also ways of anchoring the self in a complex world of experience, including investment in some beliefs more than in others. In addition they are adjustments to a social reality given by other people, including the validation for other reasonableness others give to our beliefs. Many of our most interesting beliefs are activated by a mixture of all these forces (the evidence of our senses, the commitments of our ego-involvements, and the support of other people) all at the same time.

NOTES

1. Sources on the Battle of Balaklava in the Crimean War include Dupuy and Dupuy (1970, p. 822); Seaton (1977), pp. 108-145; Warner (1973), especially pp. 56-77; and of course the poem of Tennyson (1854/1970). The larger picture of the Crimean War is discussed in Rich (1985) as well.

2. Krause (1978) was the main source used for the Jonestown case. The eyewitness summary is quoted from p. 136.

3. *Newsweek* and *Time* each on December 4, 1978, had special features, as well as their cover stories, devoted to the Jonestown massacre.

4. A good popular overview of the current state of knowledge about the human brain may be found in Restak (1984). Fascinating examples of human behavior that may result from particular brain malfunctions are found in Sacks (1985).

5. James J. Gibson is among those psychologists who have made us most aware of the intricate relationship between different sensory systems (though with a special emphasis on visual perception) and of the apparently self-reinforcing nature of perceptual activities. See, for example, Gibson (1966).

6. We do not need to take a position here on just how much language comes to predetermine the patterns of human thought. We can, with Vygotsky (1962), note the extent to which social communication forms are embodied in private thought as "interiorized speech"; and, with Whorf (1956), we can note the extent to which thought forms correspond to linguistic distinctions. But we can also, with Gibson (1966, p. 282) hold that our understanding of the world is "not necessarily coerced by linguistic labeling" and that language is more a convenient codification of experience than its prime determinant. There must be room here for an intermediate position that sees language as central for the more reflective forms of thought but as less important for more immediate apprehensions of the world.

7. Discussions of the nature of attitudes can be found in any good social psychology textbook. Other sources include Fishbein (1975); Kiesler, Collins, and Miller (1969); Oskamp (1977); Rokeach (1968); and Triandis (1971). A formal differentiation between beliefs (as a purely cognitive component) and the other components of attitudes would suggest that beliefs be separated from feelings and behavior. In reality, however, there cannot be a sharp separation. In discussions elsewhere in this chapter we consider beliefs in the broader sense (including some implications for feelings and behavior) as well as in the more restrictive purely cognitive sense.

8. Bertrand Russell's quote comes from his delightful essay "An Outline of Intellectual Rubbish," in turn contained in Russell (1950). The quotation (p. 82) is followed by numerous illustrations of how our egocentrism (and ethnocentrism and species-centeredness) tends to shape a great variety of beliefs.

9. The original grasshopper experiment was done by E. E. Smith, with later replications by Philip Zimbardo and his associates. These studies are described in Zimbardo, Ebbesen, and Maslach (1977), pp. 105–109 and 131–138. The theory of cognitive dissonance was first presented by Festinger (1957).

10. The theory of cognitive dissonance was originally intended to help us understand a wide range of psychological consistencies (Festinger, 1957). However, the most successful support for the theory comes from issues where a person's sense of selfhood is centrally involved. Self-justification is indeed a powerful force in seeking a reduction of psychological dissonance (Aronson, 1980).

11. Reasons for frequent concern about drinking water are documented by King (1985).

12. Crain, Katz, and Rosenthal (1969) provide a helpful analysis of community reactions to the fluoridation issue. A different perspective is given by Martin (1989).

13. A good source for the story of alcohol in America is Mendelson and Mello (1985). Our quotation of a "Puritan divine"—actually Increase Mather—is from p. 10 of this source.

14. The phrase here quoted is that of Gusfield (1986), p. 199. His *Symbolic Crusade* provides perceptive analyses of the meanings of alcohol in American life.

15. There are also ethnic subcultures in America with important differences in beliefs and behavior regarding alcohol. For evidence on this, see Greeley, McCready, and Theisen (1980).

16. This study was originally done by N. R. Jackman and Carolyn W. Sherif; our description has been based on Sherif, Sherif, and Nebergall (1965), pp. 133–138. So strongly marked were the results here that this study has sometimes been cited to criticize one of the most popular techniques of attitude measurement, Thurstone scaling, which rests on the assumption that scale values can be based on the ratings made by relatively impartial judges. How can there be valid judgments about scale values when persons differ so much in how they evaluate the items? Instead, what is suggested is that individuals use their own positions as an anchor for evaluating belief statements, with distance from one's own position being a critical factor in whatever rating may be given. Whatever we think on this methodological issue, we may conclude that there are often strong interrelationships between beliefs and feelings and action tendencies (which partly supports our choice, indicated above in Note 7, to use the concept of beliefs in a rather broad way in most of this chapter).

17. The study we have been citing and quoting from is that of Warriner (1958). Quotations have been from pages 165, 166, and 167, respectively.

18. The full report of this study is found in Asch (1952), pp. 450–501. Our quotations have been from pp. 461 and 467–468.

19. Our primary source for this experiment has been Milgram (1963), with the description of the distressed businessman quoted from p. 377. A fuller discussion is contained in Milgram (1974).

20. The study of the confrontation between three men who each claimed to be Jesus Christ is fully described in Rokeach (1964).

21. As we look closely at the lives of the three Christs at Ypsalanti, we note, however, that their delusional systems provided social gains as well as losses. For persons who had demonstrated a very poor ability to cope with normal human society, their delusional systems provided an insurance of care in a public mental hospital. And within the hospital, they captured more attention than a common or routine identity would command.

22. Festinger, Riecken, and Schachter (1956) is our source for the story of the Seekers. Quotations are from pp. 169 and 170, respectively. These authors give special attention to Festinger's theory of cognitive dissonance for helping to understand the events involved—especially the increased effort at proselyting after disconfirmation of a critical belief, as set forth mainly in their initial and final chapters.

Chapter 6

The Mystery of Attraction

THE WELCOME WEEK EXPERIMENT

Each year incoming freshmen at a large mid-western university are given a week of specially planned events known locally as "Welcome Week." Scheduled for the final day of this week one year was a dance with partners selected by a computer. "Here's your chance to meet someone who has the same expressed interests as yourself," said the advertising pitch. Tickets were sold at the rate of $1 per person for the first 376 male and 376 female students who appeared to be taking part in this computer dance. Students were also, without their knowing it, taking part in a social-psychological experiment.

In the process of getting properly registered for this dance, students met four people. The first person sold tickets, a second person down the same table checked identification cards and told the students to proceed to another room, where a third person met the students and gave them questionnaires, then a fourth person directed them to seats where they could fill out their questionnaires. These four persons (two males and two females, all sophomores) had another less obvious task in addition to helping students register. This was to make an independent evaluation of the physical attractiveness of each of the 752 freshmen buying tickets.

In filling out advance questionnaires, students supplied general information about themselves and their preferences. Also included were questions designed to measure four variables: self-report of popularity, nervousness, general self-esteem, and expectations of the date's attractiveness. Actually, nearly all of this information was ignored in matching partners. The only information systematically used was height; no males were matched with taller females. Aside from this, the matching was done on a purely random basis.

During the intermission at the dance, ticket stubs were collected for a $50 drawing, and all participants filled out questionnaires to rate their partners. In a follow-up several months later, the investigators contacted participants to see whether or not there had been any attempts by the computer partners to date each other after the dance. Because some couples could not be contacted later, and a few failed to show up for the dance, the final analysis involved only 317 of the original 376 couples.

As the reader may guess, the intermission ratings of dance partners suppled the basic "moment of truth" for this experiment. This was when the measures of the main variable, interpersonal attraction, were obtained. Supplementing these ratings were the follow-up data concerning whether further dating occurred.

What do we suppose led to attractiveness toward a partner, as found in this research? What types of persons found their partners most attractive, and what kinds of partners were considered to be the most attractive dates?

Elaine Hatfield and her associates who planned this field experiment had a particular set of hypotheses they were trying to test. These hypotheses generally had to do with the levels of aspiration of persons, related in turn to their own levels of social desirability. Persons who considered themselves highly desirable would have higher aspirations than others when examining a potential partner; persons who see themselves as more moderately popular would be more tolerant of partners who might be of lower levels of social desirability. Such predictions should apply to both the ratings persons make of each other at the computer dance and the likelihood of follow-up dating. Partners on a similar level of social desirability should be more likely to be satisfied with each other and to continue the relationship than persons on different levels. This pattern of interpersonal attraction is sometimes called the "matching hypothesis," since it generally predicts successful matches between persons of similar levels of desirability.

In this particular study, only one aspect of attractiveness was evaluated—physical attractiveness. It was not assumed to be the same as attractiveness in general; rather, it was used to indicate the form of attractivenesss that could be most easily assessed (by the four sophomores who helped with the dance registration procedures). The investigators expected that satisfaction with dates would be highest when persons were on similar levels of physical attractiveness, as determined by the initial ratings.

But the results did not quite turn out that way. The problem was not that the theory was wrong, for other research has generally confirmed the matching hypothesis for various forms of social desirability (including physical appearance). Nor was the problem due to an inadequate assessment of physical attractiveness, for there seemed to be a high degree of consensus in the independent judgments of the four sophomores making these ratings. Perhaps the problem was that the acquaintance of these arranged dates was so brief, and limited to a large group setting, in which the matching hypothesis did not have enough of a chance to work itself out. At any rate, only one part of the initial theory was strongly supported by the results: persons tended to be most satisfied when paired with dates of high physical attractiveness, and less satisfied when they were not. In other words, physical attractiveness came through so strongly that little else had a chance to be demonstrated by this study.

"WHAT IS BEAUTIFUL IS GOOD"

Impressed by the strength of the physical appearance variable in interpersonal attraction, some of those involved in the Welcome Week study continued to explore the ramifications of this finding. The identification of what has come to be known as the "attractiveness stereotype" is a product of this work.

A stereotype is a simplified and standardized image applied to the perception and judgment of a social object. The image is used in making quick inferences about the object in preference to the more complex realities typically involved. We all do this to some extent as a normal part of our everyday adjustment. However, in its more extreme forms, stereotyping can interfere with a realistic adjustment to the world in which we live. For example, if we use race, religion, or occupation as an automatic basis for drawing detailed conclusions about other persons, we are likely to miss the most relevant information for understanding their behavior. Might we not be doing something similar when we judge another person in terms of physical attractiveness?

A study by Karen Dion, Ellen Berscheid, and Elaine Hatfield illustrates both how this question may be explored and what pattern has been most commonly found in research results. Again using university undergraduates as their subjects, the researchers asked their help in discovering how accurately the characteristics of persons could be predicted by photographs. Each subject was given three photographs and asked to rate each of the persons pictured on a variety of personality dimensions. They were also asked to make predictions about the futures of the persons whose photographs they saw. They were told (inaccurately) that their judgments as ordinary students seeing only pictures would be compared to those of more skilled professionals who knew more about the persons pictured. In this way, the accuracy of the person perception of each subject (even though only on the basis of a single picture for each person) could be rated—or at least so the subjects were led to believe.

Actually, there were no experts to serve as a comparison group; only the subjects themselves made personality assessments. Each of the subjects (half of whom were males and half females) was asked to draw inferences about three persons whose pictures they examined. Persons pictured were approximately the same age as the subjects, and the sex of the pictured person was systematically varied. Half of the subjects of each gender rated persons of the opposite sex, and half rated persons of the same sex. More importantly, previous ratings of the photographs by other students allowed the researchers to present a subject with one picture of a person generally considered attractive, one of a moderately unattractive person, and another of a person of average attractiveness.

Among the results of this study, it should first be noted that subjects' ratings did confirm the degree of physical attractiveness represented by the pictures. The good-looking faces were rated above those of average attractiveness, which in turn were rated above less attractive faces. No surprise here. But what about the perceived personality characteristics? Did they differ from a random assortment? Indeed, yes. The more attractive persons were also perceived as being more socially sensitive, sexually warm, kind, poised, and interesting than less attractive persons. In sum, they were perceived as having all the more desirable traits. Not only were they rated higher on the personality dimensions, but they were seen to be happier and more successful in their lives. For example, physical attractiveness was significantly associated with predictions of the occupational status that might be achieved, the degree of marital happiness, and the general satisfaction in social and professional realms. In only one area was there no sharp clear advantage perceived for the more physically attractive persons; this was in the area of child rearing. Although the differences in this area were not statistically significant, the pattern here showed expectations of slightly higher competence in child rearing from a person of average attractiveness than from those who were either markedly attractive or unattractive.

All in all, these results provide rather strong support for the importance of physical appearance in forming favorable impressions of other persons. Of course, ratings from photographs do not tell us anything about actual interaction. The differences between attractive and less attractive persons might well fade as we get to know them better and as behavior becomes more important than appearance. Still, one would expect at least some continuing influence of physical attractiveness as relationships develop. Persons with pleasing physical features have some special advantages in social relationships. They would be given the benefit of any doubt concerning their inferred characteristics. This is in turn the result of the attractiveness stereotype, a phenomenon summed up by an ancient Greek poetess more than twenty-five centuries ago with the phrase, "What is beautiful is good."[3]

The study we have been discussing found no significant gender differences. Pictures of both sexes were rated by both male and female subjects. The same patterns of a physical attractiveness stereotype were found for persons of both sexes, and the gender of the persons rating the pictures did not appear to be an important factor. However, other studies that support the physical attractiveness stereotype suggest that there may be important sex differences. That is, males considered physically attractive are given special credit for features usually associated with male roles, and good-looking females are given extra credit for characteristics usually seen as feminine virtues.[4]

BUT WHAT IS BEAUTIFUL?

Studies cited so far in this chapter have taken a rather simple-minded approach to determining physical attractiveness. Persons are physically attractive when most people rate them as being attractive. We should immediately qualify this by saying that the raters were usually American college students, and the persons they rated were generally of a similar age as themselves. Although these studies showed a rather impressive consensus as to who is or is not physically attractive, this may primarily reflect judgments among American college students. And even here, we are given little guidance as to what physical stimuli lead to a person being considered beautiful or not.

Anthropologists have given us a great deal of evidence on the cultural relativity of what characteristics of the human form are considered beautiful. Also, no less an authority than Charles Darwin concluded that "it is certainly not true that there is in the mind of man any universal standard of beauty with respect to the human body." However, there is recent evidence that persons of different races and cultural backgrounds do agree to some extent on some characteristics of physical attractiveness. Furthermore, infants of less than one year in age show preferences for faces that correlate with those adults considered better looking. These preferences are unlikely to be the result of parental influences at such an early age, thus implying at least some innate basis of judgments of human beauty.[5]

Given such an array of evidence, it would be prudent to keep open the possibility that there is both a wide variation in cultural values about what constitutes human beauty and some bedrock universality for such judgments. This leads us to the following question: To the extent that there may be a common base for human judgments of beauty, can we identify what varieties of the human form it leads us to prefer?

One clue for answering this question may lie in the nature of physical differences between the sexes. It is interesting to note that anatomical differences between human males and females are greater than with most other species of mammals. Apparently this has something to do with what biologists call "sexual selection"— the development of stimuli that aid in the identification of prospective mates, leading to a preference for mates who show certain characteristics. We might therefore expect that females who clearly differ from the male form will be considered more attractive than others. Likewise, males who accentuate male features might be considered especially attractive. We must be careful here not to assume that extreme forms of sex differences would be most attractive; a moderate embodiment of sexual differentiation (such as a moderately tall man or a moderately thin woman, rather than a giant or a beanstalk figure) might be sufficient to foster a pleasing reaction. Also, we would expect that young adult forms would be emphasized in these sexual preferences, since choice of a sexual partner is especially prominant in this stage of the life cycle. Finally, given the cultural importance of the institutions of courtship and marriage, we would expect a strong intertwining of values with physical signs of sex differences. Sometimes this gives further accentuation to physical sex differences (such as corsets for women and beards for men) and sometimes not (as with some contemporary Western trends toward unisex clothing styles).

Considering the importance of questions on human beauty, it is surprising how little systematic research has been devoted to discovering what physical factors are involved in personal preferences. There have been some studies on particular aspects, but not much that systematically deals with on the nature and consequences of human beauty. One psychologist has expressed the judgment that "we know less about why certain stimuli are attractive for humans than we do about those for fish." But there are at least some important beginnings toward deciphering the riddle of what makes some persons appear especially beautiful, and a recent study by Judith Langlois and Lori Roggman at the University of Texas offers one of the more promising recent leads.[6]

Langlois and Roggman studied faces. This leaves out some of the body parts that often command attention, but the face is probably the focus of most impressions regarding personality and the imputation of motives for behavior. If we could determine what makes a face pretty, we would have a good start on answering the mystery of human beauty. And Langlois and Roggman believe that they found an answer that resolves a good portion of this mystery.[7]

In their research, Langlois and Roggman first photographed undergraduate students, then randomly selected ninety-six female and ninety-six male faces. Each face was then digitized into a 512 x 512 matrix of values for black-and-white reproductions. That is, a computer recorded measures of how light or dark each of these pieces of the face might be (with over a quarter of a million components for each face). This resulted in a quality of reproduction about halfway between a fine glossy print and the rather crudely digitized photo found in a daily newspaper. The researchers then started producing composite faces by combining and averaging the values for particular faces. They presented the faces so obtained (as well as comparable faces of real individuals) to a sample of students, who rated the physical attractiveness of each face they saw.

The procedures we have summarized allowed for different degrees of composite combination of faces. Some pictures combine two faces, others combined four faces, and still other combinations involved a greater number. Up to thirty-two faces were combined into a single composite. This is an especially important point, for the central finding of the study was that composites of sixteen or thirty-two faces were almost always considered more attractive than individual faces. In other words, the more faces involved in a combination (and thus the closer the photograph came to an average face), the more attractive was the rating given. Only a very few individual faces were rated as more attractive than higher-level composites; most individual faces were considered significantly less attractive. Langlois and Roggman concluded that attractive faces are those that represent a central tendency for the category of faces, or, as expressed in the title of their article, "attractive faces are only average."

Why should averaged characteristics of human faces be more attractive than individual faces? Before we interpret this, we need to exercise a bit of caution. For one thing, this study is quite recent, and it needs further validation. There were technical problems in the way composite faces were created; we would like to see if similar findings would occur with the use of slightly different procedures. Also, Langlois and Roggman did not systematically explore variations beyond gender in the types of faces that might be perceived. What if age and race were combined with gender to make a number of subtypes; would each subgroup have its own ideal "average" in preference to more general averaging? Or would there be some systematic biases away from the average—such as a preference for younger faces over older ones. Such questions cry out for further research.

Nevertheless, for now let us take at face value the main finding of this research: that the most average faces are generally seen as the most attractive. Why might this be so? At least two hypotheses suggest themselves, either or both of which might be supported by further research. One is that we are preprogrammed biologically with certain kinds of visual preferences: the closer we approach the most general human prototype, the more likely we are to survive the sieve of natural selection, given the highly social nature of the human species. A second hypothesis holds that we develop tastes for beauty through early socialization. According to this hypothesis, we learn to adjust both to what is expressly valued by our culture and to what is implicitly normative. Whatever kinds of human forms are most commonly observed might be seen as implicitly normative and thus preferred over less typical forms. This also could help to explain the preference for average facial features. Just how to evaluate either of these hypotheses must await further research in this area of such popular interest—but with so little systematic research.[9]

"BIRDS OF A FEATHER?"

The Welcome Week study that started this chapter suggested that, given time for interaction with one another, persons on similar levels of social desirability are more apt to be attracted to each other than those on different levels. Although we have not bothered to examine it, there is considerable evidence to support this so-called "matching hypothesis." The usual interpretation for this pattern is in terms of market forces in social exchange. In the market system of human beings wanting other human beings as friends or lovers, transactions tend to occur when both parties, given their own limited resources, can best afford the interaction. For most persons most of the time, these relationships occur with others at similar levels of peer popularity, physical attractiveness, or general social status.

One way to interpret the results regarding attraction at similar levels of social desirability is to see them as one aspect of the more general theme of similarity. As the sayings go, "like attracts like" and "birds of a feather flock together." Are there not basic psychological needs that are satisfied by attraction to someone similar to oneself?

Many research studies have documented the role of similarity in attraction. This is most clear in the case of attitude similarity. Donn Byrne and associates conducted a series of studies documenting this most precisely. They had subjects rate their attraction to a number of persons they had not met, but about whom they had detailed information on attitudes. In fact, unknown to the subjects, the persons were fictitious creations of the experimenters to represent carefully planned degrees of differences from the subjects' own expressed attitudes. These studies showed quite clearly that the degree of attitude similarity was highly predictive of the strength of interpersonal attraction.[10]

However, to say that a similarity of attitudes promotes attraction is not to say that this is equally true for all persons or for all attitudes. Some evidence suggests, for example, that in cases of heterosexual attraction males and females look for different kinds of similarity. In particular, females are more apt than males to be impressed by a prospective partner's similarity in religious attitudes; males may be more attentive to similarities of attitudes in regard to sexual behavior.[11]

Also, evidence of similarity of personality as a basis for attraction is far less clear than that of similarity of attitudes. Although most studies of friends and mates have indicated a positive correlation on personality traits, there remain several possible interpretations. Similarity of personality may be a cause or an effect of, or only indirectly associated with, attraction. Persons who are similar may be more able to provide rewards for each other or, on the other hand, persons who interact a great deal may become more similar through their association. In the first of these cases, similarity would be a cause of attraction; in the second, it would be the result. Or perhaps the association is only accidental: Persons who are similar in personality may be more apt to move in the same social circles and thereby meet each other. Most research gives us no basis for sorting out the relative importance of each of these possibilities.

There is also evidence to suggest that personalities match on bases other than similarity. There is, of course, the factor of sex; most males and females are attracted to each other on the basis of this difference. Robert F. Winch has extended the idea of attraction through personality differences to formulate a theory of complementary needs, and has presented evidence that certain patterns of personality needs (for example, dominance or nurturance) may lead to attraction toward a different rather than a similar person for marriage or close friendship. Other investigators have found results to suggest that introverts are more attracted to extroverts than to other introverts. This appears to be another exception to the more common pattern of similarity.[12]

How can such evidence for personality differences be harmonized with the more predominant evidence for similarity? One way has been suggested by the "interpersonal congruency" theory of Carl Backman and Paul Secord. Their theory holds that an individual engages in interaction with others to maximize the consistency between the following three elements: (1) one's own self–concept, (2) the behavior one shows toward others, and (3) the way others behave in return. Essentially, this suggests that we behave toward others in such a way that their response will support our own self-image. Also, these authors suggest, we are especially attracted to persons who do in fact respond in such a way as to confirm our self-images.[13]

While research reported by Backman and Secord gives strong support for a congruency theory of attraction, the same evidence also suggests a role for similarity over and above that required for interpersonal congruency. Some of this may be due to the influence of similar social backgrounds, making persons who are in a position to interact with each other more likely to be similar. However, other research reports personality similarity even after controlling for similar social backgrounds. Assuming this as an additional indication of the importance of similarity, why should this be the case? Perhaps, other things being equal, we just find it easier to associate with persons who are like ourselves. If so, this would be another manifestation of the theory of cognitive balance put forward by Fritz Heider. We adopt similar attitudes toward those things we see as "belonging" together, and similarity of self and other may be one of the ingredients for this sense of belonging. Therefore, the same high regard we (usually) have for ourselves is more apt than not to be extended to those we see as being similar to ourselves.[14]

ATTRACTION AS A PROCESS

So far we have examined two main themes regarding the understanding of interpersonal attraction: The importance of physical attractiveness and the importance of similarity. In looking at these, we have also brought in some other considerations—such as social arrangements that set the stage for who is most likely to interact with whom and important qualifications as to the conditions under which similarity might apply. Let us now try to put these themes together.

Interpersonal attraction may be seen as a process that has several phases. Some authors have summarized these phases as the following: (1) approach, or becoming aware of another person, (2) affiliation, or developing a basis for some continued interaction, and (3) attachment, or developing a basis of significant and enduring mutuality.[15]

WHAT ABOUT LOVE?

there are bonds formed in families that make them one of the most natural places to look for examples of the permanence of strongly positive relationships. What seems to be critical is the strength of mutual commitment for a continuing relationship. This can happen outside family contexts, as when really good friends make a point of keeping in contact even when they live in different cities. But there is something about the network of obligations within a family—the institutional dimension, if you will, of commitments for long-term relationships—that adds to the permanence of bonds fostered under its auspices.[19]

Finally, let us remind ourselves of a basic condition of the human species that adds to both the intensity and the permanence of our love relationships. We are a social species. We get our sense of individual identity through our association with others. We continue to find this identity supported (and changed) through our relationships. It is our relationships to particularly significant others—our closest friends, our lovers, and our family members— that give us our clearest impressions about ourselves. They also give us much of the meaning that sustains us in our day-to-day activities. We do not always think about our love for these others who are so important to us, but if some danger of loss occurs, it becomes quite clear who is included among our loved ones.

NOTES

1. The study here discussed is reported more fully in Walster and others (1966). Much of this chapter, especially its first section, is derived from Schellenberg (1974), Chapter 2 ("Liking People"). A much more thorough discussion of nearly all subjects we discuss here may be found in Berscheid (1985).

2. This study is reported in Dion, Berscheid, and Walster (1972). See also the discussion of the "attractiveness stereotype" in Berscheid and Walster (1974).

3. The poetess here mentioned is Sappho. The quoted phrase is from her *Fragments*, No. 101 (as cited by Dion, Berscheid, and Walster, 1972, p. 285).

4. This further research is reviewed in Berscheid and Walster (1974), as well as in Hatfield and Sprecher (1986).

5. Darwin's conclusion on the relativity of beauty may be found in Darwin (1871/1898), p. 597. This conclusion follows a rather detailed review of the anthropological evidence available at the time he was writing. Evidence for the impressive ability of infants in discriminating

between human faces appears in Strauss (1979) and in Quinn and Eimas (1986).

6. The quotation about our relative knowledge of attractive stimuli for fish and humans is from Hochberg (1978), p. 238. Aronson (1969) has speculated about why we know so little about the physical characteristics of attraction among humans as follows:

> It is difficult to be certain why the effects of physical beauty have not been studied more systematically. It may be that, at some levels, we would hate to find evidence indicating that beautiful women are better liked than homely women—somehow this seems undemocratic. In a democracy we like to feel that with hard work and a good deal of motivation, a person can accomplish almost anything. But, alas (most of us believe), hard work cannot make an ugly woman beautiful. Because of this suspicion perhaps most social psychologists implicitly prefer to believe that beauty is indeed only skin deep—and avoid the investigation of its social impact for fear they might learn otherwise (p. 160).

7. The research here being discussed is reported in Langlois and Roggman (1990).

8. Criticisms of the work by Langlois and Roggman include Alley and Cunningham (1991).

9. An element supporting either (or both) of these two hypotheses may be the "mere exposure" effect pointed out by Zajonc (1968). This is the tendency to prefer familiar stimuli over those that are unfamiliar.

10. Donn Byrne's work is fully discussed in Byrne (1971).

11. These gender differences are reported by Touhey (1972).

12. Winch's work is found in Winch (1958). The differences between introverts and extroverts are discussed in Hendrick and Brown (1971).

13. "Interpersonal congruency" theory is presented in Secord and Backman (1961), Backman and Secord (1962), and Secord and Backman (1964).

14. Some of the evidence for the influence of similarity over and above background similarity is contained in Schellenberg (1960). Heider's theory of cognitive balance is found in Heider (1958).

15. We borrow here, in highly summarized form, the model of attraction as a process put forward by Levinger and Snoek (1972).

16. Much of the social psychological literature on interpersonal attraction fails to give adequate attention to the social context in which relationships develop. A recent book that helps to correct this bias is Allan (1989).

17. The quote here is from Finck (1891), p. 224.

18. Work mentioned in this paragraph is developed more fully in Freud (1930/1962), Aronson (1969), Schachter and Singer (1962), and Rubin

(1970). Rubin's pioneering work measuring love has been followed up by others who have sought to measure various dimensions of love. Here the works of Hendrick and Hendrick (1986) and Sternberg (1986) are of special interest. For example, Sternberg identifies three main components of love: intimacy, passion, and commitment. Hendrick, Hendrick, and Adler (1988) offer evidence that persons tend to be attracted to others who emphasize similar dimensions of love as they themselves do.

19. Long-term relationships are discussed in much greater detail in Gottman (1979), Kelley (1979), and Duck (1986).

Chapter 7

The Mystery of Aggression

TRACKING DOWN THE KILLER INSTINCT

Sigmund Freud set forth in his psychological theories a basic idea that many other people had long felt: There is something deep within the human constitution that inclines us toward death and destruction. This is most commonly referred to as the instinct of aggression. For Freud this was a generalized unconscious urge, working at cross purposes with those values we most consciously cherish—including the dignity of human life. He saw this as the primary reason that humans engage in warfare and otherwise experience so much strife. However, when he was writing about these ideas early in this century, our knowledge of the biological basis of such a tendency toward aggression was quite sketchy. It still is, but we have learned something in the ensuing years. To what extent have we found evidence to support Freud's assumptions about human aggression?[1]

We may begin our consideration of the biological foundations of aggression with the process of natural selection. Nature selects those forms that are most successful in reproducing themselves, which implies a struggle for survival. Not all members of any species survive to reproduce. Those that do are likely to have strong inclinations both to continue alive and to reproduce, as well as skills to meet both these goals. Survival and reproduction are often competitive affairs. Faced with threats of predation on the one hand, and with limited supplies of food and opportunities for mating on the other, the network of cooperation is usually not spread forth very widely. Maternal (and paternal) instincts may be selectively fostered. Also, mechanisms of "reciprocal altruism" may develop within one's immediate circle, but altruistic behavior toward strangers of the same species is rare.

But how far does the concept of natural selection support an aggressive tendency for animals in general? Focusing on mammals in particular, it is hard to find a widespread presence of aggressive instincts. Some species appear to have them, while others do not. Those that do are those species especially prone toward crowding—either because of high birth rates or because of preferences for rather special living conditions. In such species, biologists tell us:

> Animals use aggression as a technique for gaining control over necessities, ordinarily food or shelter, that are scarce or are likely to become so at some time during the life cycle. They intensify their threats and attack with increasing frequency as the population around them grows denser. In such cases aggression is said to be a "density-dependent factor" in controlling population growth.[2]

However, in other species local population size may be naturally controlled by predation, illness, or emigration. When such factors provide effective population control, there is no reason to expect any innate tendency toward aggression.

In the special case of humans, it is easy to point to ways that our selfishness reflects our general animal natures. True, we develop cultural systems that seek to socialize us beyond our natural egocentrism and to provide bridges for our ethnocentric tendencies; but do these ever eradicate our fundamentally selfish natures? In fact, our social and cultural institutions often embody as well as restrain our competitive and aggressive tendencies—in forms as varied as market systems of exchange and armed forces of nation-states. The popularity of violence in television programming may be seen as an example of how fully we pander to our aggressive inclinations.

Some have suggested that there may have been special features of human evolution that made our species unusually prone to aggression and violence. There is, for example, the "hunting hypothesis," which emphasizes that our humanity was forged during our innumerable generations as hunters. Robert Ardrey has succinctly stated this idea as follows:

> If among all the members of our primate family the human being is unique, even in our noblest aspirations, it is because we alone through untold millions of years were continuously dependent on killing to survive.[3]

With hunting came the development of weapons, tools that could be used against other people as well as against other animals. Normally, predatory animals develop weapons that are extensions of their own bodies, such as sharp teeth or claws. As they evolve these weapon systems, they also evolve specific inhibitions against using them on their own species—such as when one animal signals submission to the dominant animal, who then refrains from a final attack. But with humans, weapons did not come through such a slow process of biological evolution; therefore, neither did inhibitions regarding their use. "No selection pressure arose in the prehistory of mankind to breed inhibitory mechanisms preventing the killing of conspecifics until, all of a sudden, the invention of artificial weapons upset the equilibrium of killing potential and social inhibitions." So writes Konrad Lorenz, a leading student of animal behavior. Lorenz adds:

> If humanity survived, as, after all, it did, it never achieved security from the danger of self-destruction. If moral responsibility and unwillingness to kill indubitably increased, the ease and emotional impunity of killing have increased at the same rate. The distance at which all shooting weapons take effect screens the killer against the stimulus situation which would otherwise activate his killing inhibitions. The deep, emotional layers of the personality simply do not register the fact that the crooking of the forefinger to release a shot tears the entrails of another man.

Certainly modern weapons of mass destruction raise this problem no less than did the first gun.[4]

Such is the case for a special "gift" of aggression in the evolution of the human species. But not all social scientists agree with Ardrey and Lorenz on these matters. Let us, in the next few paragraphs, review another interpretation.

Viewed comparatively, humans are not an especially likely species for the development of innate aggression. Their birth rates are not notably high, and they have potentials for high mobility and adaptability—making emigration a natural alternative to avoid crowding. Furthermore, as a specifically social species, humans developed biological reasons for wanting other humans around, rather than driving them off, as might be the case for more territorially jealous animals. At any rate, such were the prevailing conditions during the time that humans were being formed as a distinct species.

As we learn more about the behavior of other species, we are not as impressed with the frequency of aggression in humans. Other primates seem equally prone to violent outbursts and strategic aggression against their fellows. But is not the human animal special among primates in its carnivorous nature, and does this not make a difference? Here, too, as we learn more about other primate species, we find them less different from humans than we had supposed. Other primates also include meat in their diets. The distinction appears to be more one of degree than of kind. That man became more systematically a hunter than any other primate can be little doubted, but what is the implication here for innate tendencies for aggression? Predation upon other species in itself says nothing about patterns of aggression within the species. Omnivorous humans took to hunting and included large animals in their quarry, but there is no reason to believe that seeking to kill a mountain or deer was readily translated into seeking to kill other human beings. What is notable about early human hunting is the complex cooperation involved—not only within the hunting group, but also with those not directly involved with the hunt (mainly women and children). The food-sharing system seems to be the most impressive feature of early hunting, and this tells a story of extended cooperation rather than of aggression.

But what about the specific human weapons? Were not the tools of early hunters easily turned to attacks against other human beings? Certainly, they could have been, but there is no decisive evidence that they were. Moving closer to the present age, we find no systematic evidence associating hunting cultures with higher levels of human aggression than other societies. In fact, it is only within communities that are more settled than those of the hunter-gatherer that we find weapons made specifically for human warfare. And this has been too recent to have had much significance for biological (as distinct from cultural) evolution.

On the subject of innate restraints and inhibitions of aggression, one leading student of animal behavior believes that humans have a good supply of such inhibitions. According to Irenaus Eibl-Eibesfeldt, there seems to be a biological norm against killing humans. Apparently this complements innate gestures of submission, such as the dropping of the head and eyebrows, which appear to be universally found in human societies. Of course, the most notable forms of restraint among humans are cultural. They include formal systems of authority, highly ritualized forms of conflict, verbal substitutes for fighting, and formal mechanisms of peacemaking. Although the jury may still be out on the issue of nuclear weapons, humans have generally shown an ability to develop forms of social organization capable of controlling the destructive power of new weapons. Whatever may have been the advances in tools for aggression, so also have there been increased skills in the forms for their control. This suggests that the control of aggression must be as basic to the human constitution—if not more so—as is any impulse to hurt or destroy.[5]

Up to this point, we have spoken of aggression as a generalized tendency to hurt or do harm to others. Now, however, we must recognize that more precision is needed to do justice to the phenomenon of aggressive behavior. In particular, we need to distinguish between different kinds of aggression. Kenneth Moyer has distinguished seven kinds of animal aggression, each with its own distinctive pattern of physiological arousal. These are (1) predatory aggression, (2) inter-male aggression, (3) fear-induced aggression, (4) irritable aggression, (5) territorial defense, (6) maternal aggression, and (7) instrumental aggression. These not only differ in the stimulus situation apt to provide arousal, but usually also differ in their endocrine and neurological involvements. For example, electrical stimulation at one point in the brain of a cat may sharply increase its predatory reaction to a rat; but if the electrode is moved only slightly, the cat may ignore the rat and attack the experimenter.[7]

Do humans show such distinctions in their aggressive behavior? The distinctions between types of aggression in humans are not as clear as in, for example, cats. The complex learning processes of humans make it more difficult to distinguish behaviorally between different types of aggression. In addition, ethical considerations do not permit the kind of experimental work with humans that has been done with mice, rats, or even monkeys. Nevertheless, it does seem fairly easy to distinguish at least two main types of human aggression—irritable aggression and instrumental aggression.[8]

Irritable aggression is accompanied by feelings of anger and hostility. It may be aroused by any noxious stimulation, especially by pain or those goal-blockages psychologists refer to as frustration. It may also be triggered by stimuli that in the past have been associated with such negative experiences. Endocrine levels appear to be important factors affecting thresholds for arousal. Certain parts of the brain are critically involved (especially the hypothalamus and the amygdala), as has been shown by electrical stimulation of the human brain. Different drugs have been found to be helpful in reducing the frequency of irritable aggression for patients in whom aggression is an important personal problem.[9]

With instrumental aggression no such mapping of the physiological correlates is possible. This kind of aggression represents a learned reaction that is directed toward almost any situation in which aggression is a means to some desired end. It is largely under the control of the higher centers of the cerebral cortex, though it may be colored by associations with other kinds of aggression. For example, if a resisting shopkeeper is wounded during an armed robbery, we may see this as an example of instrumental aggression. But irritable aggression or fear-induced aggression could also be involved to an important degree. On the other hand, displays of anger may enhance certain forms of instrumental aggression. So the separation between instrumental and other forms of aggression must remain somewhat blurred for human beings.

Instrumental aggression is an especially prominent part of human behavior. The possibilities for learning here are almost unlimited—from the symbolic associations we make between present stimuli and past experiences, from the examples provided by other persons, from the consequences of our own behavior, from the consequences we see in others for their actions, and so on. Of special importance is the way aggressive behavior is shaped in the service of human groups, whose goals have been internalized by their members. When these goals conflict with those of other groups, a natural (but certainly not biologically inevitable) condition for conflict and aggression arises.[10]

Human warfare can best be seen within this context of instrumental aggression, learned to serve the goals of groups that are the sources of basic loyalties. We develop mechanisms to regulate aggression within the group, but our social systems frequently cultivate aggression toward other groups. High levels of violence may be sanctioned, especially in countering the ambitions of another tribe (or, in the modern world, another nation). This is less likely to be found between groups within the same society, although even here patterns of continual warfare may be found within some societies. Even when this is the case, as anthropologist Marvin Harris has shown, there are good sociological and ecological ways of understanding such conflicts. His studies of the Maring of new Guinea, for example, show that warfare may evolve as one part of a complex set of cultural practices indirectly serving to prevent too great a pressure on the carrying capacity of a particular environment (that is, its ability to support its population). Warfare, in his view, "has been part of an adaptive strategy associated with particular technological, demographic, and ecological conditions"; it does not require us to "invoke imaginary killer instincts or inscrutable or capricious motives to understand why armed combat has been so common in human history."[11]

ON IDEOLOGIES AND UTOPIAS

In the previous section we tried to see whether a strong tendency for within-species aggression might be biologically rooted in the human species. We spoke at the outset of an aggressive "instinct," but we have not really found evidence for this. The term instinct usually means an inherited basis for a particular behavior pattern. Nothing we have examined suggests that aggression, for humans, functions as a specific behavior pattern. It is at most a general tendency toward many specific behaviors. We must therefore conclude that our exploration of the biological foundations for aggression has not identified a particular "killer instinct" in man.[12]

But we have uncovered evidence that can be subjected to different interpretations about the biological foundations for human aggression. There are those who would maximize these biological foundations and those who would minimize them. Let us allow at least a summary statement for each of these, "maximizers" and "minimizers."

First, let us consider the case for those who emphasize the biological roots of human aggression. Genetic tendencies that favor certain kinds of behavior are selected for any species over a very long period of time. For humans, thousands of generations of hunting societies helped to develop both inclinations and skills that could be applied to fighting against other human beings. That human groups were in competition with each other for hunting territories led rather naturally to skirmishes between groups. The predominantly male leadership of hunting groups evolved into a warrior leadership, and those men who triumphed in this arena would be most successful reproductively (partly due to their prestige within the group and partly due to the women they might claim by conquest or capture). Their genes would thus disproportionately be represented in the generations to come. Also selected would be group members who are most able to function cooperatively with those close in serb groups—who could control aggression within the group and effectively pursue it against other groups. Thus we might expect to find a propensity for men, compared to women, to congregate in more systematically organized groups with stronger dominance hierarchies. We would also expect aggression and dominance to be especially associated with the masculine gender. All of these features may be seen as the inevitable products of the biological conditions within which human evolution has taken place.[ ]

But another point of view stresses some rather different features of human biological foundations. In this view, man as cooperator, not man as killer, has been the key theme of the last few million years of human evolution. Such cooperation has been based both on our natural inclinations as members of the species and on our cultural propensities developed through language, tools, and social systems. Within these social systems we have fashioned systems to divide persons by sex, race, class, tribe, and nation. We have buttressed these systems with patterns of socialization such as learning how to compete, fight, and otherwise show behavior that may be called "aggression." But such behaviors are essentially circumscribed by the social systems within which they occur. They are not free-floating expressions of some innate human nature. They are essentially the products of experience within a particular system of social and cultural arrangements. Indeed, the claim can be made, as Ashley Montagu has said, that "the direction of evolution has in man been increasingly directed toward the fuller development of cooperative behavior."[ ]

Previously in this chapter we have presented two sides of an ongoing debate about the nature of human aggression. Most readers will have in mind a clear preference for one side or the other. In so doing, they are little different from professional scholars in the sciences of human behavior. Such scholars, although more experienced in studying the evidence, also tend to come out with either a nature or a nurture emphasis in regard to the roots of human aggression. Why should this be the case?

the scientific facts, there is room for considerable agreement about the evidence. Both Konrad Lorenz and Ashley Montagu—to take two leading scientists whose perspectives on human aggression differ enormously—review similar scientific findings; it is mainly in their general interpretations that they part company.[16]

The mystery of human aggression is sufficiently deep to permit examination from many angles, ranging from genetic predispositions and brain chemistry to matters of economic organization and political leadership. Meanwhile, as this research goes on, what is to be our interim conclusion on the subject of innate roots of human aggression? There is no doubt that humans inherit genes that influence social behavior. Biological evolution has had a significant influence upon patterns such as human aggression, but so also has our cultural evolution. Indeed, our cultural forces have had feedback effects upon biological evolution. As Kenneth E. Moyer, a leading student of the biology of aggression, has said:

> As a consequence of cultural selective pressures humanity has greatly influenced the genetic substrates of its own behavioral development. This does not mean that humans have been altogether freed from the influences of genes which similarly affect the behavior of other animals, but it does mean that in humans, behavior is far less under the direction of genes than is that of other animals. Furthermore, that the educability, lack of fixity and remarkable flexibility of the human genetic constitution is such that humans are able as a consequence of their socialization to canalize the behavioral expression of genetic influence in many creative as well as destructive ways.[17]

VARIATIONS IN VIOLENCE

We move now to consider what may be empirically observed about the incidence of violence in a wide range of human relationships. What are the most prominent patterns of deadly violence found by those who have specialized in studies of human aggression?

First, we need to recognize that there have been human societies with an almost complete absence of deadly violence. For example, North American Eskimos and the aborigines of Australia knew almost nothing of violence—until they came in contact with Europeans. Violent crime occurred rarely among these peoples, and there was no conception of anything resembling warfare for their conduct of intergroup relations. This does not imply that primitive societies were generally less violent than modern ones, for opposite examples could also be cited. What it does show is that there are enormous variations among human societies in the propensity for violence, and that societies with very low levels of violence have existed.

It is interesting to note that the societies with very little violence tend to be nomadic, moving over areas of low population density, and carrying limited accumulations of property. In such circumstances, there is little to be gained by trying to seize someone else's property or territory. Furthermore, conflict could often be reduced or avoided just by moving on. Such was not the case with more settled communities that emerged following the neolithic revolution. These agricultural communities accumulated more wealth and thus became more vulnerable to violent crime from within or conquest from without. Governments grew to control— and sometimes exploit—such opportunities for violence; and the history of civilized man ever since has been a relatively bloody story.[18]

There is little evidence to support the idea that any particular group of people are by nature either fundamentally violent or peaceful. Though some societies may seem to be one or the other for long periods of time, significant changes in circumstance frequently lead to a reversal of the image. Thus the marauding Norsemen of past centuries have become the staid Scandanavians of today, and the warlike Maoris took only a few decades to be converted into peaceful Christian citizens of New Zealand. On the other hand, the polite and orderly Japanese seemed, to their enemies at least, to be rapidly transformed into a most violent people in the second quarter of the twentieth century—even though their violence proved no match to that of their enemies in the end. And the more recent change in the image of Lebanon during the 1980s from a thoroughly peaceful place to a country submerged in its own violence has been even more abrupt.

Homicide rates may be seen as one index of the varied propensity for violence found in different forms of human society. Although there are reasons for doubt about the precise numbers quoted in official crime reports, statistics for murder are generally more dependable than for other crimes. Furthermore, there is little doubt that murder rates in America are considerably above those found in most of the world. United States homicide rates are many times higher than those of most European nations, although still higher rates may be found in some Latin American countries. Within the United States, variations are equally dramatic. Homicide rates in the South are about four times as high as those in such states as Iowa or Minnesota; and rates for the District of Columbia are about three times those found in the most murder-prone of the fifty states. Generally, the highest homicide rates in America tend to be in its larger cities, with New York City accounting for almost one-tenth of all murders in the United States. Studies of homicide in major American cities have shown sharp differences in rates related to such factors as age, sex (offenders are especially likely to be young males), social class, and race (with rates for lower-status blacks especially high). Marvin Wolfgang has distilled the findings of such studies (including his own careful research of homicide in Philadelphia) with the summary statement that "the typical criminal slayer is a young man in his twenties who kills another man only slightly older." Males are involved as killers or the killed about five times as frequently as women, but, according to Wolfgang, "when a woman kills she most likely has a man as her victim"; and a woman who is killed "is most commonly slain by her husband or other close friend by a beating in the bedroom."[19]

Such variations in homicide rates, as well as in those of other crimes of violence, have led Wolfgang and other sociologists to speak of a "subculture of violence." This subculture is rooted in poverty and discrimination, in broken homes and weakened family ties, and in inconsistent patterns of childhood socialization. But more than a background of personal and social disadvantage is involved. Also present are an acceptance of violence as a means for solving personal problems and access to weapons that can be used to kill. Both of these features appear to be especially present in ghetto areas of major American cities; they are also more clearly present in American life than in most other parts of the contemporary world.

Patterns of homicide are likely to reflect important cultural differences in their particular forms as well as in overall rates. Close friends or relatives account for the victims in over one-half of American murders. Such is also true of homicide in many other societies, but with notable variations. For example, in the same African nation we may find one tribal group with a remarkable frequency for killing parents, while another group may have high rates for spouses. Different family structures with different common points of tension help to explain such variations. There are, of course, societies in which the killing of a relative is extremely rare, but in most societies relatives or friends are more likely than strangers to be murdered.[20]

Historical trends in homicide rates also show interesting variations. In the United States, homicides have shown a general increase in recent decades, this is not true for many other industrialized nations. In England, for example, homicide rates have been quite stable throughout the present century, and at a rate of less than one-twentieth that of the United States. That British murder has not always been this rare is well documented in a book by James Buchanan Given, *Society and Homicide in Thirteenth-Century England*. An analysis of medieval English records reveals homicide rates generally far above even current American rates, to say nothing of those presently found in England. An especially remarkable finding by Given is that most of the murders were done with other people; most frequently, a relative or close friend was an associate in the action. This relatively social character of medieval homicide is understandable only by seeing it as the normal form of dispute resolution at that time. In fact, concludes Given:

> For the people of thirteenth-century England, murder and violence were tools, often employed only reluctantly but still used with great frequency, for the settling of grievances and the gratification of desires. From the thief who slew his victims, to the servants who fought for their masters, to the villagers who ganged up on an obstreperous member of the community, violence was regarded as an acceptable, and often necessary, facet of life.

In his further interpretations, Givens suggests that the fundamental problem was that "the old communal mechanisms for mediating disputes were rapidly becoming outmoded and new means of resolving conflict had not yet been devised."[21]

Do we see any signs of biological factors in variations in homicide rates? The most obvious differences that reflect biological features are those regarding sex and age. Almost everywhere, young males predominate as the killers. Sex is an obvious biological fact, although what is associated with gender is highly circumscribed culturally. Still the persistent pattern of sex differences in homicide rates probably indicates something more universal than the most apparent cultural variations. That the most common male offenders are of age levels where the highest concentrations of testosterone are present may be of some importance; and it is also significant that in a fight a younger man usually has more physical strength in his muscles (as well as more testosterone in his blood) than an older person. There may well be some personality differences (including those relating to intelligence, temperamental impulsivity, and psychopathic tendency) that affect the likelihood that one person will kill another, although these are only expressed in relation to particular social circumstances. In fact, this is true for all biological factors, leaving them inextricably interwoven with those social and cultural factors that provide the most apparent sources of variation.[22]

Even more obvious is the predominance of social and cultural factors in rates for more collective forms of violence, such as social upheaval, revolution, and war. In fact, any links there may be to aggressive personalities are so overwhelmed by the aggressive natures of social movements and governments that individuals who preside over some of the most destructive episodes of recent history may actually be quite pacific in their personal inclinations. We note, for example, that the man who presided over the bloodiest chapter of American history was Abraham Lincoln. Lincoln was anything but mean-spirited in his personal behavior, but the policies he set forth for his presidency made the ensuing conflict between the North and the South inevitable.

The more collective forms of human violence may be divided into two main types: (1) those between groups within a society, usually involving the government against opposing groups seeking greater power or influence, and (2) those between societies or nations, usually considered to be wars. Both of these forms have literatures too extensive to be well summarized here. We take note, however, that many of the more scientific studies of the incidence of collective violence challenge some rather common ideas.

It is commonly thought that unrest within a society spills over into collective violence when hardships become too great to be endured. However, those researchers who have most systematically dealt with evidence for this idea have found little to support it. They have usually found a rather random relationship between any objective indices of "hardship" or widely shared "frustration" and the incidence of collective violence. What more commonly appears is that groups rising in power and influence are involved in conflict with the more established centers of power. Episodes of collective violence are correlates of major shifts in power, as rising groups test the limits of what they may achieve.[23]

Relations among nations are even more clearly understood in terms of a struggle for power and influence. Here it is the nation-state that seeks to preserve or extend its power. We may imagine that international wars might be explained as resulting from population pressures, from other forms of national deprivation, or just from some nations being more peace-loving or war-prone than others. Despite the value of such factors in justifying why a particular war was "necessary," they appear to have little predictive power for understanding the most general patterns of international warfare. What we find more clearly is that the great powers are the most frequent participants in warfare, that they are most likely to fight neighboring nations, and that the frequency of participation in war has little relation to the nature of the social or political system of a nation.[24]

Humans have always developed their identities in relation to primary units of social structure. Before the development of formal systems of government, the key units were those of kinship systems and local communities. With the development of more complex forms of social organization, an ultimate arbiter for the claims of various groups came to be developed in the form of the state. In time governments themselves came to claim primary loyalties of their peoples, although it is only in the last 250 years that nationalism has taken on the full powers that we take for granted in the modern world. With the extent of present loyalties toward the nation-state and with the weapons that have now become available to these states, the potential violence of international war dwarfs all other forms of human violence. The total deaths from just one war, World War II, are greater than all the homicides of the world in the twentieth century. And the prospects of a major nuclear war in the future are enormously more terrible.

Collective violence—especially in those forms associated with political protest and international war—is highly socialized and organized. It has little to do with the anger or aggression of individuals except insofar as these become part of some larger social system. Of course, anger and hostility become focused upon an enemy during a conflict, but studies of national stereotypes show that these hostilities tend to follow more than cause the development of international conflicts. Leaders who pursue a modern war may do it with very little emotion but with enormous attention to those they are directing and the equipment they are operating. And in the automated battlefield of the future the interaction will be primarily with computers, rather than with people.[25]

In this brave new world of modern violence, there may still be room for an atavistic aggressive impulse—but only if it is carefully engineered within a complex social system. These social systems, not the antagonisms of individual men or women, provide the most important arenas for aggression today. Consequently, the taming of aggression now requires not the control of individual impulses but the taming of the social systems at the centers of world political power.

NOTES

1. Freud's basic ideas on human aggression are spelled out in *Civilization and its Discontents* (Freud, 1930/1962), among other writings.

2. The quotation here is from Wilson (1978), p. 103; "If aggression confers no advantage," as Wilson further states, "it is unlikely to be encoded through natural selection into the innate behavioral repertoire of the species."

3. The quotation here is from Ardrey (1976), p. 11, with italics in the original.

4. Quotations from Lorenz (1966) in this paragraph are, in order, from p. 241 and 242.

5. Although Ramond Dart, who first identified the early human forms known as australopithecines, believed that these people used weapons to kill each other, others are not convinced. Says Montagu (1976, p. 129): "That australopithecines devised weapons to be used against their fellows would seem to be extremely unlikely: first, because those tools would not easily lend themselves to such usage; second, because such tools appear to have been made for practical domestic use; and third, there is no supportable evidence in fossil australopithecine bones of injuries that could have been inflicted by such tools."

6. Eibl-Eibesfeldt (1979) discusses subjects included in this paragraph, especially on pp. 188–196, 155, 91–104, and 204–217.

7. The classification given here of types of aggression is from Moyer (1971), especially pp. 27–30. Wilson (1975) and Moyer (1987) give slightly different listings of basic types. The example of different reactions from electrical stimulation of slightly different locations in the brain of a cat is cited by Moyer (1987), pp. 23–24.

8. Moyer (1987) further suggests that sex-related aggression and fear-induced aggression may be clearly seen in human behavior. He also makes this qualifying comment: "There is no theoretical reason why behavior should not be under the influence of more than one set of physiological processes. It is, in fact, probably the most common state of affairs. The possible interactions among the different kinds of aggression and other motivational states are extremely complex, and a detailed model is needed

that attempts to specify the possible behavior outcomes of various simultaneous motivational influences" (p. 21).

9. Most work in the frustration-aggression literature emphasizes the importance of how frustrating experiences may be interpreted in producing aggression. "Defining a frustration as reasonable or proper, i.e., as nonarbitrary, in essence weakens the frustrater's association with aggression; his aggressive cue value is diminished. As a consequence, he would be less likely to elicit overt aggression from the frustrated individual" (Berkowitz, 1969, pp. 24-25). Moyer (1987, pp. 143-156) discusses some possibilities of drug therapies for the control of human aggression.

10. The social learning approach of Albert Bandura (1973) is especially helpful for understanding how aggressive behavior may be learned.

11. The quotation here is from Harris (1974), pp. 79-80.

12. We have not dealt specifically with the notion of an inborn internal drive that necessarily seeks discharge in a general pattern of aggressive behavior. Both Freud (1930/ 1962) and Lorenz (1966) hold that there is evidence for such a drive, as do others who point to a need for a "catharsis" or redirection of aggressive impulses aroused by frustration (Dollard and others, 1939). Sociobiologists such as Wilson (1975, especially pp. 105-106) doubt the evidence for such a drive in humans; and recent analyses of the relationship between frustration and aggression which might bear upon a "catharsis" hypothesis have not been generally supportive (Berkowitz, 1962; Berkowitz, 1969; Bandura, 1973). Other discussions of this issue may be found in Gunn (1973) and Scott (1975).

13. Themes of this paragraph are more fully developed in Tiger (1969). Evidence for sex differences in aggression is discussed by Maccoby and Jacklin (1974), pp. 242-247. Sex differences also show in personality test measures, such as the "socialization" scale of the California Personality Inventory, which distinguishes between criminal and noncriminal populations even more clearly. See the discussion of this instrument by Wilson and Herrnstein (1985, pp. 190-198).

14. The quotation here is from Montagu (1951), p. 100. Montagu adds that man's "combativeness and competitiveness arise primarily from the frustration of his need to co-operate" (p. 101). We may not be able to identify precisely how general human cooperation became a part of our biological endowment, but we can suggest that the emphasis upon the "selfishness" of gene pools may not apply as clearly to a carrier of human culture as to other animals. Put in other words, the genetic capacities for culture may tend to counter other genetic tendencies toward more restricted loyalties. Also, contemporary evolutionists—especially those who follow a "punctuated equilibrium" theory—are less likely than Darwin (1859/1979) and other evolutionists of past generations to see most biological change as unfolding slowly through natural selection. A picture of more "quirky" shifts is given, for example, by Gould (1989).

15. We draw general insights on the sociology of knowledge, as well as the concepts of ideology and utopia, from Mannheim (1936/1966). The term "ideology" as more popularly used would include utopian tendencies as well as the more conservative frameworks here suggested.

16. One specific point on which Lorenz and Montagu clearly see the evidence differently is on the tendency of australopithecines to kill each other. In Note 5 we quoted Montagu on this subject. In contrast, Lorenz (1966, p. 239) says: "There is evidence that the first inventors of pebble tools, the African Australopithecines, promptly used their new weapons to kill not only game, but fellow members of their own species as well." Apparently the archeological facts do not speak for themselves here. Some reasons why the evidence may remain in dispute are reviewed by Leakey and Lewin (1978), especially pp. 269–272.

17. The quotation here is from Moyer (1987), p. 109. Readers who believe this is a rather wishy-washy conclusion for the subject of the biology of aggression may wish to compare this chapter with earlier statements of the author on this subject (Schellenberg, 1982, especially Chapter 3; Schellenberg 1987a).

18. We do not mean to imply here that primitive societies were generally more peaceful than civilized societies. Some were, and some were not. What we do wish to say is that the possibilities for massive violence tended to come along with those other features that we call "civilization" (including an agricultural surplus to support a dominant elite, the development of cities, and the presence of a written language).

19. Variations in American homicide rates may be found in data gathered by the Federal Bureau of Investigation and released in the form of annual Uniform Crime Reports. Homicide rates for 1990, to take a recent year, were approximately nine per one hundred thousand in the United States; for New York City the rate was about thirty-one. On general homicide rates, see also Wolfgang (1958), Wolfgang (1967), Nettler (1982), and Wilson and Herrnstein (1985). Our quotations here are from Wolfgang (1967), p. 23.

20. A good source for cultural variations in homicide patterns is Bohannan (1960), drawn upon for examples cited in this paragraph.

21. Sources here include Wolfgang (1967), especially pp. 29–35, Wilson and Herrnstein (1985), and Given (1977). The latter source estimates thirteenth century homicide rates of twelve per one hundred thousand per year for London, seventeen for the Oxford area, and forty-seven for the Warwick area. These may be compared to recent rates of less than one-half for Great Britain and about nine for the United States (again, per one hundred thousand population). The final quotations are from Given (1977), p. 213.

22. Wilson and Herrnstein (1985) give greater attention to possible biological roots of criminal behavior than do most students of crime. However, they also emphasize how difficult it is to disentangle constitu-

tional from social factors (see especially pp. 510–513). Their discussion gives special attention to the role of the family, where, of course, we find the most intimate interplay of biology with culture. They point, for example (p. 527), to unusually low crime rates in Japan, "where the norms inculcated by the family (and the general culture) emphasize obligations as much or more than rights and where families transmit a sense of collective responsibility for behavior." They add: "Some of these cross-cultural differences may reflect, to a degree, differences in constitutional factors, such as temperament, that facilitate conditioning and allow the Japanese family to be remarkably permissive and still inculcate conscience, or a concern for the well-being of others."

23. The subject of social unrest and collective violence is more fully treated by the author in Schellenberg (1982), especially Chapters 6 and 7. Other helpful sources include Graham and Gurr (1969), and Short and Wolfgang (1972).

24. Schellenberg (1982), especially Chapter 8, gives a further discussion of the incidence of warfare. See also Singer and Small (1972), Small and Singer (1982), and Wright (1942/1965). The question of the relationship of the nature of a politcial system to war frequency has recently received a great deal of attention. According to Singer and Small (1972, p. 345), nations tend to "show a remarkable flexibility in 'selecting' their partners and adversaries." However, Rummel (1985) provides evidence that more "libertarian" systems tend to be more free of both domestic violence and war; Maoz and Abdolali (1989) include in their rather complex findings clear support for a pattern of democracies tending to avoid wars with other democracies.

25. U.S. Army Chief of Staff William C. Westmoreland in 1969 gave a glimpse of what the future may have in store, when he said that "enemy forces will be located, tracked, and targeted almost instantaneously through the use of data links, computer-assisted intelligence evaluation, and automatic fire control" (quoted by Klare, 1972, p. 203). His view of the future may have been in fact largely realized in 1991, when one of the most decisive features of the brief ground campaign of the Persian Gulf War was the battlefield automation of the Allies. Of course, the deployment plans of major powers for nuclear weapons are even more fully automated than is their battlefield planning.

Chapter 8

The Mystery of Crowds

TWO CASES OF CROWDS

It was a long, hot summer. Discontent was brewing throughout the French countryside and, especially, in the streets of Paris. In Versailles the Estates General was meeting, with the Third Estate shaking the foundations of the nation by forming themselves into a National Assembly. King Louis XVI was known to disapprove, but what could he do? There were rumors, well founded, that he intended to do something; it was said that he was about to make several moves designed to strengthen royal authority. These moves might include the strengthening of foreign regiments stationed in Paris, the firing of his finance chief, Necker, who had promoted the calling of the Estates General, and the issuing of an order to dissolve the National Assembly.[1]

At noon on July 12, 1789, Paris received the news of Necker's dismissal. Crowds formed and public protest meetings were held. Uncertain of their safety on the Paris streets, the royal troops withdrew to fortified positions, and the crowd took over the city more and more. First the hated customs posts, where taxes were collected on food and wine coming into Paris, were destroyed. Then the search was on for grain and arms. Alarmed at both the intensity of the riots and the possibility of extreme countermeasures by royal military forces, the Paris members of the Third Estate formed themselves into a provisional city government and organized a citizen militia to restore order.

However, order was not restored immediately, and on July 14 the insurgency had grown in force. "To the Bastille!" became the cry of an armed throng. The Bastille, the prison-fortress that housed political prisoners, was to Paris citizens a symbol of royal oppression. Its guns could do great damage to the surrounding neighborhood, and, it was known to have recently received stocks of ammunition, which were much in demand by the insurgents. The people gathered at the Bastille and attempted to storm that gloomy fortress. Guns were fired into the crowd, killing scores of people and wounding many more. But the mob, aided by several small cannons, continued to attack. Finally, two detachments of soldiers who had defected and joined the insurgents marched up to the main gate. The drawbridge was lowered, the fortress surrendered, and the mob surged inside. The following day the local citizens began the systematic destruction of this giant edifice. The Bastille was soon removed from the sight of Parisians, while ever more indelibly marked upon French memories.

As a military event, the fall of the Bastille was of little significance. However, the political consequences were far-reaching, as this event dramatized the momentum of events that soon would sweep away the old order of French power. Almost immediately the king recognized the legitimacy of the National Assembly and of the new government for the city of Paris. But the revolution did not stop there. A process had started that was not to stop until all vestiges of royal and noble power were swept away in France.[2]

Another case of crowd behavior took place in the present century in South America—in the capital city of Ecuador on February 12, 1949, to be precise.

That day, listeners in Quito, Ecuador, heard a rather strange series of reports on the radio. The music was interrupted with the announcement of an "urgent piece of late news." An enemy in the shape of a cloud was approaching Quito after destroying a neighboring town. A "governmental minister" went on the air to urge calm. Next the "mayor" came on to promote the defense of the city against the unknown peril, and urged the evacuation of women and children. Then came the report that a monster surrounded by fire and smoke had been seen at the northern edge of the city.

This was all meant to be only a radio program. It was an adaptation to local conditions of H. G. Wells's novel *The War of the Worlds*. Perhaps those who produced the program should have anticipated that many listeners would be strongly affected by the realism of the program. There was a precedent from a decade earlier when a similar broadcast by Orson Welles had caused mass panic in New Jersey. But apparently nobody at Radio Quito anticipated the events that actually followed that broadcast.[3]

Most of the people of Quito were in the streets before the broadcasters were aware of the effectiveness of their presentation. Then the station earnestly pleaded for everyone to be calm, pointing out that the invasion had been fiction. But the crowds were not easily calmed. They began to gather around the building that housed the radio station. Soon groups set fire to the building, trapping many inside. Scores of people rushed to escape through a rear door, but others were cut off by the mob and were forced to seek refuge on a higher floor. The flames rose higher and higher, preventing any further escape. In all, fifteen persons were reportedly killed in this riot. More than a dozen others were injured. The building, which also housed the city's oldest newspaper, was almost completely destroyed. Police aid was slow to arrive, for many of the police had been out to investigate the reported invasion. Finally, army troops with tear gas had to be called on to restore order.

Here again, as in the storming of the Bastille, an attack upon a building became the objective of an aroused mob. Both of these cases—the storming of the Bastille in 1789 and of Radio Quito in 1949—are presented as examples of extreme actions taken by crowds. How can we make sense out of such behavior?

ARE CROWDS INSANE?

In *The Crowd*, published in 1895, Frenchman Gustave Le Bon, the first systematic student of crowd behavior, emphasized the irrationality and impulsiveness of crowds. When persons come together in crowds, he suggested, they lose their power of critical judgment. Instead they get carried away by the sentiments of the crowd, itself a kind of common denominator of unconscious impulses. As Le Bon expressed it, "the heterogeneous is swamped by the homogeneous, and the unconscious qualities obtain the upper hand." Crowd behavior also has a temporary and immediate character; its members, said LeBon, "will always be under the influence of the exciting causes of the moment." With such susceptibility to immediate impulses, crowds may do rather extreme things. Furthermore, they are unrestrained by a sense of responsibility, as individuals might be. "In crowds," continued Le Bon, "the foolish, ignorant, and envious persons are freed from the sense of their insignificance and powerlessness, and are possessed instead by the notion of brutal and temporary but immense strength."[4]

This does not mean, Le Bon hastened to add, that crowd behavior is necessarily always bad. Crowds may also perform very noble and heroic deeds. But whether bad or good, the deeds of a crowd always tend to be carried out in an exaggerated and uncritical manner.

Le Bon, as we have said, was the first person to try to systematically study what has since become known as "collective behavior"—including those forms of group behavior that seem relatively free from the control of established norms and institutions. Of course, group behavior is never completely free from cultural and institutional restraints, but sometimes it does appear more spontaneous than at other times. Crowd behavior (when a group is temporarily held together by some common object of attention, concerning which there is mutual stimulation through direct interaction among group members) is probably the type of collective behavior in which freedom from traditional restraints is most apparent. The storming of the Bastille and of Radio Quito seem to show these temporary attentions resulting in actions that could hardly have been forseen. Is this not the common tendency of behavior in crowds?

The writings of Le Bon, and of many others since his time, have characterized crowd behavior as highly spontaneous and variable, often tending toward extreme violence and destructiveness, and displaying gross irrationality. But other scholars have emphasized that such a picture is overdrawn. For example, historian George Rudé has made a systematic study of riots of England and France in the seventeenth and eighteenth centuries, and he finds that these crowds usually were rather selective in their efforts. In particular, they "rarely engaged in indiscriminate attacks on either properties or persons." In his concluding generalizations, Rudé says:

> In short, the crowd was violent, impulsive, easily stirred by rumor, and quick to panic; but it was not fickle, peculiarly irrational, or generally given to bloody attacks on persons. The conventional picture of the crowd painted by Le Bon and inherited by later writers is not lacking in shrewd and imaginative insight; but

it ignores the facts of history and is, in consequence, overdrawn, tendentious, and misleading.[5]

Similar views have been expressed by many who have studied more recent riots in America. For example, those who see the ghetto riots in American cities in the late 1960s as wild, irrational outbreaks on the part of the most miserable segments of American society have real difficulties in explaining some of the most interesting features of those riots. Active participants generally were not among the poorest and most disadvantaged in the areas involved. Targets of aggression were usually not random, but often highly selective. And while property destruction was often massive, crowds were seldom motivated to attack persons. For example, the riot with the greatest loss of life—in Detroit in 1967—saw no more than three persons killed by rioters; the majority of the forty-three persons who lost their lives there were killed by the police, the national guard, or the army in their attempts to impose order.[6]

In his review of recent studies of riot participation, Clark McPhail was impressed with how few consistent relationships could be found between the characteristics of individuals and their participation in a riot. This led him to suggest that the critical features for producing riots might be simply the availability of large numbers of persons with free time who can come together at the same place when events capture their attention.[7]

We are now at a point of confusion in our interpretation of riots and other forms of crowd behavior. Are these typically spontaneous and irrational outbursts of generally unruly individuals; or do they encompass a rational, even if largely unorganized, strategy? Are they symptoms of despair, or rather the cries of rising expectations of large numbers of people? Are they completely free of customary restraints of behavior, or do they embody forms that themselves become customary?

As is often the case when we seek premature closure on a subject, the above questions force an either-or kind of response when a more qualified answer is needed. Crowd behavior is characterized by suggestibility and irrationality, but this does not mean that crowds do not pursue primary objectives that might have some rational justification. They may be relatively unrestrained by conventional forms of behavior, but never completely so. And of course the crowd itself may give rise to the formation of new conventions. For example, today the French very conventionally celebrate July 14—Bastille Day—as their primary national holiday.

Probably our greatest source of confusion is our inability to predict the emergence or explain the behavior of particular crowds. Crowds do not show the predictability of behavior that is seen in most groups, where an established system of positions and roles regulates the behavior of members. This makes behavior fairly predictable in most groups, and this predictability goes a long way toward recommending such behavior to us as being rational rather than irrational.

Crowds, however, are not established groups. They are always only groups in the process of organization. If they evolve into established groups, we no longer consider them to be crowds. Usually, a crowd does not become anything other than a crowd, existing only temporarily and then vanishing when its members disperse.

While crowds are not without standards of behavior—crowd members are typically influenced by a common cultural background as well as by one another—the standards tend to be redefined and altered within the immediate situation. Thus the main features that give predictability to group behavior (established role systems and conventionalized norms) are present only in a shadowy form in crowds. This makes the concrete behavior of crowds far less predictable than that of most groups.

This lack of predictability makes us more likely to brand crowd behavior as "crazy." But the things we label as insane are no less the products of cause-and-effect than are events we see as normal and natural. They are, however, more elusive in terms of our ability to predict and control them—and are more likely to be causes of anxiety and objects of emotional labeling.

What then is our answer to the question posed by the title of this section: Are crowds insane? This question cannot be fully answered as a scientific one because it involves other issues besides matters of fact. Do we like to be in crowds? Do we like the results of crowds? Such value-laden questions are suggested by the introduction of the concept of insanity to apply possibly to the group level of crowd behavior.

However, if our purpose is not so much to approve or condemn crowd behavior, but to see it as a part of nature, we must acknowledge crowds as significant parts of our world. An important starting point in trying to understand their dynamics is to give further attention to the basic process of mutual stimulation.

THE PSYCHOLOGY OF MUTUAL STIMULATION

Whatever else we say about crowds generally, there are two key points that should be acknowledged. First, crowd behavior is purposeful, not accidental; and second, the particular purposes pursued by a crowd emerge out of the mutual stimulation of its individuals with one another.

The first point tends to negate a "madness" interpretation, or at least to point out that there is method in the madness. That is, given the goals adopted by a crowd, temporary as they may be, the behavior of a crowd in pursuing these goals may be quite effective. The crowd that stormed the Bastille, for example, carried out its purpose quite effectively, as did the mob that destroyed the building housing Radio Quito. Whether or not the objectives of a crowd are rational is of course another question. Here we must include in our judgment the kind of long-range perspective that is difficult to bring to any immediate situation, whether involving crowds or involving conventional organizations. In retrospect we see the storming of the Bastille as an incident in a purposeful revolutionary movement and the events at Quito simply as an unruly incident; but this demands a perspective beyond that of the participants themselves. The Quito rioters undoubtedly felt at the time that their retribution upon Radio Quito was well deserved, just as the Paris mob felt that they had good reasons for wanting to destroy the Bastille.

But to go now to our second point, there is a difference between the way a crowd seeks to meet its goals and the way goals are pursued in more established settings. The mutual stimulation in the immediate situation is a major ingredient in developing the goals of crowd behavior, while it is much less so in other settings. This role of mutual stimulation is really the crux of the difference. And recognition of the role of mutual stimulation in the genesis of crowd behavior should help us to understand behavior that otherwise would defy comprehension.

As we pursue the subject of mutual stimulation, we will no longer be dealing with crowds as such. We will rather take this central feature of mutual stimulation and try to identify the psychological dynamics involved.

For almost one hundred years social psychologists have performed experiments on what has come to be known as "social facilitation." This subject, incidentally, provided the earliest laboratory investigations in social psychology. In a set of rather famous early studies, Floyd Allport presented subjects with various mental tasks, such as producing free chain associations (that is, subjects were given an initial word and then asked to write other word associations below it). They did this in one of two basic conditions: "together" or "alone." The task was the same; in some cases it was done in the presence of others pursuing the same task, while in others an individual performed alone.[8]

The most general conclusion obtained from these studies was that more associations were produced in a given time in the together condition than in the alone condition. This was especially true with experimental variations that made the process of association simple and almost mechanical; in more highly mental tasks the greater productivity in a group setting was not so marked. In fact, mental productions of the highest quality tended to come from alone rather than together treatments.

These experiments were of course in no way a study of crowds. We mention them here simply for the idea of social facilitation that they suggest. The presence of other persons commonly exerts something of a stimulating effect upon an individual. We have only to add that under certain conditions the stimulating effect of the presence of others is greater than under other conditions, as we begin to see one of the important strands in the psychology of crowd behavior.

The sheer number of other persons involved may be one important element in the stimulation provided by a crowd. A large crowd has greater impact than a small number of persons. This was neatly demonstrated in a field experiment done by Stanley Milgram and others. This study was conducted with the use of 1,424 unwitting subjects on the sidewalk of one of New York City's busiest streets. Various numbers of persons (from one to as many as fifteen) would move on cue to the center of a fifty-foot length of sidewalk, then together peer up for one full minute to the sixth floor of an adjacent office building. At a window on that floor was a movie camera focused on that area of the sidewalk below. In particular, it recorded what proportion of other persons on the sidewalk stopped to look up. The results were quite clear. The impact of the group of confederates who looked up was a gradually increasing function of its size. Others stopping to gaze upward increased from 4 percent for a single experimental confederate to 40 percent in the case of a group of fifteen.[9]

Further evidence regarding the conditions under which the presence of others is especially stimulating may be found in studies of another form of collective behavior, that of rumors. We draw here especially from the work of Gordon Allport and Leo Postman. Their book, *The Psychology of Rumor*, suggests that there are two basic conditions for the spread of a rumor: First, that the theme of the rumor must have some importance to the people involved and, second, that the true facts must be ambiguous. They even suggest that these two basic conditions may be combined into a formula for the intensity of rumor activity, namely:

$$R = i \times a$$

This formula asserts that the amount of *rumor* (R) activity varies directly with the *importance* (i) of the subject to the persons concerned and the *ambiguity* (a) of their knowledge of that subject. Furthermore, Allport and Postman point out:

The relation between importance and ambiguity is not additive but multiplicative, for if either importance or ambiguity is zero there is *no* rumor. For instance, an American citizen is not likely to spread rumors concerning the market price of camels in Afghanistan because the subject has no importance for him, ambiguous though it certainly is.

Nor, they add, are important events the subject of rumors when the facts are fully known. Without either importance or ambiguity, there is no rumor.[10]

Let us now pull together these three threads: (1) the generally activating effect of the presence of other people, especially when they are present in significant numbers; (2) an event or series of events of considerable importance to the persons involved; and (3) a general ambiguity about how these events are to be interpreted or what action would constitute an appropriate response. Combining these three, the potential for mutual stimulation is very great.[11]

Crowd behavior is of course not the only form mutual stimulation may take. Falling in love may provide another example of the combination of social stimulation creating meaning and reducing ambiguity on issues of supreme importance for the persons involved. But when more than a small handful of people are involved at the same time and place, the results of mutual stimulation are usually recognized as crowd behavior.

THE POLARIZATION PHENOMENON

In his theory of collective behavior, Neil Smelzer gives central attention to the beliefs that activate persons toward collective action. Through mutual stimulation, what Smelser calls a "generalized belief" comes to be shared by members of a crowd. Such beliefs and shared attitudes help to reduce the ambiguity that people sense, provide them with a common direction for their thinking (usually including a common object for their ire), and point them in the same direction for collective action.[12]

As a group becomes involved in collective behavior, there are increased pressures for conformity—to share with others in both attitudes and behavior. But attitudes of crowd members do not just become more similar to one another; they frequently move to a more extreme position, and this is not easily seen as a result of simple pressures for conformity. However, this movement toward more extreme attitudes has now been well explored under what has become known as the "group polarization effect."[13]

Early research on this phenomenon was usually discussed as the "risky shift." First reported in research for a 1961 master's thesis at the Massachusetts Institute of Technology, this was the initially surprising finding that groups tend to support higher risk levels in decision making than individual members would. This effect, though small, was soon reliably confirmed by many investigators. Their basic experimental procedures involved first giving a questionnaire to measure individual risk preferences, then having these persons formed into groups to discuss some of the cases previously presented to them as individuals, asking for a group decision on the level of risk to be recommended. Because this group decision usually supported a higher level of risk than the mean of earlier individual recommendations, it became common to refer to groups as promoting a general "shift" toward risk.

However, as more research accumulated, the shift was not always toward more risk. A group induced shift toward caution could also be reliably produced for certain kinds of items. Gradually it became clear that the main difference in situations producing more risk and those producing more caution was to be found not in the situations themselves but in the initial inclinations of most group members. If the initial inclinations of most people are toward risk, a risky shift is likely; but if initial leanings are more on the side of caution, the group is apt to undergo a cautious shift. In fact, except for the most extreme initial positions, the *amount* of shift in either direction can be well predicted by the mean initial position of individuals. The more extreme the initial averages in the direction of *either* risk or caution, the more would the group position move in that direction. As this finding was confirmed, the "risky shift" became more accurately designated as the "group polarization effect." Groups, it appears, tend to support more extreme or more "polarized" views than those shown by the same persons as individuals.

Because of the ease of using the Choice Dilemmas Questionnaire, a readily available instrument to measure risk, the early research was focused especially upon risk-taking. But as the effect was seen in the more general terms of group polarization, the subject matter of research was broadened to all kinds of topics. Racial attitudes, views on international conflict, sex-role attitudes, simulations of jury trials, and general studies of person perception—these are a few of the areas toward which experiments in group polarization processes were applied. The usual finding of these studies was that, yes, members of a group do make a group judgement that is more extreme (in whatever direction members are initially inclined) than the mean of earlier individual judgments.

How can we explain this group polarization effect? A number of different theories have been put forward, though some have little supporting evidence. Two theories stand out among those that have accumulated strong support: the persuasive arguments theory and the social comparison theory.

The persuasive arguments theory holds that the polarization is mainly a result of the content of group discussion. There is a greater pool of arguments available for the direction in which most members are initially inclined, and these are therefore better represented in the discussion among group members. Also, more novel arguments are likely to be made in this direction, giving new reasons to justify a more extreme position. Studies have supported this interpretation by showing that group discussions are in fact usually biased in the direction of initial inclinations. Also, just presenting individuals with such a biased sampling of arguments (but without actual group discussion) induces a polarization effect. This is precisely what would be expected if the persuasiveness of arguments is the key to the group polarization effect.

The social comparison theory holds that most people share in a cultural value that supports one direction or the other for the issue at hand. In terms of this value, they want to be at least as "good" as most other members. Initially, most members think they are actually "better" (that is, closer to the cultural ideal) than most other persons; but the group discussion calls this into question. They find that others are equally inclined in that direction. In their desire to be at least as "good" as others, they shift their position further in that direction. When most members of the group are doing this, the result is to make the group's judgment more extreme than that represented by the the initial average of its members. Some studies have found a polarization effect merely by exposure to the postions of others—that is, without any group discussion at all, but only from information about the positions of others. This is strong evidence to support the social comparison explanation for the group polarization effect.

Most investigators in this area of study believe that both persuasive arguments and social comparison explanations generally apply to the phenomenon of group polarization. Furthermore, rather than acting as distinct influences or competing hypotheses, they are actually complementary in the way they work together to generate this effect. David Myers, a leading researcher of this problem, describes his view of the typical operation of these forces as follows:

> People secretly want to act in a given way, but are restrained from fully doing so by their perception of an external social norm. When several such people find themselves in a group, they soon verbalize their inclinations and discover that others are emitting similar arguments and opinions. Since information consistent with their shared inclinations is expressed and received most warmly, the discussion arguments become polarized. The net result is that when people feel a conflict between what they ought to do and what they want to do, discussion with similar others generally induces information processing in support of their internal preference and this tendency is therefore magnified.[14]

Myers is not talking specifically about crowds. He is, rather, discussing the general effects of group interaction. But what he describes is especially likely to occur in the mutual stimulation of crowds. Concentrated together in a particular place and time, united by common attention to unexpected events, sharing some of their interpretations—these characteristic features of crowds are all conditions especially likely to produce a polarizing effect.

IN CONCLUSION

We have been searching for key social psychological factors involved in crowd behavior. We have identified several:

1. a situation which combines high ambiguity and great importance for the people involved;

2. social stimulation, which becomes heightened under conditions of temporarily high density; and

3. pressures unfolding through interaction to support positions more extreme than those previously anticipated by the participants.

Identifying these factors in crowd psychology does not eliminate the mystery of crowd behavior. It does make this behavior more understandable within the concepts of social psychology, but it adds only a little to our understanding of any particular instances of crowd behavior. We are still amazed by what we sometimes observe—as in televised events where we witness history in the making through crowd behavior (such as seeing the Berlin Wall come down in November of 1989 or observing a Soviet coup fail in the streets of Moscow in August of 1991), and by what we may find ourselves doing when in a crowd.

NOTES

1. Much of the present chapter is adapted from Chapter 18 of Schellenberg (1974).

2. Any history of France—indeed, of modern Europe—will have further details about the fall of the Bastille in 1789. Our evidence for the Ecuador case to follow is derived primarily from Britt (1950).

3. The earlier American dramatization of *The War of the Worlds* (Wells, 1898/1951) is fully described in Cantril, Gaudet, and Herzog (1940).

4. Our source here is Le Bon (1895/1960). Quotations in this paragraph are from pp. 29, 37, and 50–51.

5. Our quotations here are from Rudé (1964), pp. 254 and 275.

6. Evidence on American ghetto riots may be found in Lieberson and Silverman (1965), Kerner (1968), Graham and Gurr (1969), Spilerman (1970), and Short and Wolfgang (1972)

7. See especially McPhail (1971).

8. This research is described in Allport (1920). Even earlier experiments in this line of research were reported in the closing years of the nineteenth century.

9. The study here cited is more fully described in Milgram, Bickman, and Berkowitz (1969).

10. Our key source here is Allport and Postman (1947), with material quoted from p. 34.

11. Bibb Latané's theory of social impact uses a slightly more abstract representation of some of these same ideas. According to this theory, "when some number of social sources are acting upon a target individual, the amount of impact experienced by the target should be a multiplicative function of the strength, S, the immediacy, I, and the number, N, of sources present" (Latané, 1981, p. 344). Our "importance" and "ambiguity" factors could well be interpreted as ingredients in Latane's "S"; and his "N" and "I" factors may be considered as social facilitation variables.

12. See Smelser (1963), especially pp. 79–130.

13. In our discussion of group polarization, we draw especially upon Myers (1982), Brown (1986), and Turner (1991).

14. This quotation is from Myers (1982), pp. 156–157.

Chapter 9

The Mystery of Social Order

THE HOBBESIAN QUESTION

How is social order possible?

We do not often ask this question, preferring simply to accept the social order around us as given. Rather than question this order, we seek to explain the departures from it, taking forms as varied as political revolution and criminal activity. Certainly we need an understanding of such departures from social order, but a much more profound question is why there should be such an order in the first place. This is the fundamental mystery that we pursue in the present chapter.

One person who did not take social order for granted was the seventeenth century political philosopher, Thomas Hobbes. He raised this issue so insistently that it has sometimes come to be known as the "Hobbesian question."

The answer Hobbes formulated to his own question made central use of the idea of a social contract. This idea had been around in one form or another for many centuries, implying some agreement by the populace in their governing arrangements. Hobbes applied the idea of a social contract to the whole framework of organized society, not just to a particular form of government. In doing so, he imagined humanity in what he called a "state of nature," a condition without established political or social institutions. In such a state, each person seeks only his own interests, and the result is the insecurity of a condition of perpetual war. "The life of man" in such circumstances is, in the vivid language of Hobbes, "solitary, poor, nasty, brutish, and short." But, blessed with reason, humans see the need for peace, a peace that requires a system of government. Indeed, the chaos of a state of nature would be so great that, in Hobbes' view, only a leap into political absolutism can free us from the perils of anarchy. So Hobbes used the idea of a social contract for justifying the institutions of absolute monarchy.[1]

Of course, the social contract idea could also be turned in more democratic directions, toward a justification of strictly limited and representative government with John Locke or in defense of direct democracy with Jean Jacques Rousseau. The founding documents of America's first republic—the *Declaration of Independence* and the *Constitution*—are heavily infused with social contract themes, borrowed largely from the Lockean tradition. Even today this idea is used hypothetically to explore basic questions of social ethics within a framework of democratic values.[2]

Historically speaking, the social contract represents little more than a myth. It views social order as a rational and purposeful construction of a free people. This is, of course, the democratic ideal; but the reality seldom approaches such an ideal, even in democratic societies. And in the full range of human societies for which we have historical or anthropological evidence, governing structures have most commonly been dictated after seizure from within or conquest from without. Seldom have they been systematically constructed through free elections or some other means of reflecting a general consensus of the populace.

On his part, Hobbes recognized that humans did not suddenly transform themselves from a state of nature to form a civil society. Although he argues that many parts of the world may still approach his image of the "natural condition of man" (he, writing in 1651, mentions in particular "the savage people in many places in America"), most of humanity, he admits, has developed far beyond such a condition. The main use of his "state of nature" is therefore not to describe any historical reality, but to describe a hypothetical tendency inherent in human nature. Humans by nature are selfish, Hobbes believed, and do not naturally come to consider the welfare of each other. That being the case, only a higher power in the form of the state can bring humans into peaceful and productive relationships with each other.[3]

Let us leave aside the distinctively political overtones of Hobbes's analysis, as well as the question of whether or not the social contract provides a realistic model for any actual historical events. Let us take his fundamental assumptions about the natural human condition and see whether they do not lead directly into some kind of a social order. Simplifying, with little loss of meaning, we may describe the Hobbesian state of nature as a condition in which individuals may face each other, two at a time (we'll call our mythical representatives Abner and Bert), with the following results repeatedly experienced:

1. When both Abner and Bert are mean to each other, they punish each other.

2. When both Abner and Bert are generous to each other, they both experience a situation that is tolerable but hardly very rewarding.

3. When one of these two individuals is mean and the other is generous, the mean one is rewarded and the generous one is punished.

In such a state of affairs, to be generous does not lead to reward. The predictable result is continual meanness between individuals, or what Hobbes called "a war of every man" against every other man.[4]

But would not the Abners and Berts see that, if they coordinated their actions, they could at least each stop punishing one another? By being generous together—that is, forming some coordinated plan of cooperation—they would both attain tolerable outcomes. This may not be highly rewarding, but it could at least stop the constant punishment or "war." But could they trust each other enough to do this? Would not each be tempted to feign generosity to cover up their underlying meanness in seeking to exploit each other? If so, it is easy to see that they would remain in a state of continual conflict.

We have here the fundamental question of how those standards for behavior that we call social norms may emerge. Given the situation that we have described (admittedly in rather stark and extreme terms), persons would rationally see the need for norms. They would see the futility of continual struggle against each other and note the more desirable results that could be achieved with mutual cooperation. But could they make the transition to such cooperation, given the strong temptation to exploit any moves toward generosity on the part of others? Hobbes's answer here was a rather pessimistic one—people would see the need for a normative order, but they could not bring themselves to create it on their own. It was instead necessary to create a higher power that would impose and enforce a normative order. Once such an order was established, people could live together with mutual cooperation.

It is possible to create laboratory situations that capture the essential features of the Hobbesian state of nature. In particular, we can place two persons into a situation for which the contingencies of reward and punishment are as those described earlier for Abner and Bert. If, further, they face a single opportunity to choose, and they have no good way to communicate with each other before they choose, such subjects will quite naturally choose the "mean" response to each other. On the other hand, suppose the experimenter tells them of the advantages of being generous, and, indeed, clearly implies that generosity is the "right" response; subjects then regularly show mutual generosity. This would be analogous to Thomas Hobbes's sovereign laying down the normative order. But let us consider as well a third set of experimental conditions: Persons face each other with a long series of repeated choices of a similar nature, the experimenter suggests no "right" or "wrong" responses, but subjects can talk with each other about what they are experiencing. Would they then develop a pattern of mutual generosity on their own?

There have been numerous experiments performed along the lines just described. Some pairs in some experiments find it impossible to break out of their mutual deadlock, but most subjects (with repeated choices and at least limited opportunity for advance communication) develop a pattern of mutual cooperation. This demonstrates the emergence of norms—and without the external enforcer Hobbes considered essential.[5]

It may seem presumptuous to claim that such experiments provide a reasonable model for the emergence of social order. Certainly, our bare-bones case of Abner and Bert hardly represents the range of interaction experienced by men and women in preliterate societies! Nevertheless, we can at least use such cases as mind games to imagine how various patterns of norms might in theory come to be established, thus laying the foundations for a social order.

An example may be seen in the work of Robert Axelrod. He used what is generally known as the Prisoner's Dilemma game. We need not delve into the rather curious reasons for such a designation for this structure that has become so popular for experimental games by social psychologists; suffice it to say that this is a situation for two persons very similar to that described for Abner and Bert (with the only significant addition that either of these two individuals will be more punished when his move toward generosity is exploited by the other than when they both are mean to each other). Rather than having live human subjects exposed to each other in repeated choices with such a game, Axelrod raised the question of what computer programs might be most successful in dictating what a person should choose in such a situation. That is, what definition of strategy would be most successful in achieving an individual's self-interests when involved in such a situation? To pursue this question, he sent out a call to game theorists to send him a program to be used in a tournament between computer programs. He then ran the tournament on his computer and announced the winning strategy. To the surprise of a considerable number of experts, the winning program was the simplest strategy of all, a tit-for-tat strategy. This strategy consisted of initial cooperation, followed by matching whatever behavior the other had shown on the previous occasion. It apparently provided better assurance against exploitation than most programs, and it also laid out a promise for fruitful cooperation with any others so inclined.

Axelrod concluded from his tournament results that "under suitable conditions, cooperation can indeed emerge in a world of egoists without central authority." He then proceeded to identify more formally the conditions under which this might apply. He saw the Prisoner's Dilemma as a suitable prototype for a kind of situation that might lead to the development of cooperative norms, provided the individuals involved anticipated continued interaction with one another. He has pointed to many areas of human affairs—from the planning of whom to invite to dinner parties to decisions of international relations—where events might be fruitfully interpreted in terms of such a model. He even points to interesting parallels to be found in patterns of genetic change in biological evolution (showing how selfish genes may nevertheless evolve to support certain forms of cooperation between organisms).[6]

As we have just seen, the Prisoner's Dilemma game is a rich source for exploring questions concerning the emergence of social norms. It represents quite well what Thomas Hobbes viewed as the natural and original human condition, and it allows us to go beyond Hobbes' own answer to the question of how social order is possible. But the Prisoner's Dilemma game is not the only framework within which a normative pattern might naturally arise. In her theoretical analysis of the emergence of norms, Edna Ullmann-Margalit identifies two other basic situations as especially likely to create norms. These situations arise respectively from problems of coordination and those of social inequality. Let us discuss each of these types of situations briefly.[7]

Consider two strangers approaching one another from opposite directions, both walking in the middle of the sidewalk. To avoid bumping into each other, one or both will have to move slightly to one side as they meet. But that will hardly do, if they both move in the same direction. On the other hand, if each moves slightly to the right, their problem is solved. But why to the right— why not to the left? That would serve just as well, of course, provided they both understood this plan. The problem consists of assuring that they both have the same idea. A fairly simple norm such as "when in doubt, keep to the right" serves to regulate pedestrian traffic quite well. A slightly more formal rule may be applied to the more hazardous conditions of cars on highways. Of course, there is nothing inherently correct about "keeping to the right" (motorists in Great Britain readily demonstrate this); the important thing is to know what the norm is so that there can be effective coordination.

Many elements of human culture are the products of coordination norms. There is some convenience for most people to eat and sleep at similar times, though when the times are to be typically involves some arbitrary exercise of convention. The scheduling of public activities to start on the hour or half-hour is another illustration of an arbitrary coordination of human activities. Other examples can be found in language forms, especially in the way meanings are attached to particular sounds in creating vocabularies; such conventions of rather arbitrary word meanings provide a primary base for human communication.

Less obvious than how problems of coordination may create common standards is how human inequalities may support the emergence of norms. Nevertheless, what Ullmann-Margalit calls "norms of partiality" play an extremely important role in the formation of social orders. These norms tend to preserve past inequalities by identifying certain rights for more favored persons. Such rights range from ceremonial recognitions of status to special opportunities to exercise power. Private property offers a good example. As Ullmann-Margalit points out:

> The concept of trespass, the notions of the sanctity of individual property and the rights of inheritors, and the norms associated with them, are all meant, essentially, to preserve, protect, and perpetuate the position of the "haves"—and their descendants— in states which are inherently states of inequality.[8]

When two persons in a relationship have unequal power, both may have an interest in norms that regulate that relationship. The weaker party recognizes his vulnerable position and would like some protection against arbitrary uses of power. The more powerful party finds it both costly and inconvenient if he constantly needs to reassert his power. Both therefore have an interest in the development of norms. Norms formed to guide such relations thus show a pattern that reflects the original inequality, preserving it in the interaction that follows.[9]

What we have considered in this section suggests that there are at least three conditions of human interaction that naturally lead to the creation of normative orders. One of these is the presence of self-defeating conflict, which leads to the development of norms that facilitate cooperation. Another is more simply the absence of information necessary for the mutual coordination of activities by persons whose interests are parallel; such situations yield norms of coordination. A third condition is that of any inequality that might set in motion a struggle for relative advantage—a struggle that may become costly for all involved, and that may be minimized by the development of norms of partiality. Combinations of these three general situations may also occur, leading to corresponding mixtures of normative patterns.

These norms arise naturally out of social interaction. In contrast to Hobbes's theorizing, they do not depend on the establishment of some formal authority; instead, they arise in some degree whenever and wherever people come together. Of course, formal authority may strengthen and embellish such norms; but they clearly would have been present prior to, as well as after, the emergence of civil society.

Thus our analysis of the Hobbesian question (of how social order is possible) leads us to negate his answer (which was: only through the authority provided by a sovereign power). A normative order can be expected to be present wherever we have human society, which means wherever we have human beings living together. People in interaction with one another naturally develop—through explicit agreements or, more often, through a gradual evolution of social habits—norms to create a social order for themselves.

HOW STATES BEGAN

We have just made the case that social order is possible without a formal system of government. This leads us to the next question: Why did humanity turn to formal political structures at all, if formal governments are not essential for social order?

The first point to be made here is that the creation of formal political institutions is comparatively recent (in the long story of humanity). One anthropologist has reminded us that "for 99 per cent of the approximately one million years that man has inhabited this earth, he lived, thrived, and developed without any true government whatsoever," and that

> as late as one hundred years ago half the peoples of the world— not half the population but half the tribes or nations—still ordered their lives exclusively through informal controls without benefit of political institutions.

Other anthropologists might dispute parts of this statement, arguing that some form of government (or at least what may be called political institutions) may be found in every known form of human society. Such disputes hinge largely on matters of definition. There is a sense in which even the simplest bands of hunter-gatherers have political institutions. But these are based on the kinship system or the relatively informal forms of social control within the local community. A separate political order beyond the kinship group and beyond local community organizations is present only in more complex societies. We refer to this separate political order as a "state," and the question we now pursue is how such an order came to be.[10]

George P. Murdock, the anthropologist quoted above, sets forth the basic outline of the origin of the state as follows:

> When, in consequence of Neolithic technological and economic advances, human beings found themselves for the first time living in local aggregations of appreciably more than a thousand people, they discovered that informal mechanisms of control no longer

sufficed to maintain social order. . . . The commonest solution to
this problem, achieved independently in many places and at
many different times in the last 10,000 years of man's culture
history, is the formation of a state, that is, of government or political institutions in the strict sense. A special organization is set up
to which is delegated the authority and power to supplment
informal social control with physical force.[11]

For our purposes, we may define a state as a formal organization with identified leaders, whose responsibility it is to rule over a
specified group of people in a particular area. In so ruling, these
leaders are expected to promote social order within the society and
defense against forces beyond. In pursuing these objectives, leaders
claim a priority on the legitimate use of physical force. Further, they
come to represent the central forces of society in a special way,
which provides a meaning for the state that transcends the
particular group of people in power or their specific governmental
activities. In this way an order of social reality is consolidated that
is different from the kinship system or the local community—or
even the tribe (with tribes, in turn being combinations of local
communities and related extended kin groups). This new political
order and its associated society become an important source of
social identity for its people, to some extent at the expense of older
family and local community ties, although these continue to be
powerful.

A state thus characterized can still take on an enormous range
of possible forms. These may include the ancient theocratic dynas-
ties of Egypt or the more democratic city-state of Athens; the nineteenth century British empire or the proud kingdom of Buganda in
Africa that it came to subdue; or today's reputed Great Powers or
the tiny principality of Leichtenstein. Notwithstanding such
variety, all of these forms are fundamentally different from the
stateless societies of primitive man, represented by such groups as
North American Eskimos, Australian aborigines, or the bushmen of
southern Africa.

It is conventional to divide the forms of humanity into two
main types: primitive man and civilized society. Civilized man
always comes with a state; that, indeed, is the basis of his "civil"
designation. But it is misleading to group all precivilized and
nonliterate peoples under a common "primitive" category. Particularly if we are seeking to find how states began, we must be alert to
great variations among societies that lacked the full range of charac-

teristics we see in modern nation-states. Brief comments about three tribal societies—the Crow, the Kpelle and the Shilluk—help to illustrate this point.[12]

The Crow, as did a number of other North American tribes of Plains Indians, had a tribal council composed of leading men, who selected one of their number to be head chief. But the tribal council had only minimal authority over everyday life in the villages of the Crow, and the head chief had no real powers of government. In writing generally about Plains Indians, one anthropologist comments that "nothing was more remote from native conceptions than that a chief should wield power over the property and life of the population." A much more significant force for social control was found in fraternal clubs or associations, of which the Crow had eight. Each of these associations served military, social, and religious purposes for its members and for the tribe as a whole. Any adult male could apply for membership, subject to acceptance at an annual election. Nonelective elders provided formal leadership within each association. Only on the occasion of the communal buffalo hunt—usually held each summer, with buffalo hunted by smaller groups during other parts of the year—did the Crow develop what might clearly be recognized as a system of government. On this occasion, the entire tribe congregated in one place, special coordination was necessary for a successful hunt, and means were established to obtain a greater level of discipline than usual. The tribal chief would designate one of the eight military societies to be in charge of the buffalo hunt for that year, and they could exercise such police powers as corporal punishment or confiscation of property in order to enforce their dictates during this period. However, their authority was primarily related to hunting procedures; they had no power to mete out punishment for unrelated episodes of individual violence; and once the communal hunt was over, they had no authority beyond their own members.[13]

The Kpelle in western Africa (mostly in Liberia) also had special associations, with separate groups for males and females. These secret societies served primarily religious and social purposes, and an adult could have little status in society without membership in at least one of these associations. But, in contrast to the Crow case, associations among the Kpelle were clearly of unequal status and power. One of them, the Poro society, dominated the life of the entire tribe. Although all adult males were members, there were special categories of membership for different Poro groups, and only a few persons were permitted to know the most sacred mysteries. We are told that a very high order of dignity was attached to the top Poro leader, known as the Grand Master, and that:

> Since the people believed him to be immortal, his death is kept a secret, his successor being elected in a conclave of prominent Poro men. Popular faith has it that he is able to kill and revive human beings by his magic.

The Kpelle also have a king, who in theory owns the entire tribal territory and its people. Despite this exalted status, we are told:

> Actually, he is little more than the representative of the popular will as expressed by prominent freemen. Without their consent no important decision is normally rendered, the initiative being taken by the elders of the tribe as frequently as by the supposed ruler. Specifically, it is the Poro that retrenches royal prerogative. Its Grand Master has the right of calling meetings of his own accord, of summoning or excluding the King from such assemblies according to his pleasure, and may inflict penalties, even capital punishment, without consultation of other authorities.

Among the Shilluk (along the Nile in the country now known as the Sudan) much more sacred power—but no more real authority—was placed in the person of the king. He was the leader of all the Shilluk, with both secular and spiritual powers attached to his throne. The king's position was hereditary, although the chiefs of the tribe had a hand in choosing which son of the previous king was to ascend to the throne. Chiefs represented the various lineages of the tribe, and they generally exercised greater power than the monarch. Although the king had an impressive court, he had no governmental machinery beyond the royal capital. There was no delegation of powers to officials elsewhere and no direct influence upon the everyday life of the people (other than the widespread belief that the good health of the king would promote prosperity and success throughout the kingdom).[14]

None of the three societies just mentioned have the full characteristics we have identified as those of the state; but all of them have limited characteristics of a state-like order. All three had a person who carried symbolic leadership for the tribe, but who did not have much influence on the lives of ordinary people. The chief of the tribal council among the Crow was probably in a weaker position than the king in either of the two African cases; but even these monarchs had little more than ceremonial powers. Most of what we consider normal functions of government were dispersed in these societies, although dispersed in quite different ways in each case. The Crow probably approached the image of a society without government most closely—but each year a rather clear order of tribal authority was established to control the communal buffalo hunt. The Kpelle monarch was theoretically in charge, but in practice his power was subservient to the leaders of a secret society. The Shilluk had all the trappings of a monarchical state, but without any administrative apparatus to influence what the real leaders did in villages throughout the land.

It is also instructive to take note of cases of nonliterate societies that, although we might be more likely to think of them in a "tribal" rather than a "civilized" category, nevertheless meet all the features set forth as those of the state. We briefly mention the cases of Hawaii and Buganda.[15]

When Europeans first made contact with the Hawaiian Islands in 1778, each of the four main islands was a separate kingdom. When American missionaries arrived in 1820, the entire group of islands had been consolidated into one kingdom, the founding monarch had recently died, and the newly crowned king had abolished the traditional religion with its great variety of special taboos. Such an exercise of monarchical power was possible only in a society with a centralized political system, such as had been established through force and cunning by Kamehameha I. The native Hawaiians were a highly stratified society with careful attention paid to their relative status and genealogical roots. They apparently respected the role of a king more than they revered their traditional gods—which worked to the benefit of the missionaries when the monarch promptly embraced Christianity. But the king was also assisted by an effective administrative apparatus, including (despite the absence of writing) a precise system for keeping track of tax collections.

Even more impressive was the spectacle that greeted the first Europeans to visit the kingdom of Buganda (in what is now Uganda, in East Africa). The first visitor in 1862 was struck by the orderliness of the kindgom, including the straight twelve-foot-wide roads from all provincial centers to the city of the king. Explorer Henry M. Stanley visited this place a few years later and was much impressed by what he saw at the king's court. This king (or *kabaka*, as the Baganda, the people of Buganda, called him) theoretically had absolute power, but practically he shared it with a prime minister and ten provincial governors (in turn all appointed by the king). Each governor had subgovernors, who also had their subordinates to collect taxes and carry out the orders of the realm. A total of about one million people were subject to the king, who could put thirty thousand warriors into the field at one time if needed, with thousands more in a navy (primarily to patrol the shores of Lake Victoria).

We may study evidence from other preliterate tribes (in addition to the Crow, Kpelle, Shilluk, Hawaiians, and Baganda) who were studied in the process of developing more complex political systems. To such evidence we may add historical records and archeological remains of ancient civilizations, showing the early conditions of their states. From such sources we may build a picture of factors that were most generally involved in the emergence of states. This picture does not all fit into a standardized pattern, with a few rather clear-cut causes of state formation. In fact, the state emerged independently on many different occasions and under rather diverse conditions. Still, it is possible to give at least a rough description of the factors most generally present. These can be identified as (1) an increased population size and/or diversity, (2) the centralization of political authority, and (3) certain kinds of psychological changes.[16]

States have generally arisen in societies following periods of a notable increase in the size or diversity of its population. Rapid population growth in a limited area (resulting from irrigation or other forms of intensive agriculture) may sometimes be the most obvious condition of state formation. Ancient Egypt provides a good example of this, and other ancient civilizations in river valleys suggest similar patterns. Along with increased population size is an increased diversity of the population. This may take the form of a greater economic complexity, leading to the development of cities. Sharper class divisions are likely to emerge along with growth. Sometimes another group moves into the area, creating tensions with those already living there. Any or all of these factors may be involved in an increased diversity that strains the previous framework of social organization. A more comprehensive system of social organization is the result, leading to what may be recognized as a state.[17]

Among the preliterate societies we have mentioned as examples of state-building societies, the Crow most clearly illustrate the importance of population size. Only during the annual buffalo hunt, when all Crow were brought together in one place, was a systematic governmental system in place. Here it was a special association, uniting different kinship lines, that provided a temporary system of rule. Among the Kpella the secret societies exerted their power more permanently, side-by-side with an official monarch, each effectively checking the other and limiting the further development of a state system. In eastern Africa, the Shilluk and Buganda kindgoms represent interesting contrasts in state development, though both operated within a framework of well developed clan organizations. Of the two, Buganda was more densely populated, and the king there had succeeded (over a period of several centuries) in asserting effective power over clan leaders—a process that had not occurred among the Shilluk. Both were highly hierarchical societies, as was the case with Hawaiian natives. The monarch who united the Hawaiian Islands skillfully manipulated local leaders and developed contacts with European and American fleets to help consolidate his preeminence throughout that group of islands, which had previously developed their own relatively complex social structure.

An increase in population size or complexity tends to be correlated with a centralization of political authority. Tribes with several chiefs may have a paramount chief, whose role may be largely ceremonial, but who may assume more powers under certain conditions. A largely figurehead king may develop an administrative apparatus and begin to exercise real powers, or a leading warrior may use his military leadership to establish himself in a position of political dominance. Such are among the forms of political centralization that may be involved in the emergence of the state. The important thing is not the precise form of the governmental apparatus—though most early states are recognized as kingdoms—but the way an increased centralization of political authority comes to be generally accepted in society. An increase in coercive power, through the control of armies and police forces, is a regular part of the story here. But such coercion presupposes an acceptance of the authority to have armies and to enact decrees that may be enforced by the police. Such authority cannot usually be seen as arising at any one particular point in time; rather, it grows gradually as people come to look more and more for leadership from central authority positions—and as claims from that center for increased authority fail to be disputed.[18]

Among the five societies we have used as examples, only the Crow failed to represent any elements of a central monarchy. The kings in the Kpella and Shilluk cases were effectively countered by other forces, preventing a consolidation of central power. The Baganda represent a preliterate people with a fully developed central government, and the Hawaiian Islands show a political system (at the time of first contact with Europeans and Americans) in the process of its consolidation under a single monarch.

Certain kinds of psychological changes tend to accompany the centralization of political authority. Most notable is the attachment of special powers to the person of the leader. He is given a freedom unknown in most tribal societies, and he is considered to be justified in an enormously wide range of possible actions. Although such freedom must always be limited in practice, monarchs of early states frequently stake a claim to absolute power, and most of their followers give them wide leeway for their exercise of kingly powers. In fact, religious awe toward the person of the king is often highly interwoven with political subservience. But the monarch is not the only recipient of such an increased claim to individuality. His leadership frequently inspires others to act in a similar fashion, on a smaller scale. The power of the individual thus becomes more widely recognized at the expense of more traditional relationships. Often this is accompanied by a remarkable growth in the artistic productivity of a society becoming a state, as new forms for the expression of individuality are sought and cultivated.[19]

Both the Buganda and Hawaiian cases show (especially in comparison with the other three preliterate societies we have reviewed) important psychological changes associated with the consolidation of their monarchies. The African explorer Stanley noted a widespread imitation among the Baganda of their monarch, and others were much impressed by the comparatively high cultural development of this society. European visitors were "immediately struck by the vitality, the eagerness, the intelligence, the life-enhancing quality of the Baganda"; and a young Winston Churchill called their land "the Pearl of Africa." Even more remarkable was the break with traditional religious beliefs in the Hawaiian Islands shortly after consolidation of their monarchy, suggesting that there had been an earlier period during which traditional values had eroded. A remarkable development of artistic talent (especially in poetry, dance, and music) was occurring at the same time among the Hawaiians.[20]

The factors just mentioned (increase in population size and diversity, centralization of political authority, and psychological changes that erode traditional claims) can hardly be treated as definite or precise causes of state formation. We generally find them to be preconditions, but in a variety of particular forms. Their role is further confused by the fact that all three of these general features tend to be products of state formation as well as preconditions. Once a society develops as a state, a much greater size and diversity of population may be accommodated, since the new form of social organization does not rest on kinship and local community ties. Once established, the state becomes a vehicle for further political centralization, frequently developing an elaborate governmental apparatus to preserve and enhance central power. And the cult of individuality (both for the sovereign and for more ordinary people) can continue to grow in a society that has a framework of organization beyond that of family, tribe, and village.

Once set in motion, the state tends to be a self-perpetuating form. This does not mean that states do not vanish (usually to become part of some other state), or that states, once formed, never revert to a more tribal form of organization. We mean rather that this form of social organization has shown an amazing persistence in its general growth and in its displacement of tribal societies. More is involved here than that state systems provide for their own continuation and that their bureaucracies function as self-enhancing systems—although both of these tendencies are common enough. Societies organized as states have had a special dynamic quality that eluded more traditionally organized forms of humanity. Part of this dynamism has come rather obviously from the coercive powers of the state to put large armies in the field and to administer punishments to people who disobey its dictates. But another part rests on the more voluntary identification of people with the state—accepting the state and its authority as a special embodiment of the society as a whole. There is also the openness of the state to growth and change. The state can expand to include more people with greater diversity, and even entirely new populations, without changing its basic form. By its secular powers of legislation, it can modify practices of a people to conform to standards other than those of traditional virtues. Finally, the state can provide a wider form of social order than could have been imagined by previous generations. Such social order can be wider in the simple geographical sense of covering more territory. But there is another meaning that we associate with the wider order—it provides a more dependable system of public order. This order, in turn, makes possible some of the "finer" qualities that we have come to associate with "civilization," such as a systematic development of arts and the codification of our knowledge. These too are products of the framework of social order that came with the development of civil (that is, state-led) societies.[21]

THE EXPANSION OF SOCIETY

Societies such as those of Buganda and the Hawaiian Islands established state systems without the use of a written language. For both, writing came with external contacts; and both eagerly made use of writing, once available, for their purposes. An example of the existence of a state system is seen in the conditions of tax collection in the Hawaiian Islands before the use of writing. Here, we are told:

> On the island of Kauai in Hawaii, tax information was kept principally by one man on a line of cordage about twenty-five hundred feet long. Each district had its place on the cord, and each individual taxpayer was indicated. "Knots, loops, and tufts, of different shapes, sizes, and colours" were used to discriminate between districts and individuals, as well as to indicate the manner in which the tax was paid, whether in hogs, dogs, sandalwood, taro, or whatever.

In such practices we find the beginnings of the expression of a complex symbol system in a physically permanent for n. Out of such beginnings must have developed early systems of writing in a number of different early states.[22]

When it first appeared, writing must have primarily served the interests of the state. Tax information, other kinds of economic records, historical information, and official glorification of the monarch were among the early purposes of writing. In time this form of language—which could overcome the bounds of time and space that had so limited earlier oral communication—was put to many other purposes. Writing increased the economic and ceremonial power of small elites in early civilizations, just as it expands the popular powers of the citizenry in present-day societies with free public education and mass media. In ancient civilizations it allowed members of the priesthood to make special claims about the understanding of sacred writings from a diety; in more modern civilizations it has provided for a widespread sharing of great works of the human imagination from the pens and word processors of many thousands of authors. Certainly many of the current uses of written language go far beyond the interests of governmental authorities, illustrating how far the products of civilization have expanded beyond the conditions of their origin.

City life, as well as writing, seemed to originate with the early states. Buganda illustrates what may have been a common pattern among such societies. The Buganda king's residence was at the center of a thriving city with a population estimated at over thirty thousand. The Baganda had no other cities; indeed, their preference for separate homesteads led them to avoid even villages, and in this they were rather unusual. But in their capital city they had a wide variety of people, including "the political hierarchy and bureau-cracy, the servants of the king, the hangers-on, entertainers, craftsmen, concubines, and wives." We are also told of the special-ization of labor among the Baganda, especially in the capital city, where workers no longer worked the land "but made their living as tax collectors, army officers, bards, drummers, fishermen, house builders, and executioners of the thousands sent each year to their death as human sacrifices." This last occupational specialization reminds us that political and religious authority in early states was frequently exercised with a high human cost—and with such costs unequally borne by various segments of the society.[23]

Despite the tyranny of early states, the rise of cities and the division of labor there combined to set in motion economic forces that eventually superseded the bounds of their political units. We need not go into a detailed history of the growth of trade in ancient civilizations here to recognize that large cities soon became domi-nant centers for trade and that merchants developed a degree of influence with which monarchs were forced to reckon. Eventually, such economic forces undermined the political power of early states and inspired wider organizations of political power, such as what we have come to recognize in modern nation-states.

In recent decades social scientists have come to look upon civilization as a complex product with two essential ingredients: the use of writing and the presence of cities. We have shown that each of these two primary strands of civilization is closely associated with the emergence of states. In so doing we have not intended to suggest any special order for the emergence of such key features as the effective establishment of monarchies, the develop-ment of associated priestly and military classes, the development of cities as governmental and ceremonial centers, the development of urban trading centers, and the proliferation of trades and trading. No doubt these emerged in different societies in different ways and with different emphases. However, what we know as civilized society contains *all* of these elements—as well as many more features refined from the base that these elements have provided.[24]

As the growth of civilization proceeded in various parts of the world, several general patterns of life became more emphasized. Routines of daily life become more organized by social practices of an increasingly abstract nature; the local community became less self-sufficient and more linked to a larger social order; and human affairs became more intentionally ordered, through choices made by those in power that were not simply determined by past traditions. These were among the general changes in human living that followed in the wake of societies that had organized into states and that had the additional features of writing and city life.

As contact between civilized societies increased, they borrowed heavily on the special genius of each other, as evidenced by the following examples from early eastern Mediterranean societies. The Phoenicians had special talents as merchants and sailors, and they introduced alphabetic writing to their neighbors. The Lydians assisted processes of abstract commercial exchange through a standard system of coinage for rare metals. The Hebrews provided a major impetus toward universal values in the form of a strongly ethical and radically monotheistic religion. The Greeks gave special encouragement to the arts and sciences. The Romans provided special talents for law, military science, and administration. These contributions were all brought together under Roman administration to form what we have come to know as Western Civilization.

We have not yet said much in this chapter about technology. Obviously, technological innovation has developed side-by-side with other features of civilization. In the modern world—beginning with the substitution of machine power for animal or human energy, and continuing with the substitution of machines for the mental activities of humans—technology sometimes seems to predetermine other kinds of development. But technological innovation itself would not be such a dominant force if we did not have a civilization that prepared us to think and act abstractly, embedding our work in complex organizations with the characteristics just discussed.[25]

Frequently we feel ambivalent about the products of our civilized life. Regulating our daily activities in terms of abstract quantities such as clock time or money values often seems an imposition, despite their ability to adjust our lives to those of others. Such mixed blessings must have been evident to those who first established the coinage of money (we are told that widespread prostitution accompanied coinage when first introduced by the Lydians) or the public use of time-keeping devices (a Roman poet of the third century B.C. protested the way widely used sundials "cut and hack my days so wretchedly"). Even today we protest products of modern organization that we feel are at variance with a more natural human order—called a "hassle" by some while scholars, sensing the same things, write tomes on "alienation."[26]

Is it inevitable that human society will continue to expand into ever more abstract and comprehensive forms of organization? That may appear to be the long-term trend, but the history of civilization has shown more of an ebb and flow. There have been constrictions as well as expansions in the cultural records of the past centuries.

In economic affairs there has been an increasing trend toward worldwide interdependence, especially marked during the past three centuries. This has been described with the following words:

> All old-established national industries have been destroyed or are daily being destroyed. They are dislodged by new industries, whose introduction becomes a life and death question for all civilized nations, by industries that no longer work up indigenous raw material but raw material drawn from the remotest zones; industries whose products are consumed, not only at home, but in every quarter of the globe. In place of the old wants, satisfied by the production of the country, we find new wants, requiring for their satisfaction the products of distant lands and climes. In place of the old local and national seclusion and self-sufficiency, we have intercourse in every direction, universal interdependence of nations.

Despite their contemporary ring, these words were penned almost a century and a half ago (in *The Communist Manifesto*, no less, written by Marx and Engels in 1847). This should remind us that the worldwide expansion of trade and industry is a process that has been going on for some time; it is not just a product of the late years of the twentieth century.[27]

Political life has shown a corresponding trend in recent centuries, inclining our world toward ever more comprehensive forms of political order. Today's embodiment of political order for most of the world—the nation-state—did not take its present form before the eighteenth century, when American and French republics premised their existence upon popular appeals to nationalism. Earlier, the small principality or the city-state had been the most characteristic forms of political life. Ever since neolithic times there has been a general decrease in the number of separate political units in the world, along with an increase in their typical size. It has been estimated that tens of thousands of autonomous political units existed no more than a thousand years ago; today we have fewer than two hundred nominally independent nations, and the number with an effective sovereignty is far less. Based simply on a projection of past trends of political consolidation, we would expect the political unification of the world under a single government to occur within the next few centuries.[28]

THE CHANGING FRAMEWORK OF ORDER

Aristotle, who said that man is by nature a social animal, was more correct than Thomas Hobbes, who saw society as something imposed upon naturally individualistic beings. Social order based on a normative system is much older than civilization. Indeed, it merged with the biological features of the species to form the basis of life in every primitive form of human society for which we have any evidence. It could hardly be otherwise, for most of the distinctive biological features of humans (as we saw them in the first chapter of this book) emerged to facilitate our life with others in society.[29]

Although the normative orders of simple societies varied greatly, they also had key elements in common. All were based on a kinship system, and all had their natural focus in the life lived in a local community. The kinship system included a nuclear family with its ties of marriage and descent, but it also included a wider network of relatives and the obligations due them. The local community was sometimes a migratory band, but more commonly it was a permanently established village. It was never so large to prevent everyone from knowing everybody else.

Under such circumstances, a social order could be quite compelling, even without any sanctions from formal governmental authorities. So compelling were the culturally created orders of such social systems that they came to be viewed as the natural ways to live. People saw their rhythms of ritual and work as natural extensions of the biological network in which they had their existence.

We cannot say that social order was without its problems in early human societies, but it did serve the purpose of molding the lives of its people into a working system, especially within the local community. The problems came mainly when there was contact with another group. The normative framework of one society did not apply to people of another tribe, whose claims to a common humanity might be subject to considerable doubt. It might not even apply to a neighboring village within the same tribe; in some societies there was a continual state of war between nearby communities.[30]

As local communities became larger and societies became more complex, formal systems of government came to be established. They existed side-by-side with the earlier and more informal normative orders. Usually there was not a great deal of conflict between these two forms of order; this was due in part to the mediating role commonly played by religious beliefs and practices. The new political system allowed a large number of villages to be combined into a common society. It regulated the relationships between people from different villages (usually with success) and tied them to the political and religious leadership of cities. What could not be assured by this system was a normative order beyond the society. Relations between early states were frequently characterized by bloody warfare.

In time political units became larger. This served both the interests of economic convenience (as trading relations expanded) and those of political order (as smaller units proved less defensible). In the past three centuries the dominant order has become that of nation-states, as governments have sought to foster feelings of nationalism to buttress their claims to power. A nation-state provided a system of social order over a wider territory than did earlier city-states or principalities. Such social order could not have the coherence found in primitive societies; after all, complex urban societies provide quite a different problem of social control. Still, peace generally was assured over wide ranges of territory and among populations numbering many millions. The biggest problem of social order came with relations between nation-states. As long as each claimed total sovereignty for itself, it is not surprising that disputes between nations turned into wars—with increasingly fatal consequences.[31]

This brings us to where we are now.

There is a tendency for people to view what exists at present as likely to continue indefinitely into the future. But the perspective of history offers us a less permanent view of existing systems, especially those of political units. For example, who could have imagined three centuries ago that a United States of America would come into being, drawing together Apache and Zuni, British and Scandanavians, Ashanti and Yoruba, Bavarians and Ukranians, and Chinese and Vietnamese? We might be equally surprised if we could see the political structure of the world three centuries from now.

The trend is clearly toward increasingly wider units of political order. Given the dangers of nuclear weapons, there is a very clear logic leading to a worldwide system of government—if only to lessen the dangers of international war. The general historical trend toward larger and fewer major political units points in the same direction. Unfortunately, past consolidations have come more often by war or military domination than by voluntary combinations. This, plus the way most nations today jealously guard their sovereign powers, suggests that a fully effective world state is unlikely to be peacefully created in the next century. But who can know with any assurance now what the state of the world will be by the end of the twenty-first century?

NOTES

1. The main political works of Thomas Hobbes (1588–1679) were *De Cive* (Hobbes, 1642/1949) and *Leviathan* (Hobbes, 1651/1909). Both these books outline his views on the social contract. Our quotation is from Hobbes (1651/1909), p. 97.

2. A useful interpretative essay on social contract thinking (plus important source materials from Locke, Hume, and Rousseau) may be found in Barker (1952). An influential work in ethical philosophy that builds upon earlier social contract thinking is that of Rawls (1971).

3. Just after his brief mention of natives in America showing how closely his "state of nature" may be approached, Hobbes makes it clear that his primary purpose in using this concept is to show "what manner of life there would be, where there were no common Power to feare" (Hobbes, 1651/1909, p. 97).

4. "Hereby it is manifest, that during the time men live without a common Power to keep them all in awe, they are in a condition which is called Warre; and such a warre, as is of every man, against every man. . . . Whatsoever therefore is consequent to a time of Warre, where every man is Enemy to every man; the same is consequent to the time, wherein men live without other security, than what their own strength, and their own invention shall furnish them withall" (Hobbes, 1651/1909, p. 96).

5. The experimental literature generally cited here is that dealing with the Prisoner's Dilemma game. Its discussion may be found, among other sources, in Rapoport and Chammah (1965) and Rapoport (1974); also see Luce and Raiffa (1957, p. 94 ff.) for a formal discussion of this structure in game theory terms and an explanation of why it has the name that it bears. An experiment that is more precisely based on the Abner and Bert scenario has been done, but its results have not been published, since they were used as a "filler" exercise for other data (reported in Exercise III of Schellenberg, 1988). Pairs played the roles of Abner and Bert in an abstract game presented in simple matrix form. When initially presented, without an opportunity for discussion between subjects, the predominant response was mutual meanness (although it was not so labeled for subjects). On the other hand, when discussion was allowed that permitted subjects to develop a common plan for how they might arrange their choices, the practically universal result was mutual generosity (again, though, not so labeled, since only abstract "plus" or "minus" results were given, and choices were labeled as only "X" or "Y").

6. This work is fully described in Axelrod (1984). See also Axelrod and Dion (1988). Our quotation is from Axelrod (1984), p. 20. Some of the limitations of the applicability of a tit-for-tat strategy have been suggested by Hirshleifler and Martinez Coll (1988). Let us also point out here the reason this structure came to be called the Prisoner's Dilemma. The story of two prisoners, first conceived by A. W. Tucker, has been summarized as follows (by Luce and Raiffa, 1957, p. 95):

> Two suspects are taken into custody and separated. The district attorney is certain that they are guilty of a specific crime, but he does not have adequate evidence to convict them at a trial. He points out to each that each has two alternatives: to confess to the crime the police are sure they have done, or not to confess. If they both do not confess, then the district attorney states he will book them on some very minor trumped-up charge such as petty larceny and illegal possession of a weapon, and they will both receive minor punishment; if they both confess they will be prosecuted, but he will recommend less than the most severe sentence; but if one confesses and the other does not, then the confessor will receive lenient treatment for turning state's evidence whereas the latter will get "the book" slapped at him.

7. Ullmann-Margalit (1977) uses game theory matrices (including that of the Prisoner's Dilemma) to distinguish these three basic types of situations. Are these three kinds of conditions the only ones favoring the emergence of norms? Ullmann-Margalit admits that she does not know the answer to this question, saying: "In default of conclusive arguments or

persuasive counter-examples, my hunch is that the three types of cases taken up by this study form the *core* cases in this field of inquiry" (p. viii).

8. The quotation here is from Ullmann-Margalit (1977), p. 173. It might also be pointed out that a number of different game theory matrices come within her broad category of situations with a status quo of inequality that may give rise to norms of partiality.

9. This is consistent with Thibaut and Kelley's view that norms "serve as substitutes for the exercise of personal influence and produce more economically and efficiently certain consequences otherwise dependent on personal influence processes" (Thibaut and Kelley, 1959, p. 130).

10. The anthropologist we quote here is George P. Murdock (1950), p. 716. Other sources that we have drawn upon for this section are Krader (1968) and Cohen and Service (1978).

11. The quotation is from Murdock (1950), p. 715.

12. We depend especially on Lowie (1927/1962) and Krader (1968) for information on these three societies.

13. The anthropologist quoted in this paragraph is Lowie (1927/1962), p. 104. The same book is also the source of the quotations in the following paragraph (pp. 81 and 89, respectively).

14. The belief that the Shilluk monarch's health was so important to the well-being of the tribe was ironically associated with regicide. "If the king was weak the kingdom was weak; if the king was senile the kingdom would fall into decay. Therefore the king was killed before he grew old or sick, in time to save the kingdom" (Krader, 1968, p. 38). The Shilluk clearly distinguished between the sacredness of the royal office and that of the person of the king.

15. Our information for these two cases comes primarily from Sagan (1985), with additional Hawaiian materials from Service (1975).

16. Probably the best reviews of anthropological evidence on the origins of states are those of Krader (1968) and Cohen and Service (1978). We draw upon these sources generally in the discussion that follows. Among those who emphasize a diversity of conditions that may lead to the emergence of states is Ronald Cohen, who has written that "state formation is an 'output' or effect of any one or more of a number of factors. The initial impetus could be population pressure or circumscription of a population, long distance trade, warfare and military organization, conquest, defense, internal strife, protection of privileges by a higher ranking group, or the benefits to be derived from subordination to centralized authority. . . . It is now becoming clear that there are multiple roads to statehood, that whatever sets off the process tends as well to set off other changes which, no matter how different they are to begin with, all tend to produce similar results" (Cohen and Service, 1978, p. 8). As to the similar results coming with statehood, despite possibly diverse origins, Sagan (1985, p. xxi) holds that "*every* advanced complex society had a centralized monarchy, a political bureaucracy, the systematic collection of taxes, an organized

priesthood, and a hierarchically ordered social system. . . . Further, within all complex societies, we find developed, rich cultures, full of imaginative and differentiated cultural forms."

17. Earlier theories tended to take one of these sources of increased population diversity and treat it as *the* theory of the origin of the state. For Marxists the state arose in response to class divisions, with the economically dominant class seeking political instruments to maintain their dominance; see especially Engels (1884/1942) for a fairly sophisticated presentation of this view. Others have seen conflict between ethnic groups as the key to state formation, with a newly arrived dominant group (often in the form of nomadic herders) creating a state to consolidate their power; Oppenheimer (1908/1926) represents this view. Both of these are essentially conflict theories of the origin of the state. It is also possible to see the state emerging more peacefully to handle increased population size and diversity—without emphasizing any particular forms of group conflict in its origin.

18. Service (1975) suggests a general progression from tribal societies with important individual leaders, to chiefdoms, to states—although he sees some difficulty in making a clear-cut differentiation between chiefdoms and states. Sagan (1985) is more confident in asserting a clear line of development from (a) chieftanships to (b) simple kingdoms to (c) complex kingdoms, with the state fully formed in only the last of these three stages. He further claims that "every complex centralized monarchy was built on a foundation of military conquest" (p. 316).

19. Sagan (1985) goes farther than most authorities in emphasizing psychological factors in the emergence of states. The subtitle of his book ("The Origins of Individualism, Political Oppression, and the State") shows how closely he relates social psychological qualities to the emergence of state societies. "We cannot understand the creation of the state," he asserts, "unless we understand the human drive to transcend kinship" (p. 251). This "drive" is further discussed by Sagan (largely in psychoanalytic terms) as receiving an important impetus from the personal leadership of chiefs and kings.

20. Our source for the extent to which the Baganda impressed early European visitors is Sagan (1985), p. 8.

21. We must not conclude that the development of the state was an unmixed blessing for humanity. Sagan (1985) is particularly graphic in illustrating how the most gross forms of cruelty, unknown in simpler societies, came into being with the state. Sahlins (1972) reminds us how relatively successful the hunter-gatherers could be in meeting basic economic needs, leaving us to wonder why more complex social systems were ever developed. Although the present section has been in part an answer to this question, we need make no claims for a general superiority of the results over those shown by simpler societies. However, it is probably impossible for us to make a thoroughly dispassionate judgment on this kind of issue,

being ourselves products of civilized societies. An especially sensitive discussion of this issue is found in Redfield (1953).

22. The description of Hawaiian tax record-keeping is found in Sagan (1985), p. 137.

23. The capital city of Bugunda and the different walks of life found there is described by Sagan (1985), especially pp. xv and 8 (with quotes from each of these pages).

24. The presence of writing rather naturally divides human history (based on written records) from prehistory; it is therefore quite convenient to use it as a dividing line for civilization. Childe (1936/1951) has emphasized the importance of the establishment of cities in the "urban revolution" as a foundation for civilization. A further discussion of the interrelationships of urban centers and the peasantry in traditional civilizations is found in Redfield (1953).

25. A useful discussion of the critical relationships of technology with economic organization in laying the foundations of the contemporary world is contained in Heilbroner (1962).

26. Galbraith (1975, p. 8) quotes Herodotus on the situation in Lydia where "all the young women" seem to "prostitute themselves, by which they procure their marriage portion." The ancient Roman poet quoted in this paragraph is reputed to have been Plautus. Whoever he was, his fuller comments, as quoted by Landes (1983, pp. 15–16), were as follows:

> The gods confound the man who first found out
> How to distinguish hours. Confound him, too,
> Who in this place set up a sundial,
> To cut and hack my days so wretchedly
> Into small pieces! When I was a boy,
> My belly was my sundial—one surer,
> Truer, and more exact than any of them.
> This dial told me when 'twas proper time
> To go to dinner, when I ought to eat;
> But nowadays, why even when I have,
> I can't fall to unless the sun gives leave.
> The town's so full of these confounded dials. . .

Incidentally, Landes provides a most useful history of clocks, showing their critical importance for the modern world. Max Weber (1864–1920) is among the sociologists who have most fully explored the role of formal organizations and their forms of rationality in modern society. In *The Protestant Ethic and the Spirit of Capitalism* (Weber, 1904–5/1958, p. 181) he suggests that the work routines of modern capitalism may have been taken on like a "light cloak" earlier but that they have since acquired more of the character of an "iron cage," to cite an especially famous passage from his extensive writings.

27. Our source for the quotation here from Karl Marx and Friedrich Engels is Struik (1971), p. 93.

28. After discussing a number of estimates and projections others have made concerning the extent of world political expansion, Carneiro (1978) derives 2300 A.D. as an approximate projected date when a single world state will appear. His concluding comments (p. 219) give us a concise summary of the trends toward political unification: "Viewed in its broadest perspective, the tendency of political evolution is striking. For 99.8 percent of human history people lived exclusively in autonomous bands and villages. At the beginning of the Paleolithic the number of these autonomous political units must have been small, but by 1000 B.C. it had increased to some 600,000. Then supra-village aggregation began in earnest, and in barely three millennia the autonomous political units of the world dropped from 600,000 to 157. In the light of this trend the continued decrease from 157 to 1 seems not only inescapable but close at hand."

29. Aristotle's views on the social and political nature of man are most clearly stated in the opening passages of his *Politics*.

30. Chagnon (1968) provides a thorough description of one such society where every village appears to be in a continual state of war against its neighbors. In our more civilized world, we assume that violent conflict between local communities is no longer possible; however, there are special conditions under which such conflict might still occur (Schellenberg, 1987b).

31. Aware of how bloody the wars of the twentieth century have been and how cruel some practices of its nation-states are, we hesitate to describe the long-term political trends as progress. Nevertheless, there is a sense in which we agree with Redfield (1953, p. 163) that "on the whole the human race has come to develop a more decent and humane measure of goodness." This leads us to be greatly concerned about violations of justice and public order today that would have been much more commonly and passively accepted in ages past.

Chapter 10

On Living with Mystery

How did our planet come to be formed in the first place? We know enough to infer that it was once part of a cloud of rotating gas, that parts of this cloud were drawn together to form more solid objects, including our earth and the sun, and that some of these same gases escaped to create an early atmosphere surrounding the earth. But how could this hot ball become cool enough to support life as we know it, and where did all the oxygen that we breathe every minute come from? Further, where did that original cloud of rotating gas come from? Scientists give us a variety of speculative answers to these questions—taking us through scenarios of a big bang, black holes, and the chance combination of simple atoms into macromolecules. But the evidence for such scenarios is far from our senses, and it is difficult to imagine how such cosmic forces came to make possible what we see as the world around us.

The beginning of life on our planet poses an equally profound mystery. Under what conditions did some of those complex macromolecules develop into self-reproducing systems? We may be able to get some clues in our laboratories as to how this could have happened, but the mystery remains immense. Then, once the most simple cells developed, how did they form nuclei, chromosomes, or mitochondria? And once such features existed in successful one-celled organisms, why in the world should they combine themselves to form multicelled organisms? Here again it is possible to sketch out some possible answers, but much remains unanswered by even our most brilliant microbiologists.

Next, how did life come to take the characteristic forms we now see? Here the story is a little less murky, since Charles Darwin helped us see how living things may change over time. But it was only about 130 years ago that he set forth his theory of natural selection to help explain how, as he put it, "from so simple a beginning endless forms most beautiful and most wonderful have been, and are being, evolved." But even the key of natural selection leaves much of the story of life unlocked. For example, what produced the mass extinction about seventy-five million years ago that wiped out the dinosaurs (except, some suggest, for their warm-blooded offshoots who may still fly about around us), leaving so unpromising a group as the mammals to gain rapid ascendancy? And how, among these mammals, did the kinds of brains that made consciousness possible develop? Answers to such questions are still not easily found within the enormous volume of scientific literature now available.[1]

When compared to the mysteries of our planet and its life, those dealing with the behavior of humans may seem modest. Actually, contrary to the common image of the elusiveness of evidence in the social and behavioral sciences, we can often better explain the riddles of human behavior than those of life in general or those mind-boggling questions about the nature of our cosmos. Nevertheless, much remains mysterious about such matters as the nature of individual self-consciousness, of human intelligence and systems of belief, of personal and social morality, of love and destructiveness, and of the forms of social order—and disorder—to be found among humans. Viewing such questions in terms of a social matrix that is central in the nature of the human species may help us answer some questions in these areas. But with each question answered, more riddles arise. The fundamental mysteries of human behavior remain profoundly puzzling.

The findings of modern science have reduced some of the mystery of our world. We understand physical laws of motion well enough to be able to venture to the moon and beyond. We understand some of the secrets of life well enough to begin to treat some diseases through genetic engineering. Such efforts are possible only because of an enormous wealth of fundamental knowledge, as well as the development of highly specialized applications. Our knowledge in turn is a product of systematic and careful observations that have characterized the scientific quest. Of course, science is not just a matter of systematic observation. It draws on theoretical as well as empirical roots. It depends on the discipline of logical thought and the drive toward generalization of knowledge, as well as that toward careful observation. But always at its foundation is the use of observed facts to check on the validity of ideas—what Jacob Bronowski once characterized as "the habit of truth."[2]

It is part of the conventional wisdom that a scientific understanding is less applicable to human behavior (the "soft sciences") than it is to physical things or to nonhuman forms of life (the "hard sciences"). Such conventional wisdom is in part the result of ignorance about the social and behavioral sciences and what they have been able to achieve in recent decades. To identify clearly the onset of self-recognition, to map out the details of how children learn to use language, to measure and successfully predict social attitudes, to identify stages of moral development—these are among the notable recent achievements of the behavioral sciences. We also know a great deal more than we used to about basic processes of human learning, about the dynamics of group behavior, and about the way formal organizations function.

Despite such important achievements (some of which have been described in earlier chapters of this book), there is still a nagging doubt that science can be applied as successfully to human social behavior as it can to other subject matter. This doubt is expressed by many social scientists themselves in one way or another. Why should we make such a distinction in our estimates of the prospects of science? Surely the fundamental principles of science—of controlled observation, of logical analysis, of careful generalization—are as applicable to the study of human social behavior as to anything else. What then is different?

Here we come to an important issue that divides some of the most respected professionals in the behavioral sciences. Some would say that nothing is different, except perhaps our own lack of rigor and resolve in pursuing the science of human behavior. Also, there are more unscientific ideas to contend with here than in other fields, and this complicates the task of scientists. This is especially true when it comes to communicating scientific work with the general public, which impatiently seeks easily grasped truths.

But there are other behavioral scientists who see special difficulties in their field. Some would say that human social behavior is different from any other subject matter, and that what makes it different is that humans have selves. Human behavior is always being constructed through a process of personal and social defini-

tion, and this process both makes behavior inherently less pre-
dictible and leaves our generalizations less cumulative than in other
fields of science. Some behavioral scientists are quite satisfied with
such a view, often seeing it as warranting special methodologies
(allowing us to view behavior more from the inside) as well. These
social scientists are no less scientific in their basic purposes than are
their more positivistic colleagues; but they differ in not seeing all
science as essentially the same and in having more modest aspirations for the cumulative power of scientific generalizations in areas
of distinctively human behavior.

We need not attempt to resolve the issue about the distinctiveness of the human sciences here in order to conclude that
important scientific discoveries can be, and in fact have been, made
concerning human social behavior. We have at least important
partial answers to such questions as: How do we develop a sense of
personal identity? What is the basis of our moral consciousness?
What is the source of human intelligence? How do we organize our
beliefs about the world? What especially attracts us to certain
persons more than others? How can we explain the destructiveness
of human aggression? What makes individuals in crowds often
engage in extreme behavior? How has social order developed into
its present framework?

But our answers are only partial. The more we know, the
more we see what we do not yet know. This has been frequently
illustrated in our varied explorations into social behavior. To make
this point is in no way to detract from the scientific achievements
that have been made. But it should help us recognize that scientific
answers will not fully satisfy the popular need for explanations—
and thus that numerous mythologies of social life are bound to
remain mixed with scientific views in the popular mind. Also, the
sense of wonder at what we have learned, combined with our
profound sense of ignorance regarding how much more there is to
learn, is not alone a property of the behavioral and social sciences.
Such thinking may well be the dominant spirit of any mature
science. Although he was thinking especially of the biological and
medical sciences, Lewis Thomas was speaking as well of the total
scientific enterprise when he asserted that "the most significant
contribution of twentieth-century science to the human intellect"
has been to discover how profoundly ignorant we are in the face of
the wonders of the natural world. Thomas continues:

In earlier times we either pretended to understand how things worked or ignored the problem, or simply made up stories to fill the gaps. Now that we have begun exploring in earnest, doing serious science, we are getting glimpses of how huge the questions are, and how far from being answered. Because of this, these are hard times for the human intellect, and it is no wonder that we are depressed. It is not so bad being ignorant if you are totally ignorant; the hard part is knowing in some detail the reality of ignorance.[3]

This may appear to be a rather negative note with which to end our explorations of social behavior. Our mood in this book generally has been more upbeat about our ability to solve the fundamental mysteries of social behavior. But we would be less than candid if we did not recognize that what we have learned has in no way diminished how much more there is to learn. That is true for all the sciences, and that is where we are bound to come out as we apply the scientific quest to explaining the mysteries of our own behavior. But could we do otherwise and still be true to the curious streak that lies at the heart of what is most distinctively human?

NOTES

1. The quotation from Charles Darwin (1809–1882) is from the final sentence of his most famous book (Darwin, 1859/1979, p. 460).

2. Jacob Bronowski's rich discussion of the development of the "habit of truth" in modern science is contained in Bronowski (1965).

3. Our quotations here are from Thomas (1990), p. 156.

Bibliography

Allan, Graham. 1989. *Friendship*. Boulder, CO: Westview Press.

Alley, Thomas R., and Michael R. Cunningham. 1991. "Averaged Faces Are Attractive, but Very Attractive Faces Are Not Average," *Psychological Science*, 2, 123–125.

Allport, Floyd H. 1920. "The Influence of the Group Upon Association and Thought," *Journal of Experimental Psychology*, 3, 159–182.

Allport, Gordon W., and Leo Postman. 1947. *The Psychology of Rumor*. New York: Holt.

Amsterdam, Beulah. 1972. "Mirror Self-image Reactions Before Age Two," *Developmental Psychobiology*, 5, 297–305.

Amsterdam, Beulah, and Morton Levitt. 1980. "Consciousness of Self and Painful Self-consciousness," *The Psychoanalytic Study of the Child*, 35, 67–83.

Ardrey, Robert. 1976. *The Hunting Hypothesis*. New York: Atheneum.

Aronson, Elliot. 1969. "Some Antecedents of Interpersonal Attraction," pp. 143–173. In W. J. Arnold and D. Levine (eds.), *Nebraska Symposium on Motivation*, 1969. Lincoln: University of Nebraska Press.

_____.1980. "Persuasion via Self-Justification: Large Commitments for Small Rewards," pp. 3–21. In L. Festinger (ed.), *Retrospections on Social Psychology*. New York: Oxford University Press.

Asch, Solomon. 1952. *Social Psychology*. New York: Prentice-Hall.

Axelrod, Robert. 1984. *The Evolution of Cooperation*. New York: Basic Books.

Axelrod, Robert, and Douglas Dion. 1988. "The Further Evolution of Cooperation," *Science*, 242, 1385–1390.

Backman, Carl W., and Paul F. Secord. 1962. "Liking, Selective Interaction, and Misperception in Congruent Interpersonal Relations," *Sociometry*, 25, 321–335.

Bandura, Albert. 1973. *Aggression: A Social Learning Analysis*. Englewood Cliffs, NJ: Prentice-Hall.

_____. 1977. *Social Learning Theory*. Englewood Cliffs, NJ: Prentice-Hall.

_____. 1986. *Social Foundations of Thought and Action*. Englewood Cliffs, NJ: Prentice-Hall.

Barker, Ernest. 1952. *Social Contract*. London: Oxford University Press.

Baumeister, Roy F. (ed.). 1986. *Public Self and Private Self*. New York: Springer-Verlag.

Beck, Benjamin B. 1975. "Primate Tool Behavior," pp. 413–447 In R. H. Tuttle (ed.), *Socioecology and Psychology of Primates*. The Hague: Mouton.

Benedict, Ruth. 1934. *Patterns of Culture*. Boston: Houghton Mifflin.

Berger, Peter L. 1967. *The Sacred Canopy: Elements of a Sociological Theory of Religion*. Garden City, NY: Doubleday.

Berkowitz, Leonard. 1962. *Aggression: A Social Psychological Analysis*. New York: McGraw-Hill.

_____. 1969. "The Frustration-Aggression Hypothesis Revisited," pp. 1–28. In L. Berkowitz (ed.), *Roots of Aggression*. New York: Atherton Press.

Berscheid, Ellen. 1985. "Interpersonal Attraction," pp. 413–484 In G. Lindzey and E. Aronson (eds.), *The Handbook of Social Psychology*, 3rd ed., vol. 2. New York: Random House.

Berscheid, Ellen, and Elaine Walster [Hatfield]. 1974. "Physical Attractiveness," pp. 157–215. In L. Berkowitz (ed), *Advances in Experimental Social Psychology*, vol. 7. New York: Academic Press.

Bettelheim, Bruno. 1943. "Individual and Mass Behavior in Extreme Situations," *Journal of Abnormal and Social Psychology*, 38, 417–452.

Biehler, Robert F., and Lynne M. Hudson. 1986. *Developmental Psychology: An Introduction*, 3rd ed. Boston: Houghton Mifflin.

Bohannan, Paul (ed.). 1960. *African Homicide and Suicide*. Princeton, NJ: Princeton University Press.

Bower, T. G. R. 1979. *Human Development*. San Francisco: W.H. Freeman.

Britt, Steuart H. (ed.). 1950. *Selected Readings in Social Psychology*. New York: Holt, Rinehart and Winston.

Bronowski, Jacob. 1965. *Science and Human Values*. New York: Harper.

Bronowski, Jacob, and Ursula Bellugi. 1970. "Language, Name and Concept," *Science*, 1968, 669–673.

Brown, Roger. 1965. *Social Psychology*. New York: Free Press.

_____. 1986. *Social Psychology*, 2nd ed. New York: Free Press.

Bruner, Jerome. 1983. *Child's Talk: Learning to Use Language*. New York: Norton.

Bruner, Jerome S., Rose R. Oliver, and Patricia M. Greenfield. 1966. *Studies in Cognitive Growth*. New York: Wiley.

Burton, Robert V. 1963. "The Generality of Honesty Reconsidered," *Psychological Review*, 70, 481–499.

Byrne, Donn. 1971. *The Attraction Paradigm*. New York: Academic Press.

Campbell, Donald T. 1975. "On the Conflict Between Biological and Social Evolution and Between Psychology and Moral Tradition," *American Psychologist*, 30, 1103–1126.

Cantril, Hadley, Hazel Gaudet, and Herta Herzog. 1940. *The Invasion from Mars*. Princeton, NJ: Princeton University Press.

Carneiro, Robert L. 1978. "Political Expansion as an Expression of the Principle of Competitive Exclusion," pp. 205–223. In R. Cohen and E. R. Service (eds.), *Origins of the State*. Philadelphia: Institute for the Study of Human Issues.

Cavalli-Sforza, Luigi Luca, Alberto Piazza, Paolo Menozzi, and Joanna Mounta. 1988. "Reconstruction of Human Evolution: Bringing

Together Genetic, Archaeological, and Linguistic Data," *Proceedings of the National Academy of Sciences*, 85, 6002–6006.

Chagnon, Napoleon A. 1968. *Yanomamo, the Fierce People*. New York: Holt, Rinehart and Winston.

Chein, Isidor. 1945. "On the Nature of Intelligence," *Journal of General Psychology*, 32, 111–126.

Childe, V. Gordon. 1936/1951. *Man Makes Himself*. New York: New American Library.

Chomsky, Noam. 1972. *Language and Mind*, enlarged edition. New York: Harcourt Brace Javanovich.

Cohen, Ronald, and Elman R. Service (eds.). 1978. *Origins of the State: The Anthropology of Political Evolution*. Philadelphia: Institute for the Study of Human Issues.

Coles, Robert. 1986. *The Moral Life of Children*. Boston: Atlantic Monthly Press.

Connolly, Kevin, and Jerome Bruner (eds.). 1973. *The Growth of Competence*. London: Academic Press.

Cooley, Charles H. 1902. *Human Nature and the Social Order*. New York: Scribner.

____. 1909. *Social Organization*. New York: Scribner.

____. 1927. *Life and the Student*. New York: Knopf.

Coser, Lewis A. 1971. *Masters of Sociological Thought*. New York: Harcourt Brace Jovanovich.

Courchesne, Eric, R. Yeung-Chorchesne, G. A. Press, J.R. Hesselink, and T.L. Jernigan. 1988. "Hypoplasia of Cerebellar Vermal Lobules VI and VII in Autism," *New England Journal of Medicine*, 318, 1349–1354.

Crain, Robert L., Elihu Katz, and Donald B. Rosenthal. 1969. *The Politics of Community Conflict: The Fluoridation Decision*. Indianapolis: Bobbs-Merrill.

Darwin, Charles. 1859/1979. *The Origin of Species by Means of Natural Selection*. New York: Avenel Books.

____. 1871/1898. *The Descent of Man and Selection in Relation to Sex*. New York: Appleton.

de Waal, Frans. 1982. *Chimpanzee Politics: Power and Sex among Apes*. New York: Harper and Row.

Dewey, John. 1992. *Human Nature and Conduct*. New York: Holt.

Dion, Karen, Ellen Berscheid, and Elaine Walster [Hatfield]. 1972. "What is Beautiful is Good," *Journal of Personality and Social Psychology*, 24, 285–290.

Dobzhansky, Theodosius, and Ernest Boesiger. 1983. *Human Culture: A Moment in Evolution*, edited and completed by Bruce Wallace. New York: Columbia University Press.

Dollard, John, Leonard W. Doob, Neal E. Miller, O. H. Mowrer, and Robert R. Sears. 1939. *Frustration and Aggression*. New Haven: Yale University Press.

Dornbush, Sanford M. 1955. "The Military Academy as an Assimilating Institution," *Social Forces*, 33, 316–321.

Dubos, Rene J. 1968. *So Human an Animal*. New York: Scribner.

Duck, Steve. 1986. *Human Relationships: An Introduction to Social Psychology*. London: Sage Publications.

Dupoy, R. Ernest, and Trevor N. Dupoy. 1970. *The Encyclopedia of Military History*. New York: Harper and Row.

Durkheim, Emile. 1915. *The Elementary Forms of the Religious Life*. London: George Allen and Unwin.

Dyer, Gwynne. 1985. *War*. New York: Crown Publishers.

Eibl-Eibesfeldt, Irenaus. 1975/1979. *The Biology of Peace and War*. New York: Viking Press.

Ellwood, Charles A. 1938. *A History of Social Philosophy*. New York: Prentice-Hall.

Engels, Frederick. 1884/1942. *The Origin of the Family, Private Property, and the State*. New York: International Publishers.

Felson, Richard B. 1981a. "Ambiguity and Bias in the Self Concept," *Social Psychology Quarterly*, 44, 64–69.

_____. 1981b. "Self-and Reflected Appraisal among Football Players: A Test of the Median Hypothesis," *Social Psychology Quarterly*, 44, 116–126.

Festinger, Leon. 1957. *A Theory of Cognitive Dissonance*. Evanston, IL: Row, Peterson.

Festinger, Leon, Henry W. Riecken, and Stanley Schachter. 1956. *When Prophecy Fails*. Minneapolis: University of Minnesota Press.

Field, Tiffany M., Aletha Huston, Herbert C. Quay, Lillian Troll, and Gordon E. Findley (eds.). 1982. *Review of Human Development*. New York: Wiley.

Finck, H. T. 1891. *Romantic Love and Personal Beauty: Their Development, Causal Relations, Historic and National Peculiarities*. London: Macmillan.

Fishbein, Martin. 1975. *Belief, Attitude, Intention, and Behavior*. Reading, MA: Addison-Wesley.

Forbes, James L., and James E. King. 1982a. "Vision: The Dominant Primate Modality," pp. 219–243. In J. L. Forbes and J. E. King (eds.), *Primate Behavior*. New York: Academic Press.

_____. 1982b. "Auditory and Chemoreceptive Sensitivity in Primates," pp. 245–270. In J. L. Forbes and J. E. King (eds.), *Primate Behavior*. New York: Academic Press.

_____. 1982c. "Measuring Primate Learning Abilities," pp. 289–326. In J. L. Forbes and J. E. King (eds.), *Primate Behavior*. New York: Academic Press.

_____. 1982d. "Complex Learning by Primates," pp. 327–360. In J. L. Forbes and J. E. King (eds.), *Primate Behavior*. New York: Academic Press.

Fouts, Roger S. 1975. "Capacities for Language in Great Apes," pp. 371–390. In R. H. Tuttle (ed.), *Socioecology and Psychology of Primates*. The Hague: Mouton.

Freud, Sigmund. 1913/1938. "Totem and Taboo," pp. 805–930. In A. A. Brill (ed.), *The Basic Writings of Sigmund Freud*. New York: Random House.

_____. 1930/1962. *Civilization and Its Discontents*. New York: Norton.

Fromm, Erich. 1941. *Escape from Freedom*. New York: Holt, Rinehart & Winston.

_____. 1947. *Man for Himself*. New York: Holt, Rinehart & Winston.

Furth, Hans G. 1966. *Thinking Without Language: Psychological Implications of Deafness*. New York: Free Press.

_____. 1969. *Piaget and Knowledge: Theoretical Foundations*. Englewood Cliffs, NJ: Prentice-Hall.

Galbraith, John Kenneth. 1975. *Money: Where It Came, Where It Went*. Boston: Houghton Mifflin.

Gallup, Gordon G., Jr. 1970. "Chimpanzees: Self-recognition," *Science*, 167, 86–87.

_____. 1975. "Towards an Operational Definition of Self-awareness," pp. 309–341. In R. H. Tuttle (ed.), *Socioecology and Psychology of Primates*. The Hague: Mouton.

_____. 1977. "Self-recognition in Primates," *American Psychologist*, 32, 329–338.

_____. 1982. "Self-awareness and the Emergence of Mind in Primates," *American Journal of Primatology*, 2, 237–248.

_____. 1983. "Toward a Comparative Psychology of Mind," pp. 475–510. In R. L. Mellgren (ed.), *Animal Cognition and Behavior*. New York: North Holland.

Gardner, Howard. 1976. *Frames of Mind*. New York: Basic Books.

Gardner, R. Allen, and Beatrice T. Gardner. 1969. "Teaching Sign Language to a Chimpanzee," *Science*, 165, 664–672.

Gecas, Viktor, and Michael L. Schwalbe. 1983. "Beyond the Looking-glass Self: Social Structure and Efficacy-based Self-esteem," *Social Psychology Quarterly*, 46, 77–88.

Gergen, Kenneth J. 1971. *The Concept of Self*. New York: Holt, Rinehart and Winston.

Gibson, James J. 1966. *The Senses Considered as Perceptual Systems*. Boston: Houghton Mifflin.

Gilligan, Carol. 1982. *In a Different Voice: Psychological Theory and Women's Development*. Cambridge, MA: Harvard University Press.

Given, James Buchanan. 1977. *Society and Homicide in Thirteenth-Century England*. Stanford, CA: Stanford University Press.

Goffman, Erving. 1956. "The Nature of Deference and Demeanor," *American Anthropologist*, 58, 473–502.

_____. 1959a. "The Moral Career of the Mental Patient," *Psychiatry*, 22, 123–142.

_____. 1959b. *The Presentation of Self in Everyday Life*. New York: Doubleday Anchor.

Goldenweiser, Alexander. 1931. "Totemism: An Essay on Religion and Society," pp. 363–392. In V. F. Calverton (ed.), *The Making of Man: An Outline of Anthropology*. New York: Random House.

Goodall, Jane. 1971. *In the Shadow of Man*. Boston: Houghton Mifflin.

Gordon, Chad, and Kenneth J. Gergen (eds.). 1968. *The Self in Social Interaction*, 2 vols. New York: Wiley.

Gottman, John M. 1979. *Marital Interaction*. New York: Academic Press.

Gould, Stephen Jay. 1981. *The Mismeasure of Man*. New York: Norton.

_____. 1989. "The Wheel of Fortune and the Wedge of Progress," *Natural History*, 98, 14–21.

Graham, Douglas. 1972. *Moral Learning and Development*. New York: Wiley.

Graham, Hugh Davis, and Ted Robert Gurr (eds.). 1969. *The History of Violence in America: Historical and Comparative Perspectives*. New York: Praeger.

Greeley, Andrew M., William C. McCready, and Gary Theisen. 1980. *Ethnic Drinking Subcultures*. New York: Praeger.

Greenwald, Anthony G. 1980. "The Totalitarian Ego: Fabrication and Revision of Personal History," *American Psychologist*, 35, 603–618.

Gunn, John. 1973. Violence. New York: Praeger.

Gusfield, Joseph R. 1986. *Symbolic Crusade: Status Politics and the American Temperance Movement*, 2nd ed. Urbana: University of Illinois Press.

Hall, Calvin S. 1954. *A Primer of Freudian Psychology*. Cleveland: World Publishing.

Halliday, Michael A. K. 1975. *Learning How to Mean*. London: Edward Arnold.

Harlow, Harry F., and Margaret K. Harlow. 1966. "Learning to Love," *American Scientist*, 54, 244–272.

Harris, Marvin. 1974. *Cows, Pigs, and Witches: The Riddle of Culture*. New York: Random House.

Hartshorne, Hugh, and Mark A. May. 1928. *Studies in Deceit*. New York: Macmillan.

Hatfield, Elaine, and Susan Sprecher. 1986. *Mirror, Mirror . . . The Importance of Looks in Everyday Life*. Albany: State University of New York Press.

Hearnshaw, L. S. 1979. *Cyril Burt Psychologist*. London: Hodder and Stoughton.

Heider, Fritz. 1958. *The Psychology of Interpersonal Relations*. New York: Wiley.

Heilbroner, Robert L. 1962. *The Making of Economic Society*. Englewood Cliffs, NJ: Prentice-Hall.

Hendrick, Clyde, and Steven R. Brown. 1971. "Introversion, Extroversion, and Interpersonal Attraction," *Journal of Personality and Social Psychology*, 20, 31–36.

Hendrick, Clyde, and Susan S. Hendrick. 1986. "A Theory and Method of Love," *Journal of Personality and Social Psychology*, 50, 392–402.Hendrick, Susan S., Clyde Hendrick, and Nancy L. Adler. 1988.

"Romantic Relationships: Love, Satisfaction, and Staying Together," *Journal of Personality and Social Psychology,* 54, 980–988.

Herrnstein, Richard J. 1973. I.Q. in the Meritocracy. Boston: Little, Brown.

Hirshleifer, Jack, and Juan Carlos Martinez Coll. 1988. "What Strategies Can Support the Evolutionary Emergence of Cooperation?" *Journal of Conflict Resolution,* 32, 367–398.

Hobbes, Thomas. 1642/1949. *De Cive.* New York: Appleton-Century-Crofts.

———. 1651/1909. *Leviathan.* Oxford: Oxford University Press.

Hochberg, Julian E. 1978. *Perception,* 2nd ed. Englewood Cliffs, NJ: Prentice-Hall.

Hoffman, Martin. 1975. "Developmental Synthesis of Affect and Cognition and its Implications for Altruistic Motivation," *Developmental Psychology,* 11, 607–622.

Isaac, Glynn. 1978. "The Food-sharing Behavior of Protohuman Hominids," *Scientific American,* 238:4 (April), 90–108.

James, William. 1890/1892. *Psychology.* New York: Henry Holt.

Jencks, Christopher. 1979. "The Social Basis of Unselfishness," pp. 63–86. In H. J. Gans, N. Glazer, J. R. Gusfield, and C. Jencks. (eds.), *On the Making of Americans: Essays in Honor of David Riesman.* Philadelphia: University of Pennsylvania Press.

Jencks, Christopher. 1972. *Inequality: A Reassessment of the Effect of Family and Schooling in America.* New York: Basic Books.

Jensen, Arthur R. 1972. *Genetics and Education.* New York: Harper and Row.

Kagan, Jerome. 1984. *The Nature of the Child.* New York: Basic Books.

Kelley, Harold H. 1979. *Personal Relationships: Their Structures and Processes.* Hillsdale, NJ: Lawrence Erlbaum.

Kerner, Otto (chairman). 1968. *Report of the National Advisory Commission on Civil Disorders.* New York: Bantam Books.

Kiesler, Charles A., Barry E. Collins, and Norman Miller. 1969. *Attitude Change.* New York: Wiley.

King, Jonathan. 1985. *Troubled Water.* Emmaus, PA: Rodale Press.

King, Mary-Claire, and A. C. Wilson. 1975. "Evolution at Two Levels in Humans and Chimpanzees," *Science,* 188, 107–116.

Klare, Michael T. 1972. *War Without End: American Planning for the Next Vietnams.* New York: Knopf.

Koffka, Kurt. 1924. *The Growth of the Mind.* New York: Harcourt, Brace.

Kohlberg, Lawrence. 1964. "Development of Moral Character and Moral Ideology," pp. 383–431. In M. L. Hoffman and L. W. Hoffman (eds.), *Review of Child Development Research,* vol. 1. New York: Russell Sage Foundation.

———. 1972. "A Cognitive-Developmental Approach to Moral Education," *The Humanist,* 32:6, 13–16.

———. 1978. "Revisions in the Theory and Practice of Moral Development," pp. 83–87. In W. Damon (ed.), *Moral Development.* San Francisco: Jossey-Bass.

____. 1980. "Stages of Moral Development as a Basis for Moral Education," pp. 15–98. In B. Munsey (ed.), *Moral Development, Moral Education, and Kohlberg*. Birmingham, AL: Religious Education Press.

____. 1984. *The Psychology of Moral Development: The Nature and Validity of Moral Stages*. New York: Harper and Row.

Köhler, Wolfgang. 1927. *The Mentality of Apes*, 2nd ed. New York: Harcourt, Brace.

Krause, Charles A. 1978. *Guyana Massacre*. New York: Berkley Books.

Krader, Lawrence. 1968. *Formation of the State*. Englewood Cliffs, NJ: Prentice-Hall.

Kurtines, William, and Esther B. Grief. 1974. "The Development of Moral Thought: Review and Evaluation of Kohlberg's Work," *Psychological Bulletin*, 81, 453–470.

La Barre, Weston. 1954. *The Human Animal*. Chicago: University of Chicago Press.

Landes, David S. 1983. *Revolution in Time: Clocks and the Making of the Modern World*. Cambridge, MA: Harvard University Press.

Langlois, Judith H., and Lori A. Roggman. 1990. "Attractive Faces are Only Average," *Psychological Science*, 1, 115–121.

Latané, Bibb. 1981. "The Psychology of Social Impact," *American Psychologist*, 36, 343–356.

Leakey, Richard E. 1981. *The Making of Mankind*. New York: E. P. Dutton.

Leakey, Richard E., and Roger Lewin. 1978. *People of the Lake: Mankind and Its Beginning*. Garden City, NY: Doubleday.

Le Bon, Gustave. 1895/1960. *The Crowd: A Study of the Popular Mind*. New York: Viking.

Le Douarin, Nicole. 1982. *The Neural Crest*. Cambridge, UK: Cambridge University Press.

Levinger, George, and J. Diedrick Snoek. 1972. *Attraction in Relationship: A New Look at Interpersonal Attraction*. Morristown, NJ: General Learning Press.

Lewin, Roger. 1984. *Human Evolution: An Illustrated Introduction*. New York: W. H. Freeman.

____. 1988. "American Indian Language Dispute," *Science*, 242, 1632–1633.

Lewis, Michael (ed.). 1983. *Origins of Intelligence: Infancy and Early Childhood*, 2nd ed. New York: Plenum Press.

Lewis, Michael, and Jeanne Brooks. 1974. "Self, Other, and Fear: Infants' Reactions to People," pp. 195–227. In M. Lewis and L. A. Rosenblum (eds.), *The Origins of Fear*, New York: Wiley.

Lewis, Michael, and Jeanne Brooks-Gunn. 1979. *Social Cognition and the Acquisition of the Self*. New York: Plenum Press.

Liberman, Alvin M., and Ignatius G. Mattingly. 1989. "A Specialization for Speech Perception," *Science*, 243, 489–494.

Lieberman, Philip. 1984. *The Biology and Evolution of Language*. Cambridge, MA: Harvard University Press.

Lieberson, Stanley, and Arnold R. Silverman. 1965. "The Precipitants and Underlying Conditions of Race Riots," *American Sociological Review*, 30, 887–898.

Lippmann, Walter. 1929. *A Preface to Morals*. New York: Macmillan.

Lorenz, Konrad. 1966. *On Aggression*. New York: Harcourt, Brace and World.

Lowie, Robert H. 1927/1962. *The Origin of the State*. New York: Russell and Russell.

Luce, R. Duncan, and Howard Raiffa. 1957. *Games and Decisions*. New York: Wiley.

Maccoby, Eleanor Emmons, and Carol Nagy Jacklin. 1974. *The Psychology of Sex Differences*. Stanford, CA: Stanford University Press.

MacKinnon, Donald W. 1938. "Violation of Prohibitions," pp. 491–501 In H. A. Murray, *Explorations in Personality*. New York: Oxford University Press.

Mannheim, Karl. 1936/1966. *Ideology and Utopia: An Introduction to the Sociology of Knowledge*. New York: Harcourt, Brace and World.

Maoz, Zeev, and Nasrin Abdolali. 1989. "Regime Types and International Conflict, 1816–1976," *Journal of Conflict Resolution*, 33, 3–35.

Martin, Brian. 1989. "The Sociology of the Fluoridation Controversy: A Reexamination," *Sociological Quarterly*, 30, 59–76.

Mason, William A. 1976. "Environmental Models and Mental Modes: Representational Processes in the Great Apes and Man," *American Psychologist*, 31, 284–294.

McPhail, Clark. 1971. "Civil Disorder Participation: A Critical Examination of Recent Research," *American Sociological Review*, 36, 1058–1073.

Mead, George H. 1930. "Cooley's Contribution to American Social Thought," *American Journal of Sociology*, 35, 693–706.

____. 1934. Mind, Self, and Society. Chicago: University of Chicago Press.

Mendelson, Jack H., and Nancy K. Mello. 1985. *Alcohol: Use and Abuse in America*. Boston: Little, Brown.

Milgram, Stanley. 1963. "Behavioral Study of Obedience," *Journal of Abnormal and Social Psychology*, 67, 371–378.

____. 1974. Obedience to Authority. New York: Harper and Row.

Milgram, Stanley, Leonard Bickman, and Lawrence Berkowitz. 1969. "Note on the Drawing Power of Crowds of Different Size," *Journal of Personality and Social Psychology*, 13, 79–82.

Mischel, Theodore (ed.). 1977. *The Self: Psychological and Philosophical Issues*. Totowa, NJ: Rowman & Littlefield.

Modgil, Sohan, and Celia Modgil (eds.). 1985. Lawrence Kohlberg: *Consensus and Controversy*. Philadelphia: Falmer Press.

Montagu, Ashley. 1951. *On Being Human*. New York: Henry Schuman.

____. 1976. *The Nature of Human Aggression*. New York: Oxford University Press.

Mowrer, O. Hobart. 1960. *Learning Theory and the Symbolic Processes*. New York: Wiley.

Moyer, Kenneth E. 1971. *The Physiology of Hostility*. Chicago: Markham.
____. 1987. *Violence and Aggression*. New York: Paragon House.
Mumford, Lewis. 1951. *The Conduct of Life*. New York: Harcourt, Brace and World.
____. 1961. *The City in History*. New York: Harcourt, Brace and World.
Murdock, George Peter. 1949. *Social Structure*. New York: Macmillan.
____. 1950. "Feasibility and Implementation of Comparative Community Research," *American Sociological Review*, 15, 713–720.
Myers, David G. 1982. "Polarizing Effects of Social Interaction," pp. 125–161. In H. Brandstatter, J. H. Davis, and G. Stocker-Kreichgauer (eds.), *Group Decision Making*. London: Academic Press.
Nettler, Gwynn. 1982. *Killing One Another*. Cincinnati: Anderson Publishing Company.
Oppenheimer, Franz. 1908/1926. *The State*. New York: Vanguard Press.
Oskamp, Stuart. 1977. *Attitudes and Opinions*. Englewood Cliffs, NJ: Prentice-Hall.
Piaget, Jean. 1932/1948. *The Moral Judgment of the Child*. Glencoe, IL.: Free Press.
____. 1952a. "Jean Piaget," pp. 237–256. In E. G. Boring (ed.), *A History of Psychology in Autobiography*, vol. 4. Worcester, MA: Clark University Press.
____. 1952b. *The Origins of Intelligence in Children*. New York: International Universities Press.
____. 1970. "Piaget's Theory," pp. 703–732. In P. H. Mussen (ed.), *Carmichael's Manual of Child Psychology*, 3rd ed., vol.1. New York: Wiley.
____. 1971. *Biology and Knowledge*. Chicago: University of Chicago Press.
____. 1977. *The Essential Piaget*, edited by H. E. Guber and J. J. Voneche. New York: Basic Books.
Quinn, Paul C., and Peter D. Eimas. 1986. "On Categorization in Early Infancy," *Merrill Palmer Quarterly*, 32, 331–363.
Rapoport, Anatol. "Prisoner's Dilemma—Reflections and Observations," pp. 17–34. In Anatol Rapoport (ed.), *Game Theory as a Theory of Conflict Resolution*. Dordrecht, Holland: D. Reidel.
Rapoport, Anatol, 1974. and Albert M. Chammah. 1965. *Prisoner's Dilemma*. Ann Arbor: University of Michigan Press.
Rawls, John. 1971. *A Theory of Justice*. Cambridge, MA: Harvard University Press.
Redfield, Robert. 1953. *The Primitive World and Its Transformations*. Ithaca, NY: Cornell University Press.
Restak, Richard M. 1984. *The Brain*. Toronto: Bantam Books.
Reynolds, Peter C. 1981. *On the Evolution of Human Behavior: The Argument from Animals to Man*. Berkeley: University of California Press.
Rich, John Martin, and Joseph L. DeVitis. 1985. *Theories of Moral Development*. Springfield, IL.: Charles C. Thomas.

Rich, Norman. 1985. *Why the Crimean War? A Cautionary Tale,* Hanover, NH: University Press of New England.

Riesen, Austin H. 1982. "Primate Perceptual Processes," pp. 271–286. In J. L. Forbes and J. E. King (eds.), *Primate Behavior.* New York: Academic Press.

Rogers, Charles M., and Richard K. Davenport. 1975. "Capacities of Nonhuman Primates for Perceptual Integration Across Sensory Modalities," pp. 343–352. In R. H. Tuttle (ed.), *Socioecology and Psychology of Primates.* The Hague: Mouton.

Rokeach, Milton. 1964. *The Three Christs of Ypsilanti.* New York: Knopf.

＿＿. 1968. *Beliefs, Attitudes and Values.* San Francisco: Jossey-Bass.

Rosen, Hugh. 1980. *The Development of Sociomoral Knowledge: A Cognitive-Structural Approach.* New York: Columbia University Press.

Rosenberg, Morris. 1979. *Conceiving the Self.* New York: Basic Books.

Rubin, Zick. 1970. "Measurement of Romantic Love," *Journal of Personality and Social Psychology,* 16, 265–273.

Rudé, George. 1964. *The Crowd in History: A Study of Popular Disturbances in France and England, 1730–1848.* New York: Wiley.

Rumbaugh, Duane M., E. Sue Savage-Rumbaugh, and John L. Scanlon. 1982. "The Relationship Between Language in Apes and Human Beings," pp. 361–385. In J. E. King and J. L. Forbes (eds.), *Primate Behavior.* New York: Academic Press.

Rumbaugh, Duane M., E. C. von Glasersfeld, Timothy V. Gill, Harold Warner, Pier Pisani, Josephine V. Brown, and C. L. Bell. 1975. "The Language Skills of a Young Chimpanzee in a Computer-Controlled Training Situation," pp. 391–401. In R. H. Tuttle (ed.), *Socioecology and Psychology of Primates.* The Hague: Mouton.

Rummel, R. J. 1985. "Libertarian Propositions on Violence Within and Between Nations," *Journal of Conflict Resolution,* 29, 419–455.

Russell, Bertrand. 1950. *Unpopular Essays.* New York: Simon and Schuster.

Sackett, Gene P., Virginia Gunderson, and David Baldwin. 1982. "Studying the Ontogeny of Primate Behavior," pp. 135–169. In J. E. King and J. L. Forbes (eds.), *Primate Behavior.* New York: Academic Press.

Sacks, Oliver. 1985. *The Man Who Mistook His Wife for a Hat and Other Clinical Tales.* New York: Simon and Schuster.

Sagan, Eli. 1985. *At the Dawn of Tyranny: The Origins of Individualism, Political Oppression, and the State.* New York: Knopf.

Sahlins, Marshall. 1972. *Stone Age Economics.* Chicago: Aldine-Atherton.

Schachter, Stanley, and Jerome E. Singer. 1962. "Cognitive, Social, and Physiological Determinants of Emotional State," *Psychological Review,* 69, 379–399.

Schellenberg, James A. 1960. "Homogamy in Personal Values and the 'Field of Eligibles,'" *Social Forces,* 39, 157–162.

＿＿. 1974. *An Introduction to Social Psychology,* 2nd ed. New York: Random House.

_____. 1978. *Masters of Social Psychology*. New York: Oxford University Press.

_____. 1982. *The Science of Conflict*. New York: Oxford University Press.

_____. 1987a. "On Human Dominance Systems," pp. 289–301. In D. McGuinness (ed.), *Dominance, Aggression and War*. New York: Paragon House.

_____. 1987b. *Conflict Between Communities: American County Seat Wars*. New York: Paragon House.

_____. 1988. "A Comparative Test of Three Models for Solving 'the Bargaining Problem,'" *Behavioral Science*, 33, 81–96.

Schweitzer, Albert. 1969. *Reverence for Life*. New York: Harper and Row.

Scott, John Paul. 1975. *Aggression*, 2nd ed. Chicago: University of Chicago Press.

Sears, Robert R., Lucy Rau, and Richard Alpert. 1965. *Identification and Child Rearing*. Stanford, CA: Stanford University Press.

Seaton, Albert. 1977. *The Crimean War: A Russian Chronicle*. New York: St. Martin's Press.

Secord, Paul F., and Carl W. Backman. 1961. "Personality Theory and the Problem of Stability and Change in Individual Behavior: An Interpersonal Approach," *Psychological Review*, 68, 21–32.

_____. 1964. "Interpersonal Congruency, Perceived Similarity, and Friendship," *Sociometry*, 27, 115–127.

Service, Elman R. 1975. *Origins of the State and Civilization: The Process of Cultural Evolution*. New York: Norton.

Sherif, Carolyn W., Muzafer Sherif, and Roger E. Nebergall. 1965. *Attitude and Attitude Change*. Philadelphia: W. B. Saunders.

Short, James F., Jr., and Marvin E. Wolfgang. 1972. *Collective Violence*. Chicago: Aldine/Atherton.

Shrauger, J. Sidney, and Thomas J. Schoeneman. 1979. "Symbolic Interactionist View of Self-concept: Through the Looking Glass Darkly," *Psychological Bulletin*, 86, 549–573.

Singer, J. David, and Melvin Small. 1972. The Wages of War 1816–1965: *A Statistical Handbook*. New York: Wiley.

Skinner, B. F. 1957. *Verbal Behavior*. New York: Appleton-Century-Crofts.

Small, Melvin, and J. David Singer. 1982. *Resort to Arms: International and Civil Wars, 1816–1980*. Beverly Hills, CA: Sage Publications.

Smelser, Neil J. 1963. *Theory of Collective Behavior*. New York: Free Press.

Smith, Adam. 1759/1976. *The Theory of Moral Sentiments*. London: Oxford University Press.

Snyder, Mark. 1987. *Public Appearances/Private Realities: The Psychology of Self-monitoring*. New York: W. H. Freeman.

Snyderman, Mark, and Stanley Ruthman. 1987. "Survey of Expert Opinion on Intelligence and Aptitude Testing," *American Psychologist*, 42, 137–144.

Spearman, Charles. 1923. *The Nature of "Intelligence" and the Principles of Cognition*. New York: Macmillan.

_____. 1927. *The Abilities of Man*. New York: Macmillan.

Spilerman, Seymour. 1970. "The Causes of Racial Disturbances: A Comparison of Alternative Explanations," *American Sociological Review*, 35, 627–649.

Spitz, Rene A. 1965. *The First Year of Life*. New York: International Universities Press.

Stephens, William N. 1962. *The Oedipus Complex: Cross-Cultural Evidence*. New York: Free Press.

Sternberg, Robert J. 1986. "A Triangular Theory of Love," *Psychological Review*, 93, 119–135.

Strauss, Mark S. 1979. "Abstraction of Protypical Information by Adults and 10-month-old Infants," *Journal of Experimental Psychology: Human Learning and Memory*, 5, 618–632.

Struik, Dirk J. (ed.) 1971. *Birth of the Communist Manifesto*. New York: International Publishers.

Suomi, Stephen J. 1982. "Abnormal Behavior and Primate Models of Psychopathology," pp. 171–215. In J. E. King and J. L. Forbes (eds.), *Primate Behavior*. New York: Academic Press.

Swann, Willaim B., Jr. 1985. "The Self as Architect of Social Reality," pp. 100–125. In Barry R. Schlenker (ed.), *The Self and Social Life*. New York: McGraw-Hill.

Swanson, Guy E. 1960. *The Birth of the Gods: The Origin of Primitive Beliefs*. Ann Arbor: University of Michigan Press.

Taylor, L. B., Jr. 1968. *Liftoff!* New York: Dutton.

Tennyson, Alfred. 1854/1970. "The Charge of the Light Brigade," pp. 225–227. In *Poems*, vol. 2. New York: AMS Press.

Thibaut, John W., and Harold H. Kelley. 1959. *The Social Psychology of Groups*. New York: Wiley.

Thomas, Lewis. 1990. *A Ling Line of Cells: Collected Essays*. New York: Penguin.

Thurstone, L. L. 1935. *The Vectors of Mind*. Chicago: University of Chicago Press.

Tiger, Lionel. 1969. *Men in Groups*. New York: Random House.

Touhey, John C. 1972. "Comparison of Two Dimensions of Attitude Similarity on Heterosexual Attraction," *Journal of Personality and Social Psychology*, 23, 8–10.

Triandis, Harry C. 1971. *Attitude and Attitude Change*. New York: Wiley.

Tuddenham, Read D. 1963. "The Nature and Measurement of Intelligence," pp. 469–525. In L. Postman (ed.), *Psychology in the Making*. New York: Knopf.

Turner, John C. 1991. *Social Influence*. Pacific Grove, CA: Brooks/Cole.

Ullmann-Margalit, Edna. 1977. *The Emergence of Norms*. Oxford: Oxford University Press.

Van Hooff, J. A. R. A. M. 1967. "The Facial Displays of the Catarrhine Monkeys and Apes," pp. 7–68. In D. Morris (ed.), *Primate Ethology*. Chicago: Aldine.

Voyat, Gilbert. 1982. *Piaget Systematized*. Hillsdale, NJ: Erlbaum Associates.

Vygotsky, L. S. 1962. *Thought and Language.* Cambridge, MA: MIT Press.

Walster [Hatfield], Elaine, Vera Aronson, Darcy Abrahams, and Leon Rottman. 1966. "Importance of Physical Attractiveness in Dating Behavior," *Journal of Personality and Social Psychology,* 4, 508–516.

Warner, Philip. 1973. *The Crimean War: A Reappraisal.* New York: Taplinger.

Warriner, Charles K. 1958. "The Nature and Functions of Official Morality," *American Journal of Sociology,* 64, 165–168.

Watson, John S. 1972. "Smiling, Cooing, and `The Game,'" *Merrill Palmer Quarterly,* 18, 323–339.

Weber, Max. 1904–5/1958. *The Protestant Ethic and the Spirit of Capitalism.* New York: Scribner.

Wells, Herbert George. 1898/1951. *The War of the Worlds.* London: Heinemann.

Whorf, Benjamin Lee. 1956. *Language, Thought, and Reality.* Cambridge, MA: MIT Press.

Wilson, Edward O. 1975. *Sociobiology: The New Synthesis.* Cambridge, MA: Harvard University Press.

_____. 1978. *On Human Nature.* Cambridge, MA: Harvard University Press.

Wilson, James Q., and Richard J. Herrnstein. 1985. *Crime and Human Nature.* New York: Simon and Schuster.

Winch, Robert A. 1958. *Mate Selection: A Study of Complementary Needs.* New York: Harper and Row.

Wolfgang, Marvin E. 1958. *Patterns in Criminal Homicide.* Philadelphia: University Pennsylvania Press.

_____. (ed.). 1967. *Studies in Homicide.* New York: Harper and Row.

Wright, Quincy. 1942/1965. *A Study of War.* Chicago: University of Chicago Press.

Wylie, Ruth. 1961. *The Self Concept: A Critical Survey of Pertinent Research Literature.* Lincoln: University of Nebraska Press.

_____. 1974. *The Self Concept: A Review of Methodological Considerations and Measuring Instruments,* rev. ed., vol. 1. Lincoln: University of Nebraska Press.

_____. 1979. *The Self Concept: Theory and Research on Selected Topics,* rev. ed., vol. 2. Lincoln: University of Nebraska Press.

Zajonc, Robert B. 1968. "Attitudinal Effects of Mere Exposure," *Journal of Personality and Social Psychology,* Monograph Supplement (No. 2, Part 2), 9, 1–27.

Zimbardo, Philip G., Ebbe B. Ebbesen, and Christina Maslach. 1977. *Influencing Attitudes and Changing Behavior,* 2nd ed. Reading, MA: Addison-Wesley.

Zurcher, Louis A., Jr. 1977. *The Mutable Self: A Self-concept for Social Change.* Beverly Hills, CA: Sage Publications.

Index

Abner and Bert (hypothetical case), 177–178
Abdolali, Nasarin, 159, 217
Abrahams, Darcy,222
Adler, Nancy L., 140, 215
Aggression, 141–159; biological basis, 141–150, 153–154; collective violence, 154–156; homicide patterns, 151–154; innate restraints, 143, 144–145; kinds of aggression, 145–146 (see also Ideologies and utopias and Primitive warfare)
Alcohol, see Beliefs, on food and drink
Allan, Graham, 140, 209
Alley, Thomas R., 139, 209
Allport, Floyd H., 168, 174, 209
Allport, Gordon W., 169, 174, 209
Alpert, Richard, 66, 220
Amsterdam, Beulah, 25, 26, 40, 209
Ardrey, Robert, 143, 156, 209
Aristotle, 202
Armstrong, Thomas, see Seekers
Army Alpha, 73
Army Beta, 73
Arnold, William J., 209
Aronson, Elliot, 122, 137, 139, 209, 210
Aronson, Vera, 222
Asch, Solomon, 113–115, 116, 117, 118, 123, 209
Attitudes, 105–106 (see also Beliefs)
Attraction, 125–140; as a process, 135–136; love, 136–138; physical attractiveness, 127–133; similarity and attraction, 133–135
Attractiveness stereotype, 127–129
Autism, 33
Axelrod, Robert, 179, 198, 209

Backman, Carl W., 135, 139, 209, 220
Baldwin, David, 15, 219
Bandura, Albert, 50, 66, 157, 209

Barker, Ernest, 197, 209
Bastille (case study), 161–162, 163, 167
Baumeister, Roy F., 42, 209
Beck, Benjamin B., 14, 209
Beliefs, 99–123; on authority, 102–103, 115–117; ego-enhancement function, 106–107; failing belief systems, 113–120; on food and drink, 107–113; historical cases, 99–103; identity beliefs, 117–118; nature of beliefs, 104–107
Bell, C. L., 219
Bellugi, Ursula, 14, 210
Benedict,Ruth, 13, 16, 210
Berger, Peter L., 58, 67, 68, 210
Berkowitz, Lawrence, 174, 217
Berkowitz, Leonard, 157, 210
Berscheid, Ellen, 128, 138, 210, 211
Bert, see Abner and Bert
Bettelheim, Bruno, 35, 41, 210
Bickman, Leonard, 174, 217
Biehler, Robert F., 40, 95, 96, 210
Binet, Alfred, 71–72, 73, 74, 77, 94
Boesiger, Ernest, 15, 211
Bohannan, Paul, 158, 210
Boring, Edwin G., 218
Bower T. G. R., 82, 95, 96, 210
Brain and nervous system, 2, 4, 33, 104, 146; amygdala and aggression, 146; angular gyrus and cross-modal transfer, 4; autistic children,33; basis for beliefs, 104; hypothalamus and aggression, 146; neural crest cells, 12–13; size, 2
Brandstatter, H., 218
Bridges, Ruby, see Ruby (case study)
Brill, Abraham A., 213
Britt, Steuart H., 173, 210
Bronowski, Jacob, 14, 205, 207, 210
Brooks, Jeanne, see Brooks-Gunn

Brooks-Gunn, Jeanne, 26–27, 31–32, 40, 216
Brown, Josephine V., 219
Brown, Roger 97, 174, 210
Brown, Steven R., 139, 214
Bruner, Jerome S., 87–88, 96, 97, 210, 211
Buganda (Africa), 186–187, 188 ,189, 191
Burt, Cyril, 76, 95, 214
Burton, Robert V., 66, 210
Byrne, Donn, 139, 210

Calverton, V. F., 214
Campbell, Donald T., 68, 210
Cantril, Hadley, 173, 210
Cardigan, James T., 100–101, 102, 103, 113
Carmichael, Leonard, 218
Carneiro, Robert L., 202, 210
Cavalli-Sforza, Luigi Luca, 98, 210
Chagnon, Napoleon A., 202, 211
Chammah, Albert M., 198, 218
Chein, Isidor, 95, 211
Childe, V. Gordon, 201, 211
Chomsky, Noam, 87, 97, 211
Christs (case study), 31
Churchill, Winston, 189
Cities, see Civilization
Civilization, 11, 92–93, 191–193
Cognitive development, see Intelligence
Cohen, Ronald, 199, 210, 211
Coles, Robert, 63–64, 68–69, 211
Collective violence, see Aggression
Collins, Barry E., 121, 215
Concrete operations, 79
Conditioning, 49, 86–87
Conformity, 113–117, 170; majority pressure, 114–115; obedience to authority, 115–117
Congruency, see Interpersonal congruency theory
Connolly, Kevin, 96, 211
Conscience, 43–69; biological basis of, 60–62; moral development of, 50–55; origins of morality, 43–50; religious aspects of, 55–59
Conservation (in mental functioning), 5

Cooley, Charles H., 20–22, 24, 25, 31, 35, 36, 37, 39, 67, 211, 217
Coordination norms, 180
Coser, Lewis A., 39, 211
Courchesne, Eric R., 40, 211
Crain, Robert L., 122, 211
Crimean War, 99–101, 102–103, 113
Cross-modal transfer, 4
Crow (American Indians), 184, 186, 187–188
Crowds, 161–174; historical cases, 161–163; nature of crowds, 163–166; mutual stimulation processes, 167–169 (see also Group polarization)
Culture, see Human nature
Cunningham, Michael R., 139, 209

Damon, W., 215
Dart, Raymond, 156
Darwin, Charles, 23, 44, 130, 138, 157, 204, 207, 211
Davenport, Richard K., 219
Davis, J. H., 218
Death instinct, 141
DeVitis, Joseph L., 218
de Waal, Frans, 211
Dewey, John, 22, 98, 211
Dion, Douglas, 198, 209
Dion, Karen, 128, 138, 211
Dobhansky, Theodosius, 15, 211
Dollard, John, 157, 211
Doob, Leonard W., 211
Dornbush, Sanford M., 34, 41, 212
Drinking, see Beliefs
Dubos, Rene J., 14, 212
Duck, Steve, 140, 212
Dupoy, R. Ernest, 121, 212
Dupoy, Trevor N., 121, 212
Durkheim, Emile, 57–58, 59, 67, 212, 217
Dyer, Gwynne, 41, 212

Earth, origin of, 203
Ebbesen, Ebbe B., 122, 222
Ego, 47, 49, 55 (see also Identity)
Eibl-Eibesfeldt, Irenaus, 144, 156, 212
Eimas, Peter D., 139, 218
Einstein, Albert, 82
Ellwood, Charles A., 212

Engels, Frederick, 194, 200, 202, 212
Equilibration, 81
Eysenck, Hans J., 94

Felicia (case study), 31
Felson, Richard B., 41, 212
Festinger, Leon, 108, 122, 123, 209, 212
Field, Tiffany M., 96, 212
Finck, H. T., 139, 212
Findley, Gordon E., 212
Fishbein, Martin, 121, 212
Forbes, James L., 14, 212, 219, 221
Food, *see* Beliefs
Formal operations, 79, 82
Fouts, Roger S., 14, 212
Freud, Sigmund, 20, 29, 39, 40, 43–48, 49, 55, 57, 58, 59, 65, 66, 137, 140, 141, 156, 157, 213
Fromm, Erich, 16, 65, 213
Functional hallucination (as framework for culture), 13
Furth, Hans G., 42, 96, 213

Galbraith, John Kenneth, 201, 213
Gallup, Gordon G., Jr., 25, 26, 27–28, 40, 213
Galton, Francis, 94
Gans, Herbert J., 215
Gardner, Beatrice T., 14, 213
Gardner, Howard, 76–77, 95, 213
Gardner, R., Allen, 14, 213
Gaudet, Hazel, 173, 210
Gecas, Viktor, 41, 213
Generalized other, 24
Gergen, Kenneth J., 42, 213, 214
Gestures (and language), 22–23
Gibson, James J., 121, 213
Gill, Timothy V., 219
Gilligan, Carol, 66–67, 213
Given, James Buchanan, 153, 158, 213
Glazer, Nathan, 215
Goddard, Henry H., 73, 94
Goffman, Erving, 34, 41, 59, 67, 213
Goldenweiser, Alexander, 65, 214
Goodall, Jane, 8, 14, 15, 214
Gordon, Chad, 42, 214
Gottman, John M., 140, 214
Gould, Stephen Jay, 94, 95, 157, 214

Graham, Douglas, 66, 214
Graham, Hugh Davis, 159, 173, 214
Grasshoppers, *see* Beliefs, on food and drink
Greeley, Andrew M., 122, 214
Greenfield, Patricia M., 96, 210
Greenwald, Anthony C., 41, 214
Grief, Esther B., 66, 216
Grissom, Virgil, 98
Group polarization, 170–173
Guber, Howard E., 218
Gunderson, Virginia, 15, 219
Gunn, John, 159, 214
Gurr, Ted Robert, 159, 174, 214
Gusfield, Joseph R., 122, 214, 215
Gutenberg, Johann, 93

Hall, Calvin S., 39, 214
Halliday, Michael A. K., 84–90, 97, 214
Halliday, Nigel, *see* Nigel (case study)
Hallucination, *see* Functional hallucination
Harlow, Harry F., 8, 15, 214
Harlow, Margaret K., 15, 214
Harris, Marvin, 147, 157, 214
Hartshorne, Hugh, 66, 214
Hatfield, Elaine, 125–127, 128, 138, 139, 210, 211, 214, 222
Hawaiians, 186, 187, 188, 189, 191
Hearnshaw, L. S., 95, 214
Heider, Fritz, 135, 139, 214
Heilbroner, Robert L. S., 201, 214
Hendrick, Clyde, 139, 140, 214, 215
Hendrick, Susan S., 140, 214, 215
Herrnstein, Richard J., 94, 158–159, 215
Herzog, Herta, 173, 210
Hesselink, J. R., 211
Hirshleifer, Jack, 198, 215
Hobbes, Thomas, 175–177, 178, 180, 181–182, 197, 215
Hockberg, Julian E., 139, 215
Hoffman, Lois W., 215
Hoffman, Martin L., 33, 40, 215
Homicide patterns, *see* Aggression
Hudson, Lynne., 40, 95, 96, 210
Human distinctiveness, 1–9; dependence of infants on adults, 7–9;

economic activity, 6; genetic materials, 2; language, 2–3, 12; learning ability, 4–5; physical structure, 2; reasoning ability, 5–6; sensory and perceptual processes 3–4; smiling and laughter 8–9; social organization, 7–9; social relationships, 7–9; tools, 2–3, 6
Human nature, 1–16; cultural basis, 1, 9–14 (*see also* Human distinctiveness)
Hume, David, 17
Hunting hypothesis (about source of human aggression), 142–143, 144
Huston, Aletha, 212

I (self as knower), 18, 37
Id, 48, 49
Identification, 48 (*see also* Identity)
Identity, 17–42; emergence of the self, 17–25, 37–39; identity change, 34–37, 38; studies of early identity, 25–33
Ideologies and utopias, 147–150
Incest taboos, 47
Infants, 17, 23–27, 29–33, 83–89; discrimination of others, 31–32; reactions to strangers, 31–32; social games, 29–31, (*see also* Identity)
Intelligence, 71–98; cognitive development, 77–82; community foundations, 90–94; IQ testing, 71–77, 81 (*see also* Language)
Interpersonal attraction, *see* Attraction
Interpersonal congruency theory, 134
IQ testing, *see* Intelligence
Isaac, Glynn, 15, 98, 215
Isaiah, 62, 68

Jacklin, Carol Nagy, 157, 217
Jackman, N. R., 122
Jacqueline (case study), 78–79
James, William, 18–20, 21, 22, 24, 36, 39, 42, 215
Jencks, Christopher, 68, 95, 215

Jensen, Arthur R., 94, 215
Jernigan, T. L., 211
Jesus, *see* Christs (case study)
Jones, Jim, 101–102, 103, 113
Jonestown massacre, 101–103, 113

Kagan, Jerome, 16, 60, 67–68, 96, 215
Kamehameha I, 186
Katz, Elihu, 122, 211
Keech, Marian, *see* Seekers (case study)
Kelley, Harold H., 140, 199, 215, 221
Kerner, Otto, 173, 215
Kiesler, Charles, 121, 215
King, James E., 14, 212, 219, 221
King, Jonathan, 122, 215
King, Mary-Claire, 215
Klare, Michael T., 159, 215
Koffka, Kurt, 39, 215
Kohlberg, Lawrence, 51–55, 60, 62, 64, 66, 67, 215, 216, 217
Köhler, Wolfgang, 4–5, 216
Kpelle (African tribe), 184–185, 186, 187, 188, 189
Krader, Lawrence, 199, 216
Krause, Charles A., 121, 216
Kurtines, William, 66, 216

La Barre, Weston, 14, 216
Lana (chimpanzee), 3
Landes, Davis S., 201, 216
Langlois, Judith H., 131–132, 139, 216
Language, 2–3, 12, 83–92, 191–192; early learning, 83–89; emergence in species, 90–92; writing, 191–192
Language acquisition device, 87
Language acquisition support system, 87
Latané, Bibb, 174, 216
Leakey, Richard E., 15, 98, 158, 216
Le Bon, Gustave, 163–164, 173, 216
Le Douarin, Nicole, 16, 216
Levine, David, 209
Levinger, George, 139, 216
Levitt, Morton, 40, 209
Lewin, Roger, 15, 97, 158, 216
Lewis, Felicia, *see* Felicia (case study)

Lewis, Michael, 26–27, 31–32, 40, 96, 216
Liberman, Alvin M., 97, 216
Lieberman, Philip, 90–91, 97, 216
Lieberson, Stanley, 174, 217
Life, origin of, 203–204; evolution of, 204
Light brigade, *see* Crimean War
Lincoln, Abraham, 154
Lindzey, Gardiner, 210
Lippmann, Walter, 67, 217
Locke, John, 176, 197
Looking-glass self, 20–21, 23, 25, 35, 37
Lorenz, Konrad, 143, 150, 156, 157, 158, 217
Louis XVI, 161
Lowie, Robert H., 199, 217
Luce, R. Duncan, 198, 217

Maccoby, Eleanor, 157, 217
MaKinnon, Donald W., 66, 217
Majority pressure, *see* Conformity
Mannheim, Karl, 158, 217
Maoz, Zeev, 159, 217
Martin, Brian, 122, 217
Martinez Coll, Juan Carlos, 198, 215
Marx, Karl, 194, 202
Maslach, Christina, 121, 222
Mason, William A., 6, 14, 217
Matching hypothesis, 126–127, 133
Mather, Increase, 122
Mattingly, Ignatius G., 97, 216
May, Mark A., 66, 214
McCready, William C., 122, 214
McGuinness, Diane, 220
McPhail, Clark, 165, 173, 217
Me (self as known), 18–19, 37
Mead, George H., 20, 22–24, 25, 29, 36, 37, 39, 42, 98, 217
Mellgren, P. L., 213
Mello, Nancy., 122, 217
Mendelson, Jack H., 122, 217
Menozzi, Paolo, 210
Mental hospitals, 34
Michael (case study), 33
Milgram, Stanley, 115–116, 117, 118, 123, 168, 174, 217
Military socialization, 34

Miller, Neal E., 211
Miller, Norman, 121, 215
Mirror techniques (for studying self-recognition) 25–28
Mischel, Theodore, 42, 217
Modgil, Celia, 66 217
Modgil, Sohan, 66, 217
Montagu, Ashley, 14, 148, 150, 156, 157, 158, 217
Moral development, *see* Conscience
Moral judgment, *see* Conscience
Morality, *see* Conscience
Morris, Desmond, 221
Mounta, Joanna, 210
Mowrer, O. Hobart, 97, 211, 217
Moyer, Kenneth E., 145, 150, 156–157, 158, 218
Mumford, Lewis, 58–59, 67, 68, 218
Munsey, Brenda, 216
Murdock, George Peter, 47, 65–66, 182–183, 199, 218
Murray, Henry A., 217
Mussen, Paul H., 218
Myers, David G., 172–173, 174, 218

Nature vs. nurture, 81–82
Nebergall, Roger E., 122, 220
Necker, Jacques, 161
Neural crest cells, *see* Brain and nervous system
Nervous system, *see* Brain and nervous system
Nettler, Gwynn, 158, 218
Norms, *see* Conscience *and* Social order

Obedience, *see* Conformity
Object permanence (in mental functioning), 5
Oedipus complex, 45–47
Oliver, Rose R., 210
Oppenheimer, Franz, 200, 218
Oskamp, Stuart, 121, 218

Paranoid schizophrenics, 117–118
Partiality norms, 180–181
Paul (case study), 32–33
Peaceful societies, 150–151 (*see also* Primitive warfare)

Physical attractiveness, *see* Attraction
Piaget, Jacqueline, *see* Jacqueline (case study)
Piaget, Jean, 20 29, 39, 40, 50–51, 54, 60, 66, 77–82, 95, 96, 213, 218, 222
Piazza, Alberto, 210
Pisani, Pier, 219
Plautus, 201
Polarization effects, *see* Group polarization
Postman, Leo, 169, 174, 209, 221
Press, G. A., 211
Primal horde, 44
Primitive warfare, 146–147
Printing press, 93
Prisoner's Dilemma game, 179–180

Quay, Herbert C., 212
Quinn, Paul C., 139, 218
Quito, *see* Radio Quito (case study)

Radio Quito (case study), 162–163, 167
Raglan, Fitzroy S., 99–100
Raiffa, Howard, 198, 217
Rapoport, Anatol, 198, 218
Rau, Lucy, 66, 220
Rawls, John, 197, 218
Redfield, Robert, 201, 202, 218
Restak, Richard M., 121, 218
Reynolds, Peter C., 13, 14, 15, 16, 218
Rich, John Martin, 66, 218
Rich, Norman, 121, 219
Riecken, Henry W., 123, 212
Riesen, Austin H., 14, 219
Riesman, David, 215
Risky shift, *see* Group polarization
Rogers, Charles M., 14, 219
Roggman, Lori A., 131–132, 139, 216
Rokeach, Milton, 117–118, 121, 122, 219
Romantic love, *see* Attraction
Rosen, Hugh, 66, 219
Rosenberg, Morris 42, 219
Rosenblum, L. A., 216
Rosenthal, Donald B., 122, 211
Rottman, Leon, 222
Rousseau, Jean Jacques, 176, 197

Rubin, Zick, 137, 140, 219
Ruby (case study), 63–65
Rudé, George, 164–165, 173, 219
Rumbaugh, Duane M., 14, 219
Rummel, Rudolph J., 159, 219
Rumors, 169
Russell, Bertrand, 106, 122, 219
Ruthman, Stanley, 95, 220
Ryan, Leo, 101

Sackett, Gene P., 15, 219
Sacks, Oliver, 121, 219
Sagan, Eli, 199, 200, 201, 219
Sahlins, Marshall, 200, 219
Sananda, *see* Seekers (case study)
Sappho, 138
Savage-Rumbaugh, Sue, 14, 219
Scanlon, John L., 219
Schachter, Stanley, 123, 137, 139, 212, 219
Schellenberg, James A., 39, 65, 138, 139, 158, 159, 173, 198, 202, 219–220
Schlenker, Barry R., 221
Schoeneman, Thomas J., 41, 220
Schwalbe, Michael L., 41, 213
Schweitzer, Albert, 68, 220
Science, 93–94, 204–207
Scott, John Paul, 157, 220
Sears, Robert R., 66, 211, 220
Seaton, Albert, 121, 220
Secord, Paul F., 135, 139, 209, 220
Seekers (case study), 118–120
Self, *see* Identity
Self-monitoring, 36
Sensorimotor stage, 79
Service, Elman R., 199, 200, 210, 211, 220
Sexual selection, 130–131
Sherif, Carolyn W., 122, 220
Sherif, Muzafer, 122, 220
Shilluk (African tribe), 184, 185, 186, 187, 188, 189
Short, James F., Jr., 159, 173, 220
Shrauger, J. Sidney, 41, 220
Significant symbols, 23
Silverman, Arnold P., 174, 217
Simon, Theodore, 72, 77
Singer, J. David, 159, 220
Singer, Jerome E., 139, 219

Skinner, B. F., 97, 220
Small, Melvin, 159, 220
Smelser, Neil J., 170, 174, 220
Smith, Adam, 67, 220
Smith, E. E., 122
Snoek, J. Diedrick, 139, 216
Snyder, Mark, 36, 42, 220
Snyderman, Mark, 95, 220
Social contract, 176–177
Social facilitation, 168
Social learning theory, 50
Social norms, *see* Conscience *and* Social order
Social order, 175–202; emergence of norms, 177–182; emergence of states 182–191; growth in complexity of norms 195–197; the Hobbesian question, 175–182; worldwide interdependence, 194–195, 197
Social science, distinctiveness of, 205–206
Socialization, *see* Conscience; Identity; *and* Intelligence
Spearman, Charles, 76, 95, 220
Spilerman, Seymour, 173, 221
Spitz, Rene., 15, 40, 221
Sprecher, Susan, 138, 214
Stanford-Binet, 73
Stanley, Henry M., 186, 189
Stephens, William N., 46, 65, 221
Stern, Wilhelm L., 72
Sternberg, Pobert J., 140, 221
Stocker-Kreichgauer, G., 218
Strauss, Mark S., 139, 221
Struik, Dirk J., 221
Subculture of violence, 152
Sultan (chimpanzee), 4–5
Suomi, Stephen J., 15, 221
Superego, 47–48, 49, 55
Swann, William B., Jr., 41, 221
Swanson, Guy E., 67, 221
Symbolic interactionism, 24–25

Taylor, L. B., Jr., 98, 221
Technology, 3, 6, 193
Tennyson, Alfred, 100–101, 121, 221
Terman, Lewis M., 73, 94
Theisen, Gary, 122, 214
Thibaut, John W., 199, 221

Thomas, Lewis, 206–207, 221
Thurstone, Louis L., 76, 95, 122, 221
Tiger, Lionel, 157, 221
Totemism, 44–45, 57
Touhey, John C., 139, 221
Triandis, Harry C., 121, 221
Troll, Lillian, 212
Tuddenham, Read D., 94, 95, 221
Turner, John C., 174, 221
Tuttle, Russell H., 209, 213, 219

Ullmann-Margalit, Edna, 180–181, 198–199, 221
Unanswered questions, 206–207
Utopias, *see* Ideologies and utopias

Van Hooff, J. A. R. A. M., 15, 221
Vicki (chimpanzee), 28
Violence, *see* Aggression *and* Subculture of violence
Voneche, J. J., 218
von Glasersfeld, E. C., 219
Voyat, Gilbert, 39, 221
Vygotsky, L. S., 121, 222

Wallace, Bruce, 211
Walster, Elaine, *see* Hatfield, Elaine
Warfare, *see* Aggression *and* Primitive warfare
Warner, Harold, 219
Warner, Philip, 121, 222
Warriner, Charles K., 112, 122, 223
Washoe (chimpanzee), 2–3
Watson, John S., 29–31, 40, 222
Weber, Max, 201, 222
Welcome Week (study), 125–127
Wells, Herbert George, 162–163, 173, 222
Welles, Orson, 163
Westmoreland, William C., 159
Whorf, Benjamin Lee, 16, 42, 121, 222
Wilson, A. C., 14, 215
Wilson, Edward O., 156, 157, 222
Wilson, James Q., 157, 158–159, 222
Winch, Robert F., 134, 139, 222
Wolfgang, Marvin E., 152, 158, 159, 173, 220, 222
Wright, Quincy, 159, 222
Writing, *see* Language

Wylie, Ruth, 42, 222

Yeung-Chorchesne, R., 211
Young, John, 98

Zajonc, Robert B., 139, 222
Zimbardo, Philip G., 122, 222
Zurcher, Louis, Jr., 41, 222